iPad®
For Seniors
FOR
DUMMIES®
5TH EDITION

by Nancy Muir

WILEY

Wiley Publishing, Inc.

iPad® For Seniors For Dummies®, 5th Edition

Published by
John Wiley & Sons, Inc.
111 River Street
Hoboken, NJ 07030-5774
www.wiley.com

Copyright © 2013 by John Wiley & Sons, Inc., Hoboken, New Jersey

Published by John Wiley & Sons, Inc., Hoboken, New Jersey

Published simultaneously in Canada

For general information on our other products and services, please contact our Customer Care Department within the U.S. at 877-762-2974, outside the U.S. at 317-572-3993, or fax 317-572-4002.

For technical support, please visit www.wiley.com/techsupport.

Wiley publishes in a variety of print and electronic formats and by print-on-demand. Some material included with standard print versions of this book may not be included in e-books or in print-on-demand. If this book refers to media such as a CD or DVD that is not included in the version you purchased, you may download this material at http://booksupport.wiley.com. For more information about Wiley products, visit www.wiley.com.

Library of Congress Control Number: 2012949720

ISBN 978-1-118-49708-1 (pbk); ISBN 978-1-118-52103-8 (ebk); ISBN 978-1-118-52110-6 (ebk); ISBN 978-1-118-52148-9 (ebk)

Manufactured in the United States of America

10 9 8 7 6 5 4 3 2 1

WILEY

iPad®
For Seniors
FOR
DUMMIES®
5TH EDITION

Tautology

About the Author

Nancy Muir is the author of over 100 books on technology and business topics. In addition to her writing work, Nancy runs a website on technology for seniors called `TechSmartSenior.com` and a companion website for her iPad books in the For Dummies series, `iPadMadeClear.com`. She writes a regular column on computers and the Internet on Retirenet.com. Prior to her writing career Nancy was a manager at several publishing companies, and a training manager at Symantec.

Dedication

To all the seniors who are bold enough to leap into the iPad adventure.

Author's Acknowledgments

I was lucky enough to have Blair Pottenger, the absolute best editor in the world, assigned to lead the team on this book and as usual he did a stellar job. Thanks also to Dennis Cohen for his able work as technical editor, and to Amanda Graham, the book's copy editor, for checking all the details. Last but never least, thanks to Kyle Looper, an outstanding Acquisitions Editor, for hiring me to write this and many other books.

Publisher's Acknowledgments

We're proud of this book; please send us your comments at http://dummies.custhelp.com. For other comments, please contact our Customer Care Department within the U.S. at 877-762-2974, outside the U.S. at 317-572-3993, or fax 317-572-4002.

Some of the people who helped bring this book to market include the following:

Acquisitions and Editorial

Project Editor: Blair J. Pottenger

Acquisitions Editor: Kyle Looper

Copy Editor: Amanda Graham

Technical Editor: Dennis Cohen

Editorial Manager: Kevin Kirschner

Editorial Assistant: Leslie Saxman

Sr. Editorial Assistant: Cherie Case

Cover Photo: © SelectStock/iStockphoto.com

Cartoons: Rich Tennant (www.the5thwave.com)

Composition Services

Project Coordinator: Sheree Montgomery

Layout and Graphics: Carrie A. Cesavice, Jennifer Creasey, Corrie Niehaus

Proofreader: Wordsmith Editorial

Indexer: Potomac Indexing, LLC

Publishing and Editorial for Technology Dummies

Richard Swadley, Vice President and Executive Group Publisher

Andy Cummings, Vice President and Publisher

Mary Bednarek, Executive Acquisitions Director

Mary C. Corder, Editorial Director

Publishing for Consumer Dummies

Kathleen Nebenhaus, Vice President and Executive Publisher

Composition Services

Debbie Stailey, Director of Composition Services

Contents at a Glance

Introduction 1

Part I: Making the iPad Yours 7
Chapter 1: Buying Your iPad 9
Chapter 2: Looking Over the Home Screen 27
Chapter 3: Getting Going 55
Chapter 4: Making Your iPad More Accessible 69

Part II: Taking the Leap Online 89
Chapter 5: Browsing the Internet with Safari 91
Chapter 6: Working with E-mail in Mail 115
Chapter 7: Getting Social with FaceTime, Twitter, and iMessage 133
Chapter 8: Shopping the iTunes Store 147
Chapter 9: Expanding Your iPad Horizons with Apps 161

Part III: Having Fun and Consuming Media 175
Chapter 10: Using Your iPad as an E-Reader 177
Chapter 11: Playing with Music on iPad 205
Chapter 12: Playing with Photos 217
Chapter 13: Getting the Most Out of Video Features 237
Chapter 14: Playing Games 247
Chapter 15: Finding Your Way with Maps 261

Part IV: Managing Your Life and Your iPad 281
Chapter 16: Keeping On Schedule with Calendar 283
Chapter 17: Working with Reminders and Notifications 303
Chapter 18: Managing Contacts 317
Chapter 19: Talking to Your iPad with Siri 337
Chapter 20: Making Notes 351
Chapter 21: Troubleshooting and Maintaining Your iPad 365

Index 381

Table of Contents

Introduction 1

About This Book 1
Foolish Assumptions 1
Why You Need This Book 2
How This Book Is Organized 2
Where to Go from Here 4

Part 1: Making the iPad Yours 7

Chapter 1: Buying Your iPad 9

Discover What's New in iOS 6 9
Choose the Right iPad for You 12
Decide How Much Memory Is Enough 13
Choose between Wi-Fi Only or Wi-Fi and 3G/4G 15
Understand What You Need to Use Your iPad 17
Know Where to Buy Your iPad 18
Consider iPad Accessories 19
Explore What's in the Box 22
Take a First Look at the Gadget 24

Chapter 2: Looking Over the Home Screen 27

See What You Need to Use iPad 28
Turn On iPad and Register It 29
Meet the Multi-Touch Screen 30
Goodbye Click-and-Drag, Hello Tap-and-Swipe 32
Display and Use the Onscreen Keyboard 36
Use the Split Keyboard 39
Flick to Search 40
Update the Operating System to iOS 6.0 41
Learn Multitasking Basics 43
Explore Multitasking Gestures 44
Examine the iPad Cameras 44

Customize the Side Switch 46
Explore the Status Bar 46
Take Inventory of Built-in Apps 47
Lock iPad, Turn It Off, and Unlock It 52

Chapter 3: Getting Going **55**
Charge the Battery 56
Make iPad Settings Using iTunes 57
Sync the iPad to Your Computer Using iTunes 59
Sync Wirelessly 60
Understand iCloud 61
Get an iCloud Account 62
Make iCloud Sync Settings 63
View the User Guide Online 65

Chapter 4: Making Your iPad More Accessible **69**
Set Brightness 70
Change the Wallpaper 71
Turn On Zoom 72
Invert Screen Colors 74
Set Up VoiceOver 75
Use VoiceOver 78
Adjust the Volume of Ringers and Alerts 79
Use Mono Audio 80
Have iPad Speak Auto-text 81
Turn On Large Text 83
Turn On and Work with AssistiveTouch 84
Use Dictation on the Third-Generation iPad 85
Focus Learning with Guided Access 86

Part II: Taking the Leap Online **89**

Chapter 5: Browsing the Internet with Safari **91**
Connect to the Internet 92
Explore Safari 93
Navigate among Web Pages 95
Use Tabbed Browsing 97
View Browsing History 98

Search the Web 100

Add and Use Bookmarks 102

Save Links and Web Pages to Safari Reading List 104

Use Safari Reader 105

Add Web Clips to the Home Screen 107

Save an Image to Your Photo Library 108

Post Photos from Safari 109

Send a Link 110

Make Private Browsing and Cookie Settings 111

Print a Web Page 112

Understand iCloud Tabs 113

Chapter 6: Working with E-mail in Mail 115

Add an iCloud, Gmail, Yahoo!, AOL, or Microsoft Hotmail Account ... 116

Set Up a POP3 E-mail Account 118

Open Mail and Read Messages 119

Reply To or Forward E-mail 121

Create and Send a New Message 123

Format E-mail 124

Search E-mail 126

Delete E-mail 127

Organize E-mail 127

Create a VIP List 128

**Chapter 7: Getting Social with FaceTime, Twitter,
and iMessage 133**

Understand Who Can Use FaceTime 134

Get an Overview of FaceTime 134

Make a FaceTime Call with Wi-Fi or 3G/4G 135

Accept or End a FaceTime Call 138

Switch Views 139

Experience Twitter on iPad 140

Set Up an iMessage Account 141

Use iMessage to Address, Create, and Send Messages 142

Clear a Conversation 145

Chapter 8: Shopping the iTunes Store **147**

Explore the iTunes Store 148

Find a Selection 150

Preview Music, a Movie, or an Audiobook 152

Buy a Selection 154

Rent Movies 156

Shop Anywhere Else 158

Enable Auto Downloads of Purchases from Other Devices ... 159

Chapter 9: Expanding Your iPad Horizons with Apps **161**

Explore Senior-Recommended Apps 162

Search the App Store 164

Get Applications from the App Store 166

Organize Your Applications on Home Screens 167

Organize Apps in Folders 169

Delete Applications You No Longer Need 170

Update Apps 172

Part III: Having Fun and Consuming Media **175**

Chapter 10: Using Your iPad as an E-Reader **177**

Discover How iPad Differs from Other E-Readers 178

Find Books at iBooks 178

Explore Other E-Book Sources 181

Buy Books 182

Navigate a Book 184

Work with Interactive Books 186

Adjust Brightness 188

Change the Font Size and Type 188

Search in Your Book 190

Use Bookmarks and Highlights 191

Use My Notes and Study Cards in Textbooks 194

Check Words in the Dictionary 195

Organize Your Library 196

Organize Books in Collections 198

Download Magazine Apps to Newsstand.................................199
Buy Issues.................................201
Read Periodicals.................................202

Chapter 11: Playing with Music on iPad.................................205
View the Library Contents 206
Create Playlists.................................207
Search for Audio 208
Play Music and Other Audio 210
Shuffle Music.................................212
Adjust the Volume.................................213
Understand Ping.................................214
Use AirPlay.................................215

Chapter 12: Playing with Photos 217
Take Pictures with the iPad Cameras.................................218
Import Photos from an iPhone, iPod, or a Digital Camera.................221
Save Photos from the Web.................................222
View an Album 223
View Individual Photos.................................224
Edit Photos.................................225
Organize Photos in Camera Roll.................................227
Share Photos with Mail, Twitter, and Facebook.................................228
Share Photos Using Photo Stream 229
Print Photos 231
Run a Slideshow 231
Display Picture Frame 233
Delete Photos.................................233
Play around with Photo Booth.................................235

Chapter 13: Getting the Most Out of Video Features.................237
Capture Your Own Videos with the Built-in Cameras.................................238
Play Movies, Podcasts, or TV Shows with Videos 239
Turn on Closed-Captioning.................................242
Go to a Movie Chapter.................................243
Delete Video Content from the iPad.................................244

Chapter 14: Playing Games..........................247

Open an Account in Game Center.......................248

Create a Profile 249

Add Friends...252

Purchase and Download Games 253

Master iPad Game-Playing Basics......................255

Play against Yourself 257

Play Games with Friends in Game Center.............258

Share High Scores with Friends.........................259

Chapter 15: Finding Your Way with Maps..........261

Go to Your Current Location.............................262

Change Views...263

Zoom In and Out 265

Go to Another Location 266

Drop a Pin...269

Add and View a Bookmark 270

Delete a Bookmark 271

Find Directions...272

View Information about a Location.....................275

Add a Location to a Contact.............................276

Share Location Information..............................277

Get Turn-by-Turn Navigation Help 279

Part IV: Managing Your Life and Your iPad 281

Chapter 16: Keeping On Schedule with Calendar 283

View Your Calendar..284

Add Calendar Events 288

Add Events Using Siri......................................290

Create Repeating Events 290

Add Alerts...291

Search Calendars 293

Subscribe to and Share Calendars......................294

Delete an Event...297

Display Clock..298

Add or Delete a Clock..299

Set an Alarm..300

Use Stopwatch and Timer..301

Chapter 17: Working with Reminders and Notifications 303

Create a Task in Reminders 304

Edit Task Details 305

Schedule a Reminder..306

Create a List..308

Sync with Other Devices and Calendars...............................309

Mark as Complete or Delete a Reminder...............................310

Set Notification Types 311

View Notification Center 313

Go to an App from Notification Center 314

Clear Notifications 315

Get Some Rest with Do Not Disturb.....................................315

Chapter 18: Managing Contacts 317

Add a Contact..318

Sync Contacts with iCloud 321

Assign a Photo to a Contact 322

Add Twitter or Facebook Information 324

Designate Related People..326

Set Ringtones 327

Search for a Contact 328

Go to a Contact's Website..330

Address E-mail Using Contacts..332

Share a Contact...333

View a Contact's Location in Maps 334

Delete a Contact 335

Chapter 19: Talking to Your iPad with Siri 337

Activate Siri 337

Understand All that Siri Can Do 340

Call Contacts via FaceTime...342

Create Reminders and Alerts 343

Add Tasks to Your Calendar 344

Play Music 345

Get Directions 345

Ask for Facts 347

Search the Web 348

Send E-mail or Messages 349

Get Helpful Tips 349

Chapter 20: Making Notes 351

Open a Blank Note and Enter Text 351

Create a New Note 355

Use Copy and Paste 355

Display the Notes List 357

Move among Notes 358

Search for a Note 359

E-mail a Note 360

Delete a Note 361

Print a Note 363

**Chapter 21: Troubleshooting and
Maintaining Your iPad 365**

Keep the iPad Screen Clean 365

Protect Your Gadget with a Case 367

Extend Your iPad's Battery Life 368

Find Out What to Do with a Nonresponsive iPad 370

Make the Keyboard Reappear 371

Update Software 371

Restore the Sound 372

Get Support 374

Find a Missing iPad 376

Backup to iCloud 378

Index **381**

*I*f you bought this book (or are even thinking about buying it), you've probably already made the decision to buy an iPad. The iPad is set up to be simple to use, but still, you can spend hours exploring the preinstalled apps, finding how to change settings, and syncing the device to your computer or through iTunes or iCloud. I've invested those hours so that you don't have to — and I've added advice and tips for getting the most out of your iPad.

This book helps you get going with the iPad quickly and painlessly so that you can move directly to the fun part.

About This Book

This book is specifically written for mature people like you, folks who may be relatively new to using a tablet device and want to discover the basics of buying an iPad, working with its preinstalled apps, and getting on the Internet. In writing this book, I've tried to consider the types of activities that might interest someone who is 50 years old or older and picking up an iPad for the first time.

Foolish Assumptions

This book is organized by sets of tasks. These tasks start from the beginning, assuming that you've never laid your

Introduction

Conventions Used in This Book

This book uses certain conventions to help you find your way around, including

➡ Text you type in a text box is in **bold**. Figure references, such as "see **Figure 1-1**," are also in bold, to help you find them.

➡ Whenever I mention a website address, or *URL*, I put it in a different font, `like this`.

➡ Figure callouts draw your attention to actions you need to perform. In some cases, points of interest in a figure might be indicated. The text tells you what to look for; the callout line makes it easy to find.

 Tip icons point out insights or helpful suggestions related to tasks in the step lists.

New icons highlight what features of iOS 6 are new and exciting, in case you're moving up from an earlier version.

hands on an iPad, and guide you through basic steps in nontechnical language.

This book covers both the Wi-Fi only and the Wi-Fi and 3G/4G iPad features. I'm also assuming that you'll want to download and use the iBooks e-reader app, so I tell you how to do that in Chapter 9 and cover its features in Chapter 10.

Why You Need This Book

The iPad is cool and perfect for many seniors because it provides a simple, intuitive interface for activities such as checking e-mail and playing music. But why should you stumble around, trying to figure out its features? Using the simple step-by-step approach in this book, you can get up to speed with the iPad right away and overcome any technophobia you might have.

How This Book Is Organized

This book is conveniently divided into several handy parts to help you find what you need (and give you a chuckle at the cartoons that start off each part):

⟹ **Part I: Making the iPad Yours:** If you're about to buy your iPad or are ready to get started with the basics of using it, this part is for you. These chapters highlight the newest features in third-generation iPad and the latest iOS version (at the time of this writing, it was iOS 6) and help you explore the different specifications, styles, and price ranges for all iPad models. You find out how to set up your iPad out of the box, including

• Opening an iCloud account to register and push content to all your computer and phone devices automatically.

• Opening an iTunes account to buy entertainment content and additional apps.

These chapters also provide information for exploring the iPad Home screen when you first turn it on, and useful accessibility features to help out if you have hearing, learning, or vision challenges, including the Dictation feature on the third-generation iPad for speaking text rather than typing it.

➠ **Part II: Taking the Leap Online:** In Part II, you find out how to connect to the Internet and use the built-in Safari browser and work with iCloud tabs, a new feature of iOS 6. You putter with the preinstalled Mail app and set up your iPad to access e-mail from your existing e-mail accounts. In this part, you also get to shop online for multimedia content, such as movies (which are stellar on the new Retina display in the third-generation iPad) and music, and additional fun iPad apps. You explore the Messages app, and the exciting FaceTime app, used for making video calls to other people who use the iPad, a Mac, the iPhone 4 or later, or the iPod touch.

➠ **Part III: Having Fun and Consuming Media:** The iPad has been touted by some as a device for consuming media such as music, podcasts, and movies. Preinstalled on the iPad are a Music app for playing music and the Videos and YouTube apps for watching video content. In addition, I explain in this part how to use iBooks, the free e-reader app from Apple. You also explore playing games on your iPad, which — trust me — is a lot of fun. Finally, explore playing around with the Maps app (newly revamped in iOS 6 with features such as navigation and 3-D) to find your favorite restaurant or bookstore with ease. You also discover the wonderful possibilities for using still and video cameras on iPad 2 and third-generation iPad, including the new Shared Photo Stream feature in iOS 6. Finally, you explore the amazingly fun things you can do with Photo Booth and videos in Chapters 12 and 13, respectively.

In this part you also explore the Newsstand app for subscribing to and reading magazines.

➡ **Part IV: Managing Your Life and Your iPad:** For the organizational part of your brain, the iPad makes available Calendar, Contacts, and Notes apps, all of which are covered in this part. I also introduce you to the awesomely cool Siri feature, which is like an assistant for finding everything from a taxi stand to the weight of Saturn. I also offer advice about keeping your iPad safe and troubleshooting common problems that you might encounter, including using the Find My iPad feature to deal with a lost or stolen iPad. You can also use the iCloud service to back up your content or restore your iPad.

The Reminders app and Notification Center feature introduced in iOS 5 are great for keeping you on schedule. Reminders is a great to-do list feature that allows you to enter tasks and details about them, and can also display tasks from your online calendars. Notification Center sends you alerts for items you ask to be notified about.

Where to Go from Here

You can work through this book from beginning to end or simply open a chapter to solve a problem or acquire a specific new skill whenever you need it. The steps in every task quickly get you to where you want to go, without a lot of technical explanation.

Note: At the time I wrote this book, all the information it contained was accurate for the Wi-Fi only and Wi-Fi and 3G original iPads, the Wi-Fi only and Wi-Fi and 3G iPad 2s, the Wi-Fi only and Wi-Fi and 4G third-generation iPads, version 6 of the iOS (operating system) used by the iPad, and version 10.6 of iTunes. Apple is likely to introduce new iPad models and new versions of the iOS and iTunes between book editions. If you've bought a new iPad and its hardware, user interface, or the version of iTunes on your computer looks a little different, be sure to check out what Apple has to say at www.apple.com/ipad. You'll no doubt find updates on the company's latest releases. Also, if you don't set up iCloud to automatically update your iPad, perform updates to the operating system on a regular basis, as described in Chapter 2. When a change is very substantial, we may add an update or bonus information that you can download at this book's companion website, www.dummies.com/go/ipadforseniors.

Part I
Making the iPad Yours

The 5th Wave   By Rich Tennant

"Other than this little glitch with the landscape view, I really love my iPad."

Buying Your iPad

You've read about it. You've seen on the news the lines at Apple Stores every time a new generation iPad is released. You're so intrigued that you've decided to get your own iPad to have fun, explore the online world, read e-books, organize your photos, and more.

Trust me: You've made a good decision because the iPad redefines the computing experience in an exciting, new way. It's also an absolutely perfect fit for many seniors.

In this chapter, you discover the different types of iPad models and their relative advantages, as well as where to buy this little gem. After you have one in your hands, I help you explore what's in the box and give an overview of the little buttons and slots you'll encounter — luckily, the iPad has very few of them.

Discover What's New in iOS 6

Apple's iPad gets its features from a combination of hardware and its software operating system (called *iOS*, the term is short for iPhone Operating System, in case you want to impress your friends). The most current operating system is iOS 6, though small updates appear all the time, so by the time you're reading this, you might have 6.2, 3, or 4! If you've seen the

Get ready to . . .

➡ Discover What's New in iOS 6

➡ Choose the Right iPad for You

➡ Decide How Much Memory Is Enough

➡ Choose between Wi-Fi Only or Wi-Fi and 3G/4G

➡ Understand What You Need to Use Your iPad

➡ Know Where to Buy Your iPad

➡ Consider iPad Accessories

➡ Explore What's in the Box

➡ Take a First Look at the Gadget

original iPad or iPad 2 in action or you own one, it's helpful to understand which new features the third-generation iPad device brings to the table (all of which are covered in more detail in this book). In addition to features on the original iPad and iPad 2, the third-generation iPad offers

➡ **Retina display:** This awesomely crisp display provides 3.1 million pixels, which, trust me, is a lot.

➡ **An improved dual-core A5X chip:** This chip gives your iPad much faster performance and quad-core graphics.

➡ **An improved 5-megapixel iSight camera:** The rear-facing iSight camera offers advanced optics, an illumination sensor, a face detection feature that makes people you capture clearer, and the capability to capture video in 1080p, all discussed in more detail in Chapters 12 and 13.

➡ **Dictation:** You can use the Dictation feature to speak input to your iPad rather than typing. This comes in handy in apps such as Maps, Mail, and Notes.

➡ **Available 4G LTE:** Whereas iPad 2 is offered in a 3G version, the third-generation iPad can take advantage of 4G and even 4G LTE, the latest in cellular communication technology, which simply means you can get a very fast, strong connection to the Internet if you're near a 4G–enabled locale. Unfortunately, because 4G is a relatively recent technology, right now you have to live near a major city to take full advantage of it.

 Throughout this book, I highlight features that are available only if you're using the third-generation iPad or iPad 2, so you can deduce what features won't work on an original iPad and so can use this book no matter which version of the device you own.

Any iPad device can use iOS 6 if you update the operating system (discussed in detail in Chapter 2); this book is based on version 6 of the iOS. This update to the operating system added a few new features, including

➡ **Brand new Maps app:** The Maps app has been totally rebuilt in iOS 6. Graphics are crisper, and you have more control over panning, tilting, and zooming. You can use Maps to get turn-by-turn navigation now, as well as traffic information in real time.

➡ **Siri:** This is a technology that was introduced with iPhone 4S. You can talk to Siri and ask questions from the practical (Where's the nearest gas station?) to the fun (Where can I buy a used sailboat?).

➡ **Sharing:** You can share photos with your Facebook friends, share links from Safari, share high scores from Game Center, or update your status using Notification Center or Siri.

➡ **Shared Photo Streams:** The Photo Stream feature isn't new to iOS 6, but the capability to share photos with a select group of people is. This feature uses iCloud to share with other Apple devices, or to share photos with anybody online.

➡ **FaceTime over cellular:** You can now use the FaceTime video calling feature to call others over cellular networks (if you have a 3G/4G iPad model) as well as over Wi-Fi.

➡ **Guided Access:** This accessibility feature allows you to focus your iPad to just certain sites or apps to help you or those you're helping have an easier learning experience.

➡ **Find My Friends:** You can use this feature to share your location with others and receive alerts when friends leave or arrive at a certain location.

➡ **Better than ever apps:** Several apps such as Mail, Safari, and Apple's online stores have been spiffed up to offer a few neat, new features.

Choose the Right iPad for You

iPads don't come in different sizes. Though there are slight differences in thickness and weight among the different generations, if you pick up an iPad (see **Figure 1-1**), you're not likely to be able to tell one model from another on first glance, except that some are black and some are white. Though the three generations have slightly different heft and the second- and third-generation iPads have camera holes on the back, their differences are primarily under the hood.

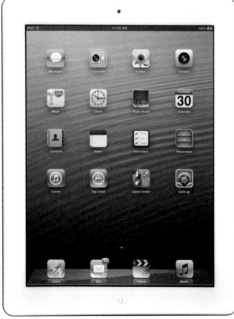

Figure 1-1

If you're in the market for a new iPad, Apple currently offers discounted iPad 2s and new third-generation iPads. iPad 2s and third-generation models have three variations:

➡️ Black or white

➡️ Amount of built-in memory

➡️ Method used for connecting to the Internet: Wi-Fi only, Wi-Fi and 3G (iPad 2), or Wi-Fi and 3G/4G (third-generation iPad)

Your options in the first bullet point are pretty black and white, but if you're confused about the other two, read on as I explain these variations in more detail.

 Some people feel that the white model of the third-generation iPad is less effective at taking advantage of the Retina display. The black model in effect disappears, letting the crisp image really pop. Still, color selection is subjective, so I say get the one that appeals to you.

Decide How Much Memory Is Enough

Memory is a measure of how much information — for example, movies, photos, and software applications, or *apps* — you can store on a computing device. Memory can also affect your iPad's performance when handling tasks such as streaming favorite TV shows from the World Wide Web or downloading music.

 Streaming refers to watching video content from the web (or from other devices) rather than playing a file stored on your computing device. You can enjoy a lot of material online without ever downloading its full content to your hard drive — and given that every iPad model has a relatively small amount of memory, that's not a bad idea. See Chapters 11 and 13 for more about getting your music and movies online.

Your memory options with an iPad are 16, 32, or 64 gigabytes (GB). You must choose the right amount of memory because you can't open the unit and add memory, as you usually can with a desktop computer. Also, you can't insert a *flash drive* (also known as a *USB stick*) to add backup capacity because iPad has no USB port — or CD/DVD drive, for that matter. However, Apple has thoughtfully provided iCloud, a service you can use to save space by backing up content to the Internet (you can read more about that in Chapter 3).

 With an Apple Digital AV Adapter accessory, you can plug into the Dock Connector slot to attach an HDMI–enabled device such as an external hard drive for additional storage capacity. See Chapter 13 for more about using these AV features (most of which are just hitting the market). As of this writing, ViewSonic is offering three new HDMI projectors; DVDO is offering an HD Travel Kit for smartphones and tablets; and Belkin has introduced a new line of tools for HDTV streaming, for example.

So how much memory is enough for your iPad? Here's a rule of thumb: If you like lots of media, such as movies or TV shows, and you want to store them on your iPad (rather than experiencing or accessing this content online on sites such as Hulu or Netflix), you might need 64GB. For most people who manage a reasonable number of photos, download some music, and watch heavy-duty media such as movies online, 32GB is probably sufficient. If you simply want to check e-mail, browse the web, and write short notes to yourself, 16GB *might* be enough.

 Do you have a clue how big a gigabyte (GB) is? Consider this: Just about any computer you buy today comes with a minimum of 250–500GB of storage. Computers have to tackle larger tasks than iPads do, so that number makes sense. The iPad, which uses a technology called *flash* for memory storage, is meant (to a great extent) to help you experience online media and e-mail; it doesn't have to store much and in fact pulls lots of content from online.

In the world of memory, 16GB for any kind of storage is puny if you keep lots of content and graphics on the device.

What's the price for more memory? For the third-generation iPad, a 16GB Wi-Fi unit (see the next task for more about Wi-Fi) costs $499; 32GB jumps the price to $599; and 64GB adds another $100, setting you back a whopping $699.

Choose between Wi-Fi Only or Wi-Fi and 3G/4G

One variation on price and performance for the iPad is whether your model has Wi-Fi or Wi-Fi and 3G/4G. Because iPad is great for browsing online, shopping online, e-mailing, and so on, having an Internet connection for it is important. That's where Wi-Fi and 3G/4G enter the picture. Both technologies are used to connect to the Internet. You use *Wi-Fi* to connect to a wireless network at home or at your local coffee shop, grocery store, or an airport that offers Wi-Fi. This type of network uses short-range radio to connect to the Internet; its range is reasonably limited, so if you leave home or walk out of the coffee shop, you can't use it. (These limitations are changing as some towns are installing community-wide Wi-Fi networks.)

The *3G* and *4G* cellphone technologies allow an iPad to connect to the Internet via a widespread cellular-phone network. You use it in much the same way you make calls from just about anywhere using your cellphone. 3G is available on iPad 2; 4G is available on third-generation iPad, and as the latest cellular connection technology, it may not always be available in every location. You'll still connect to the Internet when 4G service isn't available, but without the advantage of the superfast 4G technology.

You can buy an iPad with only Wi-Fi or one with both Wi-Fi *and* 3G/4G capabilities. Getting a 3G or 4G iPad costs an additional $130 (see **Table 1-1**), but it also includes GPS so you can get more accurate driving directions. You have to buy an iPad model that fits your data connection provider — either AT&T or Verizon in the United States.

Also, to use your 3G/4G network, you have to pay AT&T or Verizon a monthly fee. The good news is that neither carrier requires a long-term contract, as you probably had to commit to with your cellphone and its data connection — you can pay for a connection during the month you visit your grandkids, for example, and then get rid of it when you arrive home. AT&T offers prepaid and postpaid options, but Verizon offers only a prepaid plan. AT&T offers plans that top out at 5GB of data connection, and Verizon offers several levels, including 3GB, 5GB, and 10GB. Note that if you intend to *stream* videos (watch them on your iPad from the Internet), you can eat through these numbers quickly.

Table 1-1 Third-Generation iPad Models and Pricing		
Memory Size	*Wi-Fi Price*	*Wi-Fi and 4G Price*
16GB	$499	$629
32GB	$599	$729
64GB	$699	$829

Of course, these two carriers could change their pricing and options at any time, so go to these links for more information about iPad data plans: AT&T is at www. att.com/shop/wireless/devices/ipad.jsp, and Verizon is at www.verizonwireless.com/ b2c/splash/ipad.jsp.

The folks at Sprint now offer the iPhone 4S and, at this time, a pretty plausible rumor is going around that they will eventually offer iPad to their customers as well. Check their website (http://sprint.com) when you're ready to sign up to see what they have to offer.

So how do you choose? If you want to wander around the woods or town — or take long drives with your iPad continually connected to the Internet to get step-by-step navigation info from the newly rebuilt Maps app — get 3G and pay the price. But if you'll use your iPad mainly at home or using a Wi-Fi *hotspot* (a location where Wi-Fi access to the Internet is available, such as an Internet cafe), don't bother with 3G. And frankly, you can now find *lots* of hotspots out there, including restaurants, hotels, airports, and more.

 You can use the hotspot feature on a smartphone, which allows iPad to use your phone's 3G or 4G connection to go online if you pay for a higher-data-use plan that supports hotspot usage with your phone service carrier. Check out the features of your phone to turn hotspot on.

 Because 3G and 4G iPads are also GPS devices, they know where you are and can act as a navigation system to get you from here to there. The Wi-Fi–only model uses a digital compass and triangulation method for locating your current position, which is less accurate; with no constant Internet connection, it won't help you to get around town. If getting accurate directions is one iPad feature that excites you, get 3G/4G and then see Chapter 15 for more about the Maps feature.

Understand What You Need to Use Your iPad

Before you head off to buy your iPad, you should know what other devices, connections, and accounts you'll need to work with it optimally. At a bare minimum, you need to be able to connect to the Internet to take advantage of most of iPad's features. You can open an iCloud account to store and share content online, or you can use a computer to download photos, music, or applications from non-Apple online sources such as stores or sharing sites like your local library and transfer them to your iPad through a process called *syncing*. You can also use a computer or iCloud to register your iPad the first time you start it, although you can have the folks at the Apple Store handle registration for you if you have one nearby.

Can you use iPad without owning a computer and just use public Wi-Fi hotspots to go online (or a 3G/4G connection if you have such a model)? Yes. However, to be able to go online using a Wi-Fi–only iPad and to use many of its built-in features at home, you need to have a home Wi-Fi network available. You also need to use iCloud or sync to your computer to get updates for the iPad operating system.

Apple's *iPad User Guide* recommends that you have

➡ A Mac or PC with a USB 2.0 port and one of the following operating systems:

 • Mac OS X version 10.5.8 or later

 • Windows 8, 7, Windows Vista, or Windows XP Home or Professional with Service Pack 3 or later

➡ iTunes 10.7 or later, available at www.itunes. com/download

➡ An Apple ID and iTunes Store account

➡ Internet access

➡ An iCloud account

Apple has set up its iTunes software and the iCloud service to give you two ways to manage content for your iPad — including movies, music, or photos you've downloaded — and specify how to sync your calendar and contact information. Chapter 3 covers those settings in more detail.

Know Where to Buy Your iPad

As of this writing, you can buy an iPad at the Apple Store and from several brick-and-mortar stores such as Best Buy, Walmart, Sam's Club, and Target, and at online sites such as MacMall.com. You can also buy 3G/4G models (models that require an account with a phone service provider) from AT&T and Verizon.

If you get your iPad from Apple, either at a retail store or the online store, here's the difference in the buying experience:

➠ The Apple Store advantage is that the sales staff will
help you unpack your iPad and make sure it's working
properly, register the device (which you have to do
before you can use it; see Chapter 2 for more about
this process), and help you learn the basics of using
it. Occasional workshops are offered to help people
learn about using the iPad. Apple employees are
famous for being helpful to customers.

➠ Apple Stores aren't on every corner, so if visiting one
isn't an option (or you just prefer to go it alone), you
can go to the Apple Store website (`http://store.`
`apple.com/us/browse/home/shop_ipad/`
`family/ipad`) and order one to be shipped to you —
and even get it engraved, if you wish. Standard
shipping typically is free, and if there's a problem,
Apple's online store customer service reps will help
you solve the problem or replace your iPad.

Consider iPad Accessories

At present, Apple offers a few accessories you might want to check out
when you purchase your iPad (or purchase down the road), including

➠ **iPad Case/Smart Cover:** Your iPad isn't cheap and,
unlike a laptop computer, it has an exposed screen
that can be damaged if you drop or scratch it. Investing
in the iPad Case or Smart Cover (note that the Smart
Cover works only with iPad 2 or third-generation
iPad) is a good idea if you intend to take your iPad
out of your house — or if you have a cat or grandchildren. The iPad Smart Cover (see **Figure 1-2**)
costs about $40 for polyurethane and $70 for
leather, and other cases vary in price depending on
design and material.

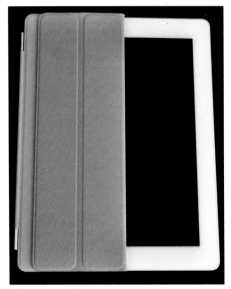

Figure 1-2

➡ **iPad Camera Connection Kit:** Because there's no USB port on an iPad, you can't use a USB connection to upload photos from your digital camera to your iPad. If you want to send digital photos directly to your iPad, you can use this handy kit. It will set you back about $30 for the privilege.

➡ **iPad Dock:** The iPad is light and thin, which is great, but holding it all the time can get tedious. The iPad Dock lets you prop up the device so that you can view it hands-free and then charge the battery and sync to your computer. At about $30, it's a good investment for ease and comfort. Be sure to get the dock that matches your iPad model.

➡ **iPad Keyboard Dock:** The iPad provides an onscreen keyboard that's passable, especially if you position it to view material in *landscape* orientation (with the long side across the top). However, if you're a touch typist who wants to write long notes or e-mails, or if you have larger hands and have trouble pressing the virtual keys on the screen, the iPad Keyboard Dock (which works with the original iPad held in portrait orientation) or the Apple Wireless Keyboard might be the answer. The iPad Keyboard Dock costs about $30, and the Apple Wireless Keyboard costs about $70. You can also explore Bluetooth keyboards from other manufacturers.

➡ **Apple Digital AV Adapter:** To connect devices to output high definition media, you can buy this adapter for about $40. More and more devices are coming out that use this technology, such as projectors and TVs. See **Figure 1-3.**

Figure 1-3

➡ **Apple Component AV Cable or Apple Composite VA Cable:** These accessories sell for about $40 and let you connect your iPad 2 or third-generation iPad to certain TV or stereo systems.

➡ **Printers:** Several printers from companies such as Hewlett-Packard, Canon, and Epson work with iPad's native printing capability to handle wireless printing. These printers range from about $100 to $250, and you can browse all models at the online

Apple Store (http://store.apple.com).
AirPrint Activator 2 and Printopia are Macintosh
apps that can make any printer shared on a network
accessible to your iPad.

 Several companies produce iPad accessories such as
cases and more will undoubtedly pop up, so feel free
to do an online search for different items and prices.

 Don't bother buying a wireless mouse to connect
with your iPad via Bluetooth — the iPad recognizes
your finger as its primary input device, and mice
need not apply. However, you can use a stylus to tap
your input.

Explore What's in the Box

When you fork over your hard-earned money for your iPad, you'll be
left holding one box about the size of a package of copy paper. Here's
a rundown of what you'll find when you take off the shrink wrap and
open the box:

⟾ **iPad:** Your iPad is covered in a thick, plastic sleeve-
thingie that you can take off and toss (unless you
think there's a chance you'll return it, in which case
you might want to keep all packaging for 14 days —
Apple's standard return period).

⟾ **Documentation (and I use the term loosely):**
Notice, under the iPad itself, a small, white envelope
about the size of a half-dozen index cards. Open it
and you'll find:

• *A tiny pamphlet:* This pamphlet, named *Important
Product Information Guide,* is essentially small print
(that you mostly don't need to read) from folks
like the FCC.

• *A label sheet:* This sheet has two white Apple logos
on it. (I'm not sure what they're for, but my

husband and I use one sticker to differentiate my iPad from his.)

- *A small card:* This card displays a picture of the iPad and callouts to its buttons on one side, and the other side contains brief instructions for setting it up and information about where to find out more.

➥ **Dock Connector to USB Cable:** Use this cord (see **Figure 1-4**) to connect the iPad to your computer, or use it with the last item in the box, the USB Power Adapter.

➥ **10W USB Power Adapter:** The power adapter (refer to **Figure 1-4**) attaches to the dock connector cord so that you can plug it into the wall and charge the battery.

Dock Connector
to USB Cable   10W USB Power Adapter

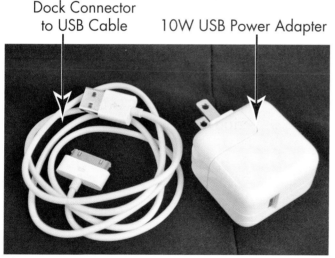

Figure 1-4

That's it. That's all there is in the box. It's kind of a study in Zen-like simplicity.

Take a First Look at the Gadget

The little card contained in the documentation (see the preceding task) gives you a picture of the iPad with callouts to the buttons you'll find on it. In this task, I give you a bit more information about those buttons and other physical features of the iPad. **Figure 1-5** shows you where each of these items is located.

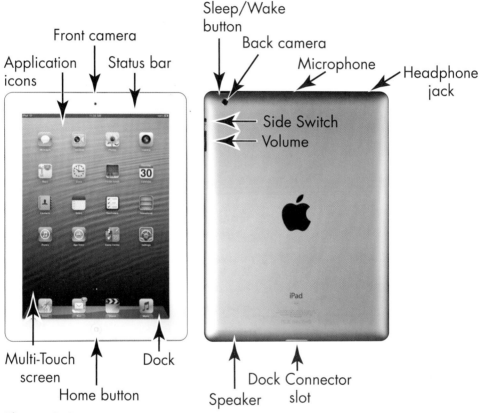

Figure 1-5

Here's the rundown on what the various hardware features are and what they do:

➡ **(The all-important) Home button:** On the iPad, you can go back to the Home screen to find just about anything. The Home screen displays all your installed and preinstalled apps and gives you access to your iPad settings. No matter where you are or what you're doing, push the Home button, and you're back at home base. You can also double-push the Home button to pull up a scrolling list of apps so you can quickly move from one to another.

➧ **Sleep/Wake button:** You can use this button (whose functionality I cover in more detail in Chapter 2) to power up your iPad, put it in Sleep mode, wake it up, or power it down.

➧ **Dock Connector slot:** Plug in the Dock Connector to USB Cable to charge your battery or sync your iPad with your computer (which you find out more about in Chapter 3).

➧ **Cameras:** The iPad 2 and third-generation iPad offers front- and rear-facing cameras, which you can use to shoot photos or video. The rear one is on the top-right corner (if you're looking at the front of the iPad), and you need to be careful not to put your thumb over it when taking shots. (I have several very nice photos of my fingers already.)

➧ **Side Switch:** In case you hadn't heard, the iPad screen rotates to match the angle you're holding it. If you want to stick with one orientation even if you spin the iPad in circles, you can use this little switch to lock the screen, which is especially handy when reading an e-book. You can also customize the function of the Side Switch using iPad General Settings to make the switch lock screen rotation rather than mute sound, which it does by default (see Chapter 2 for instructions).

➧ **(A tiny, mighty) Speaker:** One nice surprise when I first got my iPad was hearing what a great little monaural sound system it has and how much sound can come from this tiny speaker. The speaker is located on the bottom edge of the screen, below the Home button.

➡ **Volume:** Tap the volume switch, called a *rocker,* up for more volume and down for less. With iOS 5 and later, you can use this rocker as a camera shutter button when the camera is activated.

➡ **Headphone jack and microphone:** If you want to listen to your music in private, you can plug in a 3.5mm minijack headphone (including an iPhone headset if you have one, which gives you bidirectional sound). A tiny microphone makes it possible to speak into your iPad to do things such as make phone calls using the Internet, video calling services, or other apps that accept audio input.

Looking Over the Home Screen

I won't kid you: You have a slight learning curve ahead of you because iPad is different from other computing devices you may have used (although, if you own an iPhone or iPod touch, you've got a huge head start). That's mainly because of its Multi-Touch screen and onscreen keyboard — no mouse necessary. The iPad doesn't have a Windows or Mac operating system: It does have a modified iPhone operating system, so some of the methods you may have used on computers before (such as right-clicking) don't work in quite the same way on the touchscreen.

The good news is that getting anything done on the iPad is simple after you know the ropes. In fact, using your fingers instead of a mouse to do things onscreen is a very intuitive way to communicate with your computing device.

In this chapter, you turn on your iPad and register it and then take your first look at the Home screen. You also practice using the onscreen keyboard, see how to interact with the touchscreen in various ways, get pointers on working with cameras, and get an overview of built-in applications.

Get ready to . . .

→ See What You Need to Use iPad

→ Turn On iPad and Register It

→ Meet the Multi-Touch Screen

→ Goodbye Click-and-Drag, Hello Tap-and-Swipe

→ Display and Use the Onscreen Keyboard

→ Use the Split Keyboard

→ Flick to Search

→ Update the Operating System to iOS 6

→ Learn Multitasking Basics

→ Explore Multitasking Gestures

→ Examine the iPad Cameras

→ Customize the Side Switch

→ Explore the Status Bar

→ Take Inventory of Built-in Apps

→ Lock iPad, Turn It Off, and Unlock It

Have a soft cloth handy, like the one you might use to clean your eyeglasses. Despite a screen that has been treated to repel oils, you're about to deposit a ton of fingerprints on your iPad — one downside of a touchscreen device.

See What You Need to Use iPad

You need to be able, at a minimum, to connect to the Internet to take advantage of most iPad features, which you can do using a Wi-Fi network or by paying a fee and using a phone provider's network if you bought a 3G or 4G model. You might want to have a computer so that you can download photos, videos, music, or applications and transfer them to or from your iPad through a process called *syncing*. With iOS 5, a new Apple service called iCloud arrived, which, when you turn the feature on, syncs content from all your Apple iOS devices, Mac, and PC wirelessly, so anything you buy on your iPhone, for example, will automatically be pushed to your iPad.

You can register your iPad the first time you start it, using iCloud or by syncing with your computer via a cable, although you can have the folks at the Apple Store handle registration for you if you have one nearby.

Can you use iPad if you don't own a computer and you use public Wi-Fi hotspots to go online (or a 3G/4G connection if you have one of those models)? Yes. However, to be able to go online using a Wi-Fi–only iPad and to use many of its built-in features at home, you need to have a Wi-Fi network available.

Apple has set up both iCloud and its iTunes software to help you manage content for your iPad — which includes the movies, TV shows, music, or photos you've downloaded — and specify where to transfer your calendar and contact information from. Chapter 3 covers these settings in more detail.

Turn On iPad and Register It

1. The first time you turn on your iPad, you have to register it. You can do this using a physical connection to a computer with the latest version of iTunes installed. To register using iTunes on your computer, hold the iPad with one hand on either side, oriented like a pad of paper.

2. Press and hold the Sleep/Wake button on the top of your iPad until the Apple logo appears. In another moment, a screen appears asking if you'd like to register via iCloud or use iTunes. If you choose via iCloud, you can simply follow directions to register. If you want to use iTunes, tap the iTunes option and proceed.

3. Plug the Dock Connector to USB Cable that comes with your device into your iPad.

4. Plug the other end of the cable into a USB port on a computer. Both your computer and the iPad think for a few moments while they exchange data.

5. Sign in to your iTunes account in the dialog that appears on your computer screen, and then follow the simple onscreen instructions to register your iPad and choose whether to use iCloud (see Chapter 3 for more about this feature); choose a language and country; choose a network; agree to terms and conditions; choose to use the Find My iPad service; choose to use the Dictation feature (available only on third-generation iPads); select whether to automatically send information about your iPad to Apple; and choose whether to allow location services to use your current location. (If you're not sure about these options, you can accept or decline any of them and change them later; these steps are covered in Chapter 3, and various settings are discussed throughout this book.) When you're done, your iPad Home screen appears and you're in business.

6. Unplug the Dock Connector to USB Cable.

 If you buy your iPad at an Apple Store, an employee will register it for you, and you can skip this whole process.

 You can choose to have certain items transferred to your iPad from your computer when you sync, including music, videos, downloaded apps, contacts, audiobooks, calendars, e-books, podcasts, and browser bookmarks. You can also transfer to your computer any content you download directly to your iPad using the iTunes, iTunes U, Newsstand, iBooks, and App Store apps. See Chapters 8 and 9 for more about these features.

 If you have set up iCloud when registering or after registering (see Chapter 3), updates to your operating system will be pushed to your iPad without you having to plug it into a computer running iTunes. Apple refers to this feature as *PC Free*, simply meaning that your device has been liberated from having to use a physical connection to get upgrades.

Meet the Multi-Touch Screen

When the iPad Home screen appears (see **Figure 2-1**), you see a pretty background and two sets of icons. One set appears in the Dock, along the bottom of the screen. The *Dock* contains the Safari, Mail, Photos, and Music app icons by default, though you can add up to two other apps to it. The Dock appears on every Home screen. Other icons appear above the Dock and are closer to the top of the screen. (I cover all these icons in the "Take Inventory of Built-in Apps" task, later in this chapter.) Different icons appear in this area on each Home screen. You can add new apps to populate as many as 11 additional Home screens and move apps from one Home screen to another (see Chapter 9 for more about this).

Application icons

The Dock

Figure 2-1

 Treat the iPad screen carefully. It's made of glass and will smudge when you touch it (and will break if you throw it at the wall).

The iPad uses *touchscreen technology:* When you swipe your finger across the screen or tap it, you're providing input to the device just as you use a mouse or keyboard with your computer. You hear more about the touchscreen in the next task, but for now, go ahead and play with it for a few minutes — really, you can't hurt anything. Use the pads of your fingertips (not your fingernails) and follow these steps:

1. Tap the Settings icon. The various settings (which you read more about throughout this book) appear, as shown in **Figure 2-2.**

Figure 2-2

2. To return to the Home screen, press the Home button.

3. Swipe a finger or two from right to left on the screen. If downloaded apps fill additional Home screens, then this action moves you to the next Home screen. Note that the little dots at the bottom of the screen, above the Dock icons, indicate which Home screen is displayed. The tiny magnifying glass on the far left of the dots represents the Spotlight search screen.

4. To experience the screen rotation feature, hold the iPad firmly while turning it sideways. The screen flips to the horizontal orientation. To flip the screen back, just turn the device so it's oriented like a pad of paper again.

 You can customize the Home screen by changing its *wallpaper* (background picture) and brightness. You can read about making these changes in Chapter 4.

Goodbye Click-and-Drag, Hello Tap-and-Swipe

You can use several methods for getting around and getting things done in iPad using its Multi-Touch screen, including

➡ **Tap once.** To open an application on the Home screen, choose a field such as a search box, select an item in a list, select an arrow to move back or forward one screen, or follow an online link, tap the item once with your finger.

➡ **Tap twice.** Use this method to enlarge or reduce the display of a web page (see Chapter 5 for more about using the *Safari* web browser) or to zoom in or out in the Maps app.

➡ **Pinch.** As an alternative to the tap-twice method, you can pinch your fingers together or move them apart on the screen (see **Figure 2-3**) when you're looking at photos, maps, web pages, or e-mail messages to quickly reduce or enlarge them, respectively.

Figure 2-3

You can use the three-finger tap to zoom your screen to be even larger or use multitasking gestures to swipe with 4 or 5 fingers (see the "Explore Multitasking Gestures" task later in this chapter). This method is handy if you have vision challenges. Go to Chapter 4 to discover how to turn on this feature using Accessibility settings.

➡ **Drag to scroll (known as *swiping*).** When you press your finger to the screen and drag to the right or left or drag up or down, the screen moves (see **Figure 2-4**). Swiping to the right on the Home screen, for example, moves you to the *Spotlight* screen (the iPad search screen). Swiping up while reading an online newspaper moves you down the page; swiping down moves you back up the page.

Figure 2-4

➡ **Flick.** To scroll more quickly on a page, quickly flick your finger on the screen in the direction you want to move.

➡ **Tap the Status bar.** To move quickly to the top of a list, web page, or e-mail message, tap the Status bar at the top of the iPad screen.

➡ **Press and hold.** If you're using Notes or Mail or any other application that lets you select text, or if you're on a web page, pressing and holding text selects a word and displays editing tools you can use to select, cut or copy, and paste the text.

Try these methods now by following these steps:

1. Tap the Safari button to display the web browser. (You may be asked to enter your network password to access the network.)

2. Tap a link (typically colored text or a button or image) to move to another page.

3. Double-tap the page to enlarge it; then pinch your fingers together on the screen to reduce its size.

4. Drag one finger around the page to scroll up or down or side to side.

5. Flick your finger quickly on the page to scroll more quickly.

6. Press and hold your finger on black text that isn't a link. The word is selected and the Copy/Define tool is displayed, as shown in **Figure 2-5.** (This step is tricky, so if you don't get it right the first time, don't worry — I cover text editing in more detail in Chapter 20.)

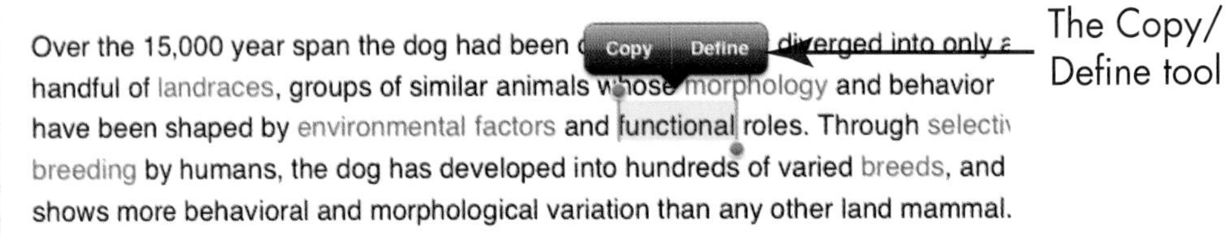

Over the 15,000 year span the dog had been [Copy] [Define] diverged into only a handful of landraces, groups of similar animals whose morphology and behavior have been shaped by environmental factors and functional roles. Through selectiv breeding by humans, the dog has developed into hundreds of varied breeds, and shows more behavioral and morphological variation than any other land mammal.

The Copy/ Define tool

Figure 2-5

7. Press and hold your finger on a link or an image. A menu appears with commands you select to open the link or picture, open it in a new tab, add it to your Reading List (see Chapter 5), or copy it. If you press and hold an image, the menu also offers the Save Image command.

8. Position your fingers slightly apart on the screen and then pinch your fingers together to reduce the page; with your fingers already pinched together, place them on the screen and then move them apart to enlarge the page.

9. Press the Home button to go back to the Home screen.

Display and Use the Onscreen Keyboard

1. The built-in iPad keyboard appears whenever you're in a text-entry location, such as a search field or writing an e-mail message. Tap the Notes icon on the Home screen to open this easy-to-use notepad and try out the keyboard.

2. Tap the note page; the onscreen keyboard appears.

3. Type a few words using the keyboard. To make the keyboard display as wide as possible, rotate your iPad to landscape (horizontal) orientation, as shown in **Figure 2-6**.

Tap in the note...

then use the Dictation key...   or keyboard to enter text

Figure 2-6

4. If you make a mistake while using the keyboard — and you will when you first use it — press the Delete key (it's in the top-right corner, with the little *x* on it) to delete text to the left of the insertion point.

5. To create a new paragraph, press the Return button just as you would do on a regular computer keyboard.

6. To type numbers and symbols, press the number key (labeled *.?123*) on either side of the spacebar (refer to **Figure** 2-6). The characters on the keyboard change. If you type a number and then tap the spacebar, the keyboard returns to the letter keyboard automatically. To return to the letter keyboard at any time, simply tap one of the letter keys (labeled *ABC*) on either side of the spacebar.

7. Use the Shift buttons just as you would on a regular keyboard to type uppercase letters or alternate characters. Tapping this once causes just the next letter you type to be capitalized.

8. Double-tap the Shift key to turn on the Caps Lock feature so that all letters you type are capitalized until you turn the feature off. Tap the Shift key once to turn off Caps Lock. (You have to turn this feature on using iPad General Settings under Keyboard.)

9. To type a variation on a symbol (for example, to see alternate currency symbols when you press the dollar sign on the numeric keyboard), hold down the key; a set of alternate symbols appears (see **Figure 2-7**). Note that this trick works with only certain symbols.

A set of alternate symbols

Figure 2-7

10. Tap the Dictation key (refer to **Figure 2-6**) to activate the Dictation feature and then speak your input. This works in several apps such as Mail, Notes, and Maps. Tap the Dictation key again (or tap in the Note) to turn off the Dictation feature.

11. To hide the keyboard, press the Keyboard key in the bottom-right corner.

12. Press the Home button to return to the Home screen.

 You can undock the keyboard to move it around the screen. To do this, press and hold the Keyboard button on the keyboard and from the pop-up menu that appears, choose Undock. Now by pressing the Keyboard button and swiping up or down, you can move the keyboard up and down on the screen. To dock the keyboard again at the bottom of the screen, press and hold the Keyboard button and choose Dock from the pop-up menu.

 To type a period and space, just double-tap the spacebar.

Use the Split Keyboard

1. With iOS 5 came the *split keyboard* feature. This allows you to split the keyboard so that each side appears nearer the edge of the iPad screen. For those who are into texting or typing with your thumbs, this feature makes it easier to reach all the keys from the sides of the device. Open an application such as Notes where you can use the onscreen keyboard.

2. Tap in an entry field or page that displays the onscreen keyboard.

3. Place two fingers in the middle of the onscreen keyboard and spread them toward the left and right. The keyboard splits, as shown in **Figure 2-8.**

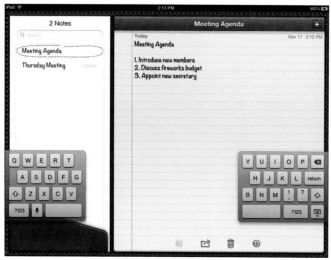

Figure 2-8

4. Now hold the iPad with a hand on either side and practice using your thumbs to enter text.

5. To rejoin the keyboard, place two fingers on each side of the keyboard and swipe to join them together again.

 When the keyboard is docked and merged at the bottom of your screen, you can also simply press the Keyboard key and swipe upward simultaneously. This undocks and splits the keyboard. To revert this, you can press the Keyboard key and swipe downward. The keyboard is docked and merged.

Flick to Search

1. The search feature in iPad helps you find photos, music, e-mails, contacts, movies, and more. Press and drag from left to right on the Home screen or tap the small magnifying glass symbol furthest to the left at the bottom of the Home screen to display the Spotlight screen. (You can also, from the primary Home screen, press the left side of the Home button to move one screen to the left.)

2. Tap in the Search iPad field (see **Figure** 2-9); the keyboard appears.

Search iPad field

Figure 2-9

3. Begin entering a search term. In the example in **Figure 2-10**, after I typed the letter *S*, the search results displayed a contact, a couple of built-in apps, and some music I had downloaded, as well as a few e-mail messages. As you continue to type a search term, the results narrow to match it.

Figure 2-10

4. Tap an item in the search results to open it.

Update the Operating System to iOS 6.0

1. This book is based on the latest version of the iPad operating system at the time of writing: iOS 6.0. To be sure you have the latest and greatest features in iPad, update your original, iPad 2, or third generation iPad to the latest iOS now (and periodically, to receive minor upgrades to 6.0).

If you have set up an iCloud account on your iPad, updates will happen automatically, or you can update over a Wi-Fi or 3G/4G connection by going to Settings⇨General⇨Software Update. To use a physical connection to a computer to update the iOS, plug the 30-pin end of the Dock Connector to USB Cable into your iPad and plug the smaller USB end into your computer USB port.

2. When iTunes opens, click your iPad (in the Devices section of the Source List on the left side of the screen) and then click the Summary tab if it isn't already displayed (see **Figure** 2-11).

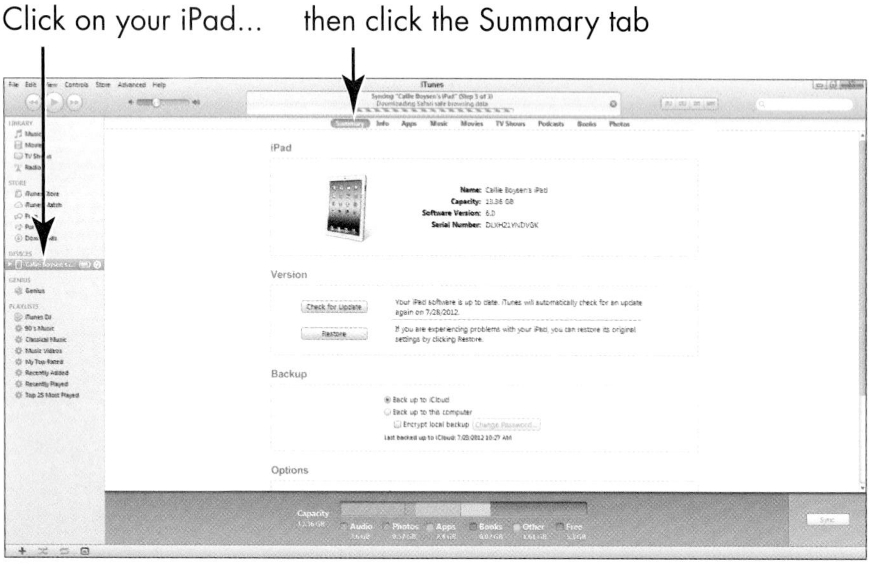

Click on your iPad...   then click the Summary tab

Figure 2-11

3. Read the note next to the Check for Update button to see whether your iOS is up to date. If it isn't, click the Check for Update button. iTunes checks to find the latest iOS version and walks you through the updating procedure.

A new iOS version may introduce new features for your iPad. If a new iOS appears after you buy this book, go to the companion website at www.ipadmadeclear. com for updates on new features introduced in major updates.

Learn Multitasking Basics

1. *Multitasking* lets you easily switch from one app to another without closing the first one and returning to the Home screen. First, open an app.

2. Double-press the Home button.

3. On the horizontal bar that appears beneath the Dock at the bottom of the screen (see **Figure 2-12**), flick to scroll to the left or right to locate another app you want to display.

Figure 2-12

4. Tap the app to open it.

 At the left end of the multitasking bar are controls for volume and playback, as well as a button that locks and unlocks screen rotation so that the screen changes based on how you are holding your iPad, or mutes the sound, depending on which feature you've set the side switch to activate (you do that in the General Settings).

Explore Multitasking Gestures

Multitasking involves jumping from one app to another. Introduced in iOS 5, the Multitasking Gestures feature allows you to use four or five fingers to multitask. You can turn on these gestures by tapping Settings on the Home screen, and then in the General Settings, tap the On/Off button for Multitasking Gestures.

Here are the three gestures you can then use:

➡ Swipe up with four or five fingers on any Home screen to reveal the multitasking bar.

➡ Swipe down with four or five fingers to remove the multitasking bar from the Home screen.

➡ With an app open, swipe left or right using four or five fingers and you move to another app.

Examine the iPad Cameras

iPad 2 introduced front- and back-facing cameras to the iPad hardware feature list. You can use the cameras to take still photos (covered in more detail in Chapter 12) or shoot videos (covered in Chapter 13).

 There's good news and bad news. The good news is that the third-generation iPad introduced a superclear Retina display and 5-megapixel rear-facing iSight camera for viewing and taking the best iPad-generated photos and video yet. The bad news is that, if you own a first generation iPad, you have no cameras at all.

For now, take a quick look at your camera by tapping the Camera app icon on the Home screen. The app opens, as shown in **Figure 2-13**.

Take photo or start recording

Options button to display grid

Previously captured image or video

Switch between front and rear cameras

Camera/Video slider

Figure 2-13

You can use the controls on the screen to

⟶ Switch between the front and rear cameras.

⟶ Change from still-camera to video-camera operation by using the Camera/Video slider.

⟶ Take a picture or start recording a video.

⟶ Turn on a grid to help you autofocus on still-photo subjects.

⟶ Open previously captured images or videos.

When you view a photo or video, you can share it by posting it to Facebook or sending it in a tweet, message, or e-mail. You can also print the image, use it as wallpaper, assign it to a contact, run a slide-show, or edit it. See Chapters 12 and 13 for more detail about using the iPad cameras.

Customize the Side Switch

Starting with iOS 4.3, you can customize the Side Switch on the top-right side of your iPad (in portrait orientation). Use these steps to set up the switch to control screen rotation or mute the sound:

1. From the Home screen, tap the Settings icon.

2. Under General settings, tap either the Lock Rotation or Mute option in the Use Side Switch To section to choose which feature you want the switch to control.

3. Press the Home button to return to the Home screen.

4. Move the side switch up or down to toggle between the settings you chose: lock or unlock screen rotation or mute or unmute sound.

Explore the Status Bar

Across the top of the iPad screen is the *Status bar* (see **Figure 2-14**). Tiny icons in this area can provide useful information such as the time, battery level, and wireless-connection status. **Table 2-1** lists some of the most common items you find on the Status bar:

| iPad | 3:30 PM | 79% |

Figure 2-14

Table 2-1	Common Status Bar Icons	
Icon	*Name*	*What It Indicates*
	Wi-Fi	You're connected to a Wi-Fi network.
	Activity	A task is in progress — a web page is loading, for example.
11:53 AM	Time	You guessed it: You see the time.
	Screen Rotation Lock	The screen is locked and doesn't rotate when you turn the iPad.
	Play	A media element (such as a song or video) is playing.
82%	Battery Life	The charge percentage remaining in the battery. The indicator changes to a lightning bolt when the battery is charging.

 If you have GPS, 3G, 4G, or Bluetooth service or a connection to a virtual private network (VPN), a corresponding symbol appears on the Status bar whenever one of these features is active. The GPS and 3G/4G icons appear only with 3G- or 4G-enabled iPad models. (If you can't even conceive of what a virtual private network is, my advice is not to worry about it.)

Take Inventory of Built-in Apps

The iPad comes with certain functionality and applications — or *apps*, for short — built in. When you look at the Home screen, you see icons for each app. This task gives you an overview of what each app does. (You can find out more about every one of them as you read different chapters in this book.) The icons in the Dock (see the "Meet the Multi-Touch Screen" task, earlier in this chapter) are, from left to right

➡ **Safari:** You use the Safari web browser (see **Figure 2-15**) to navigate on the Internet, create and save bookmarks of favorite sites, and add web clips to your Home screen so that you can quickly visit favorite sites from there. You may have used this web browser (or another such as Internet Explorer) on your desktop computer.

Figure 2-15

➡ **Mail:** You use this application to access mail accounts that you have set up in iPad. Your e-mail is then displayed without you having to browse to the site or sign in. Then you can use tools to move among a few preset mail folders, read and reply to mail, and download attached photos to your iPad. Read more about e-mail accounts in Chapter 6.

➡ **Videos:** This media player is similar to Music but specializes in playing videos and offers a few features specific to this type of media, such as chapter breakdowns and information about a movie's plot and cast. With iOS 6 this app is placed on the Dock.

➡ **Music:** Music is the name of your audio media player. Though its main function is to play music, you can use it to play podcasts or audiobooks as well.

Apps with icons above the Dock and closer to the top of the Home screen include

⟶ **Messages:** For those who have been waiting for instant messaging on iPad, the iMessage feature comes to the rescue. Using the Messages app, you can engage in live text- and image-based conversations with others via their phones or other devices that use messaging.

⟶ **Calendar:** Use this handy onscreen daybook to set up appointments and send alerts to remind you about them.

⟶ **Notes:** Enter text or cut and paste text from a website into this simple notepad app. You can't do much except save notes or e-mail them — the app has no features for formatting text or inserting objects. You'll find Notes handy, though, for simple notes on the fly.

⟶ **Reminders:** This is a useful app that centralizes all your calendar entries and alerts to keep you on schedule, as well as allowing you to create to-do lists.

⟶ **Maps:** In this cool Apple mapping program, you can view classic maps or aerial views of addresses, find directions from one place to another by car, foot, or public transportation, and view your maps in 3-D.

⟶ **Clock:** This app, new with iOS 6, allows you to display clocks from around the world, set alarms, and use timer and stopwatch features.

⟶ **Photos:** The photo application in iPad (see **Figure 2-16**) helps you organize pictures in folders, e-mail photos to others, use a photo as your iPad wallpaper, and assign pictures to contact records. You can also run slideshows of your photos, open albums, pinch or unpinch to shrink or expand photos, and scroll photos with a simple swipe. New for iPad with iOS 6, you can use the Photo Stream feature via iCloud to share photos among your friends.

➠ **Contacts:** In the address book feature (see **Figure** 2-17), you can enter contact information (including photos, if you like, from your Photos or Cameras app) and share contact information by e-mail. You can also use the search feature to find your contacts easily.

Figure 2-16

Figure 2-17

➠ **Game Center:** The Game Center app helps you browse games in the App Store and play them with other people online. You can add friends and track your scores. See Chapter 14 for more about Game Center.

➠ **iTunes:** Tapping this icon takes you to the iTunes store, where you can shop 'til you drop (or until your iPad battery runs out of juice) for music, movies, TV shows, audiobooks, and podcasts and then download them directly to your iPad. (See Chapter 8 for more about how iTunes works.)

➠ **App Store:** At the Apple Store online, you can buy and download applications that do everything from enabling you to play games to building business presentations. Some of these are even free!

➠ **Newsstand:** Similar to an e-reader for books, Newsstand is a handy reader app for subscribing to and reading magazines, newspapers, and other periodicals.

➠ **FaceTime:** The FaceTime video calling app lets you use the iPad 2 and third-generation iPad video cameras to talk face-to-face with someone who has an iPad 2 or third-generation iPad, Mac (running OS X 10.6.6 or later), fourth-generation iPod touch, or iPhone 4 or later. Chapter 7 fills you in on FaceTime features.

➠ **Camera:** As you may have read earlier in this chapter, the Camera app is control central for the still and video cameras built into the iPad 2 and later.

➠ **Photo Booth:** This fun app, which has been supplied with Mac computers for some time, lets you add effects to photos you take using your iPad camera in weird and wonderful ways.

→ **Settings:** Settings isn't exactly an app, but it's an icon you should know about, anyway: It's the central location on the iPad where you can specify settings for various functions and do administrative tasks such as set up e-mail accounts or create a password.

 The iBooks application isn't bundled with the iPad out of the box. Though iBooks is free, you have to download it from the App Store. Because the iPad has been touted as an outstanding *e-reader* — a device that enables you to read books on an electronic device, similar to the Amazon Kindle — you should definitely consider downloading the app as soon as possible. (For more about downloading applications for your iPad, see Chapter 9. To work with the iBooks e-reader application itself, go to Chapter 10.)

Lock iPad, Turn It Off, and Unlock It

Earlier in this chapter, I mention how simple it is to turn on the power to your iPad. Now it's time to put it to *sleep* (a state in which the screen goes black, though you can quickly wake up the iPad) or to turn off the power to give your new toy a rest. Here are the procedures you can use:

→ **Press the Sleep/Wake button.** The iPad goes to sleep: The screen goes black and is locked.

 If you bought a Smart Cover with your iPad 2 or third-generation iPad or a third-party case with Smart Cover functionality, just fold the cover over the front of the screen and iPad goes to sleep; open the cover to wake up the iPad. See Chapter 1 for more about iPad accessories.

→ **Press the Home button or slide the Sleep/Wake slider.** The iPad wakes up. Swipe the onscreen arrow on the Slide to Unlock bar (see **Figure 2-18**) on the bottom of the screen to unlock the iPad.

Figure 2-18

⟶ **Press and hold the Sleep/Wake button until the Slide to Power Off bar appears at the top of the screen, and then swipe the bar.** You've just turned off your iPad.

 The iPad automatically enters sleep mode after a few minutes of inactivity. You can change the time interval at which it sleeps by adjusting the Auto-Lock feature in Settings. See this book's companion Cheat Sheet at www.dummies.com/cheatsheet/ipadfor seniors to review tables of various settings.

Getting Going

*Y*our first step in getting to work with the iPad is to make sure that its battery is charged. Next, if you want to find free or paid content for your iPad from Apple, from movies to music to e-books to audiobooks, you might want to open an iTunes account.

After you have an iTunes account and the latest iTunes software on your computer, you can connect your iPad to your computer and sync them to exchange content between them (for example, to transfer your saved photos or music to the iPad). You can also use the wireless sync feature to exchange content over a wireless network.

If you prefer, you can take advantage of the new iCloud service from Apple to store and *push* (send or share) all kinds of content and data to all your Apple devices — wirelessly.

This chapter also introduces you to the *iPad User Guide*, which you access using the Safari browser on your iPad. The guide essentially serves as your iPad Help system, to provide advice and information about your magical new device.

Get ready to . . .

➡ Charge the Battery

➡ Make iPad Settings Using iTunes

➡ Sync the iPad to Your Computer Using iTunes

➡ Sync Wirelessly

➡ Understand iCloud

➡ Get an iCloud Account

➡ Make iCloud Sync Settings

➡ View the *User Guide* Online

Charge the Battery

1. My iPad showed up in the box almost fully charged, and let's hope yours did, too. Because all batteries run down eventually, one of your first priorities is to know how to recharge your iPad battery. Go get your iPad and its connector cord and power adapter.

2. Gently plug the USB end (the smaller of the two connectors) of the Dock Connector to USB Cable into the USB Power Adapter.

3. Plug the other end of the cord into the cord connector slot on the iPad (see **Figure 3-1**).

Attach the USB connector...
to the power adapter.   Then plug this
end into the iPad.

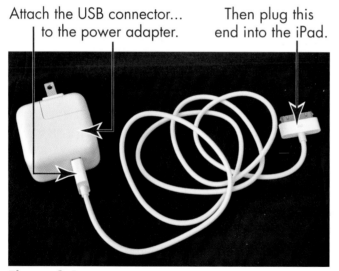

Figure 3-1

4. Unfold the two metal prongs on the power adapter (refer to **Figure 3-1**) so they extend from it at a 90-degree angle; and then plug the adapter into an electrical outlet.

If you buy the iPad Dock accessory ($29.00), you can charge your iPad while it's resting in the Dock. Just plug the larger connector into the back of the Dock instead of at the bottom of the iPad.

Make iPad Settings Using iTunes

1. Before you can use iTunes to manage your iPad, you have to download the latest version of iTunes by going to www.apple.com/itunes. You should also create an iTunes account, providing a payment method so you can use iTunes on your computer or the iTunes app on your iPad to purchase apps and content. Next, open your iTunes software on your computer. (On a Windows 7 computer, choose Start⟹All Programs⟹iTunes; on a Windows 8 computer, begin typing iTunes from the Start screen and then click iTunes in the search results; on a Mac, click the iTunes icon in the Dock or Launchpad.)

2. iTunes opens, and if you've connected it to your computer using the Dock Connector to USB cable, your iPad is listed in the Devices section of the Source List on the left, as shown in **Figure 3-2**. Click your iPad, and a series of tabs displays. The tabs offer information about your iPad and settings to determine how to download music, movies, or podcasts, for example. (You can see the simple choices on the Music tab in **Figure 3-3**.) The settings relate to the kind of content you want to download and whether you want to download it automatically (when you sync) or manually. See **Table 3-1** for an overview of the settings that are available on each tab.

Click on your iPad...   to display this series of tabs

Figure 3-2

Figure 3-3

3. Make all settings for the types of content you plan to obtain on your computer. **Table 3-1** provides information about settings on the different tabs.

Table 3-1	iPad Settings in iTunes
Tab Name	**What You Can Do with the Settings on the Tab**
Summary	Perform updates to the iPad software and set general syncing options.
Info	Specify which information to sync: Contacts, Calendars, e-mail accounts, Bookmarks, or Notes.
Apps	Sync with iPad the apps you've downloaded to your computer and manage the location of those apps and folders.
Tones	Sync ringtones and sound effects from the iTunes Tones Store.
Music	Choose which music to download to your iPad when you sync.
Movies	Specify whether to automatically download movies.
TV Shows	Choose shows and episodes to sync automatically.
Podcasts	Choose podcasts and episodes to sync automatically.
iTunes U	Set up how to sync content from the free iTunes U app for educational content.
Books	Choose to sync all, or only selected, books and audiobooks to your iPad.
Photos	Choose the folders from which you want to download photos or albums.

Sync the iPad to Your Computer Using iTunes

1. After you specify which content to download in iTunes (see the preceding task), you can use the Dock Connector to USB Cable to connect your iPad and computer at any time and sync files, contacts, calendar settings, and more. After iTunes is downloaded to your computer and your iTunes account is set up, plug the data connection cord into your iPad (using the wider connector).

2. Plug the other end of the cord into a USB port on your computer.

3. iTunes opens and shows an item for your iPad in the Source List on the left (refer to **Figure 3-2**). Your iPad screen shows the phrase *Sync in Progress*.

4. When the syncing is complete, the Lock screen returns on the iPad; iTunes shows a message above the series of tabs (refer to **Figure 3-2**), indicating that the iPad sync is complete and that you can disconnect the cable. Any media you chose to transfer in your iTunes settings, and any new photos in the photos folder on your computer, have been transferred to your iPad.

Sync Wirelessly

1. You can also use the iTunes Wi-Fi Sync setting to allow cordless syncing if you are within range of a Wi-Fi network that has a computer connected to it with iTunes installed. Tap Settings⇨General⇨iTunes Wi-Fi Sync.

2. In the dialog shown in **Figure** 3-4, tap Sync Now to sync with a computer connected to the same Wi-Fi network.

Tap this option

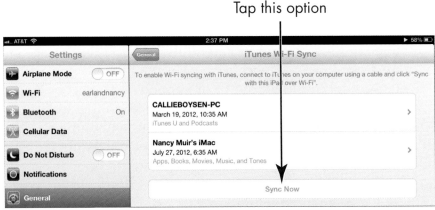

Figure 3-4

 If you have your iPad set up to sync wirelessly to your Mac or PC and both are within range of the same Wi-Fi network, iPad will appear in your iTunes Source list. This allows you to sync and manage syncing from within iTunes.

Understand iCloud

There's an alternative to syncing content using iTunes. When iOS 5 launched in fall 2011, it introduced iCloud, a service that allows you to back up all your content and certain settings such as bookmarks to online storage. That content and those settings are then pushed automatically to all your Apple devices through a wireless connection.

All you need to do is get an iCloud account, which is free, and then make settings on your devices for which types of content you want pushed to each. After you've done that, any content you create or purchase on one device — such as music, apps, books, and TV shows, as well as documents created in Apple's iWork apps, photos, and so on — can be synced among your devices automatically.

When you get an iCloud account, you get 5GB of free storage; content you purchase through Apple (such as apps, books, music, and TV shows) won't be counted against your storage. If you want additional storage, you can buy an upgrade from one of your devices. 10GB costs $20 per year; 20GB is $40 per year; and 50GB is $100 a year. Most people will do just fine with the free 5GB of storage.

To upgrade your storage, go to iCloud in Settings, tap Storage & Backup, and then tap Manage Storage. In the dialog that appears, tap Buy More Storage. Tap the amount you need and then tap Buy.

 You can make settings for backing up your content to iCloud in the iCloud section of Settings. Here you can back up content automatically or manually.

 If you pay $25 a year for the iTunes Match service, you can sync any amount of content in your iTunes library to your devices, which may be a less expensive way to go than paying for added iCloud storage. Visit `www.apple.com/itunes/itunes-match.com` for more information.

Get an iCloud Account

Before you can use iCloud, you need an iCloud account, which is tied to the Apple ID you probably already have. You can turn on iCloud when first setting up your iPad or use Settings to sign up using your Apple ID.

1. When first setting up your iPad (either a third-generation iPad or an iPad 2), in the sequence of screens that appear, you'll see the one in **Figure** 3-5. Tap Use iCloud.

Figure 3-5

2. In the next dialog, tap Back Up to iCloud.

Your account is now set up based on the Apple ID you entered earlier in the setup sequence.

Here are the steps to set up iCloud on your iPad if you didn't do so when first setting up iPad:

1. Tap Settings and then tap iCloud.

2. Tap the On/Off button to turn on iCloud.

3. Enter your Apple ID and password and tap the Sign In button. (See **Figure 3-6.**) (If you don't have an Apple ID, tap the Get a Free Apple ID button and follow the instructions to get your ID.) A dialog appears, asking whether you'd like to merge your iPad calendars, reminders, and bookmarks with iCloud. Tap OK.

Figure 3-6

4. A dialog may appear asking if you want to allow iCloud to use the location of your iPad. Tap OK. Your account is now set up.

Make iCloud Sync Settings

When you have an iCloud account up and running (see the preceding task), you have to specify which types of content should be synced with your iPad via iCloud. Note that content you purchase and download will be synced among your devices automatically via iCloud.

1. Tap Settings and then tap iCloud.

2. In the iCloud settings shown in **Figure** 3-7, tap the On/ Off button for any item that's turned off that you want to turn on (or vice versa). You can sync Mail, Contacts, Calendars, Reminders, Bookmarks, and Notes.

Select the content to sync via iCloud

Figure 3-7

3. To turn Photo Stream, Documents & Data, or Storage & Backup on or off (so you can sync photos, documents created in iWork, or settings data, respectively), tap those options on the list (refer to **Figure** 3-7) and then tap the On/Off button for each particular setting in the subsequent screen.

4. To enable automatic downloads of music, apps, and books, tap iTunes & App Stores in the Settings pane (see **Figure** 3-8).

Tap this option...   then select content to automatically
download via iCloud

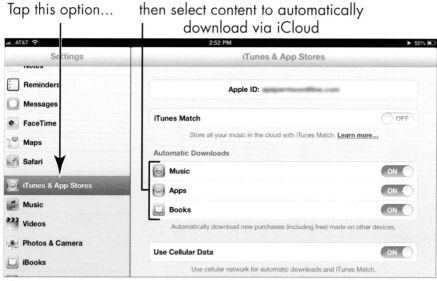

Figure 3-8

5. Tap the On/Off button for Music, Apps, or Books to set up automatic downloads of any of this content to your iPad via iCloud.

 If you want to allow iCloud to provide a service for locating a lost or stolen iPad, tap the On/Off button in the Find My iPad field to activate it. This service helps you locate, send a message to, or delete content from your iPad if it falls into other hands.

View the User Guide Online

1. The *iPad User Guide* is equivalent to the Help system you may have used on a Windows or Mac computer. You access the guide online as a bookmarked site in the Safari browser. From the iPad Home screen, tap the Safari icon.

2. Tap the Bookmark icon. On the Bookmarks menu that appears (see **Figure 3-9**), tap iPad User Guide.

Tap this option

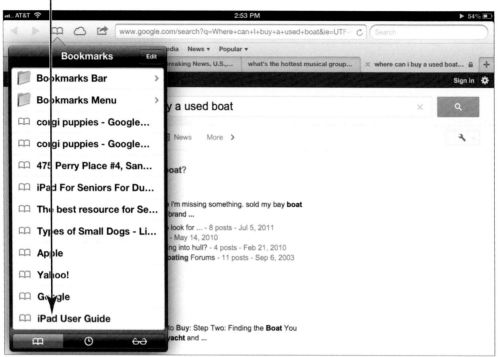

Figure 3-9

3. Tap a topic on the left to display subtopics, as shown in
   Figure 3-10.

Tap this option...   to display its subtopics

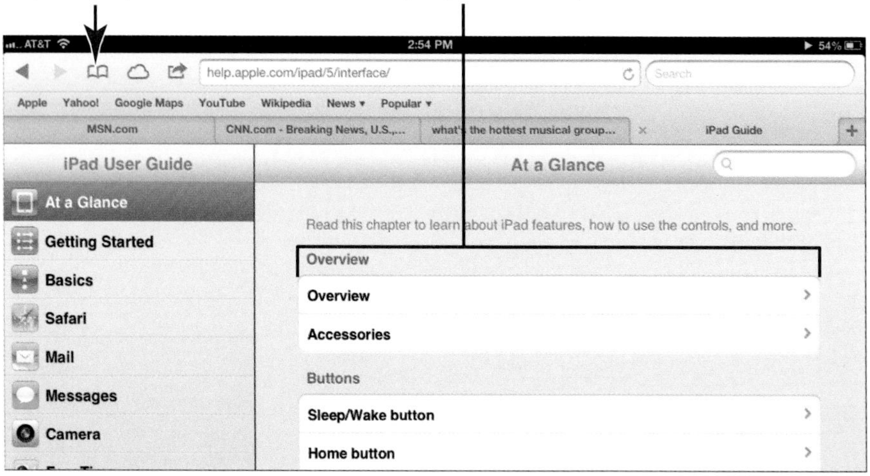

Figure 3-10

4. Tap a subtopic to display information about it, as shown in **Figure 3-11.**

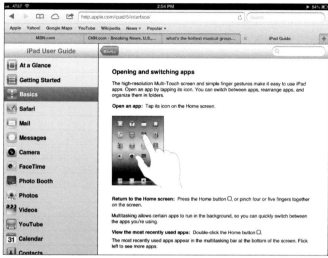

Figure 3-11

5. Tap any link in the subtopic information to access additional topics.

6. Press the Home screen button to return to the Home screen.

 To find the PDF version of the *iPad User Guide* on your browser, see `http://manuals.info.`
`apple.com/en_us/ipad_user_guide.pdf.`

Making Your iPad More Accessible

*i*Pad users are all different; some face visual, dexterity, or hearing challenges. If you're one of these folks, you'll be glad to hear that iPad offers some handy accessibility features.

To make your screen easier to read, you can adjust the brightness or wallpaper. The Zoom feature lets you enlarge the screen even more than the standard unpinch gesture on the touchscreen does. The black-and-white screen option even offers a black background with white lettering that some people find helpful when reading text. You can also set up the VoiceOver feature to read onscreen elements out loud. iPad uses the Speak Auto-text feature to tell you whenever text you enter in any iPad application is autocorrected or capitalized. You can also set a larger text size for your iPad to bring text into better focus.

If hearing is your challenge, you can do the obvious and adjust the system volume. The iPad also has a setting for mono audio that's useful when you're wearing headphones. Rather than breaking up sounds in a stereo effect, this setting puts all the sound in each

Get ready to . . .

➡ Set Brightness

➡ Change the Wallpaper

➡ Turn On Zoom

➡ Invert Screen Colors

➡ Set Up VoiceOver

➡ Use VoiceOver

➡ Adjust the Volume of Ringers and Alerts

➡ Use Mono Audio

➡ Have iPad Speak Auto-text

➡ Turn On Large Text

➡ Turn On and Work with AssistiveTouch

➡ Use Dictation on the Third-Generation iPad

➡ Focus Learning with Guided Access

ear. If you have more trouble hearing in one ear than in the other, this option can help make sounds clearer.

Turn on the AssistiveTouch Control Panel to help you make gestures and choices if you struggle with the touchscreen interface. If typing text is painful or difficult for you, consider the Dictation feature, which enables you to speak text instead of typing.

Finally, the Guided Access feature introduced with iOS 6 provides help for those who have difficulty focusing on one task. The Guided Access feature also provides a handy mode for showing presentations of content in situations where you don't want users to flit off to other apps, as in a school or a public kiosk.

Set Brightness

1. Especially when using iPad as an e-reader, you may find that a slightly dim screen reduces strain on your eyes. To adjust screen brightness, tap the Settings icon on the Home screen.

2. In the Settings screen shown in **Figure 4-1,** tap Brightness & Wallpaper.

3. To control brightness manually, tap the Auto-Brightness On/Off button (refer to **Figure 4-1**) to turn off this feature.

4. Tap and drag the Brightness slider to the right to make the screen brighter, or to the left to make it dimmer.

5. Press the Home button to close the Settings dialog.

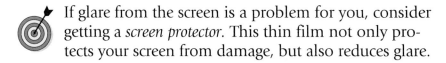

If glare from the screen is a problem for you, consider getting a *screen protector.* This thin film not only protects your screen from damage, but also reduces glare.

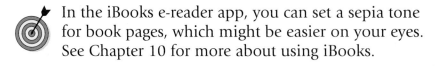

In the iBooks e-reader app, you can set a sepia tone for book pages, which might be easier on your eyes. See Chapter 10 for more about using iBooks.

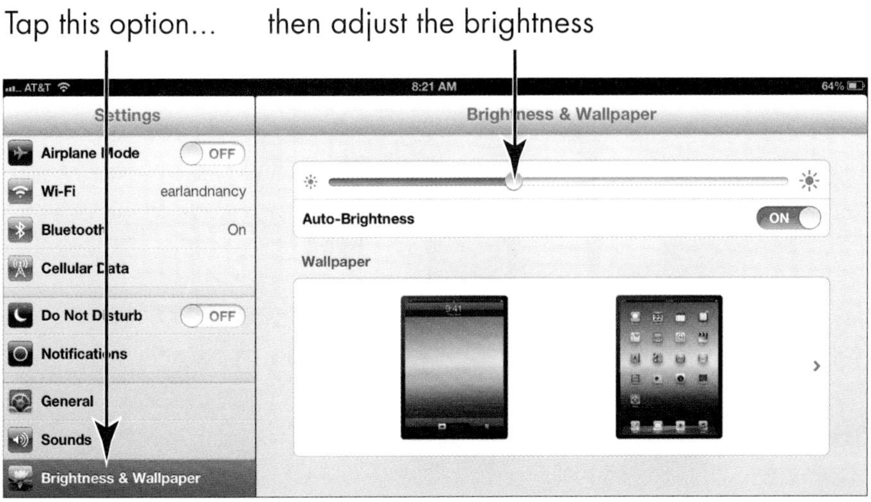

Tap this option...   then adjust the brightness

Figure 4-1

Change the Wallpaper

1. The picture of a blue pool of water — the default iPad back-ground image — may be pretty, but it may not be the one that works best for you. Choosing different wallpaper may help you to better see all the icons on your Home screen. Start by tapping the Settings icon on the Home screen.

2. In the Settings dialog, tap Brightness & Wallpaper.

3. In the Brightness & Wallpaper settings that appear, tap the arrow to the right of the iPad images displayed in the Wallpaper section (refer to **Figure** 4-1) and then tap Wallpaper.

4. The wallpaper options shown in **Figure** 4-2 appear. Tap one to select it.

Tap a wallpaper sample

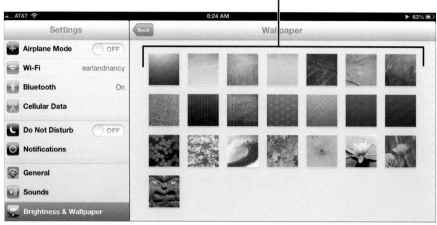

Figure 4-2

5. In the preview that appears (see **Figure** 4-3), tap Set Lock Screen (the screen that appears when you lock the iPad by tapping the power button), Set Home Screen, or Set Both.

Tap to set one or both screens

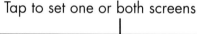

Figure 4-3

6. Press the Home button to return to your Home screen with the new wallpaper set as the background.

Turn On Zoom

1. The Zoom feature enlarges the contents displayed on the iPad screen when you double-tap the screen with three fingers. Tap the Settings icon on the Home screen and then tap General. In the General settings, tap Accessibility. The Accessibility pane, shown in **Figure** 4-4, appears.

Tap this option

Figure 4-4

2. Tap Zoom (refer to **Figure** 4-4).

3. In the Zoom pane shown in **Figure** 4-5, tap the Zoom On/Off button to turn on the feature. The screen zooms in.

Tap to turn on Zoom

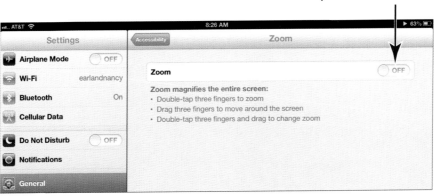

Figure 4-5

4. Press three fingers on the screen and drag to move around it.

5. Double-tap with three fingers again to go back to regular magnification.

6. Double-tap the screen using three fingers; it enlarges.

7. Press the Home button to close Settings.

 The Zoom feature works almost everywhere in iPad: in Photos, on web pages, in your Mail, in Music and Videos — give it a try!

Invert Screen Colors

1. The Invert Colors accessibility setting reverses colors on your screen so that backgrounds are black and text is white. To turn on this feature, tap the Settings icon on the Home screen.

2. Tap General and then tap Accessibility.

3. In the Accessibility dialog, tap the Invert Colors On/Off button to turn on this feature (see **Figure** 4-6).

Tap to turn on Invert Colors

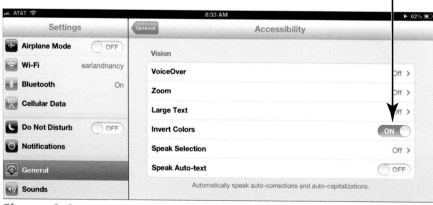

Figure 4-6

4. The colors on the screen reverse. Press the Home button to leave Settings.

 The Invert Colors feature works well in some places and not so well in others. For example, in the Photos application, pictures appear almost as photo negatives. Your Home screen image will likewise look a bit strange, and don't even think of playing a video with this feature turned on! However, if you need help reading text, White on Black can be useful in several applications.

Set Up VoiceOver

1. *VoiceOver* reads the names of screen elements and settings to you, but it also changes the way you interact with iPad. In Notes, for example, you can have VoiceOver read the name of the Notes buttons to you and, when you enter notes, it reads words or characters you've entered. It can also tell you whether features such as Autocorrect are on. To turn on VoiceOver, tap the Settings icon on the Home screen. Tap General and then Accessibility.

2. In the Accessibility pane shown in **Figure** 4-7, tap VoiceOver.

Tap this option

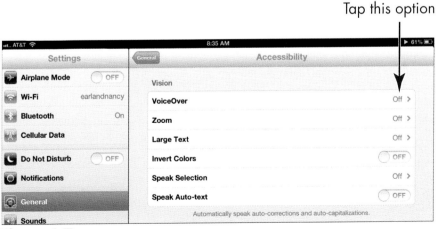

Figure 4-7

3. In the VoiceOver pane shown in **Figure** 4-8, tap the VoiceOver On/Off button at the top to turn on this feature. You see a dialog noting that turning on VoiceOver changes gestures that you use to interact with the iPad. Tap OK once to select the button, and then tap OK twice to proceed.

With VoiceOver on, you must first single-tap to select an item such as a button, which causes VoiceOver to read the name of the button to you. Then, double-tap the button to activate its function. (VoiceOver reminds you about this if you turn on Speak Hints, which is helpful when you first use VoiceOver but soon becomes annoying.)

Tap to turn on VoiceOver

Figure 4-8

4. Tap the VoiceOver Practice button to select it, and then double-tap the button to open VoiceOver Practice. (This is the new method of tapping that VoiceOver activates.) Practice using gestures such as pinching or flicking left, and VoiceOver tells you what action each gesture initiates.

5. Tap the Done button and then double-tap it to return to the VoiceOver dialog. Tap the Speak Hints field, and VoiceOver speaks the name of each tapped item. Double-tap the slider to turn off Speak Hints.

6. If you want VoiceOver to read words or characters to you (for example, in the Notes app), tap and then double-tap Typing Feedback.

7. In the Typing Feedback dialog, tap to select the option you prefer. The Words option causes VoiceOver to read words to you, but not characters, such as "dollar sign" ($). The Characters and Words option causes VoiceOver to read both, and so on.

8. Press the Home button to return to the Home screen. Read the next task to find out how to navigate your iPad after you have turned on VoiceOver.

 You can change the language that VoiceOver speaks. In General settings, choose International and then Language and select another language. This action, however, also changes the language used for labels on Home icons and various settings and fields in iPad.

 You can use the Triple-Click Home Accessibility setting to help you more quickly turn the VoiceOver and Invert Colors features on and off. In the Accessibility dialog, tap Triple-Click Home. In the dialog that appears, choose what you want a triple-click of the Home button to do: Turn on Guided Access (the default); Toggle VoiceOver on or off; toggle Invert Colors on or off; toggle the Zoom feature on or off; or toggle on the AssistiveTouch Control Panel. Now a triple-click with a single finger on the Home button provides you with the option you selected wherever you go in iPad.

Use VoiceOver

After VoiceOver is turned on, you need to figure out how it works. I won't kid you; using it is a bit tricky at first, but you'll get the hang of it! Here are the main onscreen gestures you should know how to use:

⟹ **Tap an item to select it.** VoiceOver then speaks its name.

⟹ **Double-tap the selected item.** This action activates the item.

⟹ **Flick three fingers.** It takes three fingers to scroll around a page with VoiceOver turned on.

Table 4-1 provides additional gestures to help you use VoiceOver. I suggest that, if you want to use this feature often, you read the VoiceOver section of the iPad online *User Guide,* which goes into a great deal of detail about the ins and outs of using VoiceOver.

Table 4-1	VoiceOver Gestures
Gesture	*Effect*
Flick right or left.	Select the next or preceding item.
Tap with two fingers.	Stop speaking the current item.
Flick two fingers up.	Read everything from the top of the screen.
Flick two fingers down.	Read everything from the current position.
Flick three fingers up or down.	Scroll one page at a time.
Flick three fingers right or left.	Go to the next or preceding page.
Tap three fingers.	Speak the scroll status (for example, line 20 of 100).
Flick four fingers up or down.	Go to the first or last element on a page.
Flick four fingers right or left.	Go to the next or preceding section (as on a web page).

If tapping with two or three fingers seems difficult for you, try tapping with one finger from one hand and one or two from the other. When double- or triple-tapping, you have to perform these gestures as quickly as you can for them to work.

 Check out some other settings for VoiceOver, including a choice for Braille, language Rotor for language choices, the ability to navigate images, and a setting to have iPad speak notifications.

Adjust the Volume of Ringers and Alerts

1. Though individual applications such as Music and Videos have their own volume settings, those settings work relative to your system volume setting. You can set your iPad system volume higher to help you better hear what's going on. You can simply press the volume rocker controls on the top-right side of your iPad (when it's in portrait orientation) to increase or decrease volume.

However, this doesn't change the volume of ringers and alerts unless you change one additional setting. Tap the Settings icon on the Home screen.

2. Tap Sounds.

3. In the Sounds pane that appears (see **Figure** 4-9), tap and drag the slider to the right to increase the volume, or to the left to lower it.

Adjust iPad ringer and alert volume here

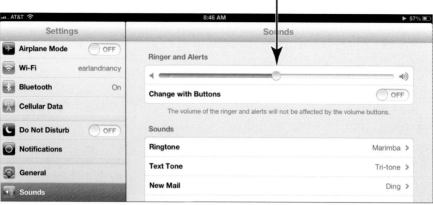

Figure 4-9

4. Press the Home button to close Settings.

 In the Sounds pane, you can manage what kind of sound plays when certain events occur (such as receiving new mail or Calendar alerts). If you need an audio clue when you lock or unlock your iPad or click keys on the onscreen keyboard, just tap the On/Off button for one of those items at the bottom of the Sounds panel to turn it on.

Use Mono Audio

1. Using the stereo effect in headphones or a headset breaks up sounds so that you hear a portion in one ear and a portion in the other ear, to simulate the way your ears process sounds. However, if you're hard of hearing or deaf in one ear, you're hearing only a portion of the sound in your hearing ear, which can be frustrating. If you have such hearing challenges and want to use iPad with a headset connected, you should turn on Mono Audio. When it's turned on, you can set up iPad to play all sounds in each ear. Tap the Settings icon on the Home screen.

2. In the General settings, tap Accessibility.

3. In the Accessibility pane shown in **Figure 4-10,** tap the Mono Audio On/Off button to turn on the feature.

4. Tap and drag the slider to L for sending sound to only your left ear or R for only the right ear.

5. Press the Home button to close Settings.

 If you have hearing challenges, another good feature that iPad provides is support for closed-captioning. In the video player, you can use the closed-captioning feature to provide onscreen text representing dialogue and actions in a movie (if it supports closed-captioning) as it plays. For more about playing videos and turning on closed-captioning, see Chapter 13.

Tap to turn on Mono Audio

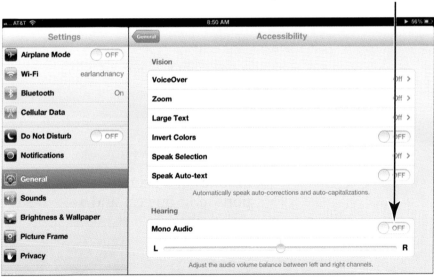

Figure 4-10

Have iPad Speak Auto-text

1. The *Speak Auto-text* feature speaks autocorrections and autocapitalizations (you can turn on both these features using Keyboard settings). When you enter text in an application such as Pages or Mail, the app then makes either type of change, while Speak Auto-text lets you know what change was made. To turn on Speak Auto-text, tap the Settings icon on the Home screen.

2. Under the General settings, tap Accessibility.

3. In the Accessibility pane shown in **Figure 4-11,** tap the Speak Auto-text On/Off button to turn on the feature.

Tap to turn on Speak Auto-text

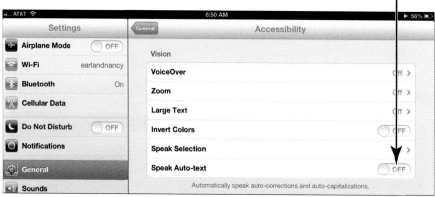

Figure 4-11

4. Press the Home button to leave Settings.

 Why would you want iPad to tell you whenever an autocorrection has been made? If you have vision challenges and you know that you typed *ain't* when writing dialogue for a character in your novel, but iPad corrected it to *isn't,* you would want to know. Similarly, if you type the poet's name *e.e. Cummings* and autocapitalization corrects it (incorrectly), you need to know immediately so that you can change it back again.

Turn On Large Text

1. If having larger text in apps such as Contacts, Mail, and Notes would be helpful to you, you can turn on the Large Text feature and choose the text size that works best for you. To turn on Large Text, tap the Settings icon on the Home screen.

2. Under the General settings, tap Accessibility.

3. In the Accessibility pane, tap the Large Text button to turn on the feature.

4. In the list of text sizes shown in **Figure** 4-12, tap the one you prefer.

Tap a text size to select it

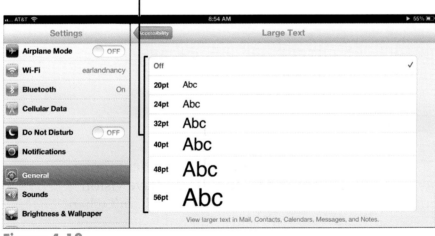

Figure 4-12

5. Press the Home button to close the Settings dialog.

 Note that enlarging text doesn't enlarge all labels in iPad such as items on menus.

Turn On and Work with AssistiveTouch

1. The AssistiveTouch Control Panel helps those who have challenges working with the touchscreen to provide input to iPad using custom gestures. To turn on AssistiveTouch, tap Settings on the Home screen and then tap General and then Accessibility.

2. In the Accessibility pane, tap AssistiveTouch. In the pane that appears, tap the On/Off button for AssistiveTouch to turn it on (see **Figure 4-13**). The AssistiveTouch Control Panel (the gray square) appears on the top left side of the screen and it will appear in the same location in whatever apps you display on your iPad, though you can tap and drag it to a different corner.

Tap to turn on AssistiveTouch

Figure 4-13

3. Tap the AssistiveTouch Control Panel to display options, as shown in **Figure 4-14**.

Figure 4-14

4. You can tap Gestures, Favorites, or Device on the panel to see additional choices, or tap Home to go directly to the Home screen. After you've chosen an option, tapping the Back arrow takes you back to the main panel.

Table 4-2 shows the major options available in the AssistiveTouch Control Panel.

Table 4-2	AssistiveTouch Controls
Control	**Purpose**
Gestures	Choose the number of fingers to use for gestures on the touchscreen.
Favorites	Displays a set of gestures with only the Pinch gesture preset; you can tap any of the other blank squares to add your own favorite gestures.
Device	You can rotate the screen, lock the screen, turn volume up or down, mute or unmute sound, or shake iPad to undo an action using the presets in this option.
Home	Sends you to the Home screen.

Use Dictation on the Third-Generation iPad

1. Dictation is a simple but powerful feature that allows you to tap a button on the onscreen keyboard and speak text rather than typing it in several apps, including Mail, Notes, Contacts, Calendar, Messages, and Reminders. With an app where you want to enter text open, tap in the text entry area to display the onscreen keyboard.

2. Tap the Dictation key on the keyboard, and the Dictation icon shown in **Figure** 4-15 appears.

Dictation icon indicating Dictation feature is active

Dictation key

Figure 4-15

3. Speak the text you want to include in the document. Keeping to about a paragraph of text at a time is a good rule of thumb.

4. Tap the Dictation icon to stop recording. Wait a moment, and the text appears in your document.

 Dictation accepts spoken punctuation such as "comma" and "period;" however, it accepts only limited directions such as "new paragraph" to move to the next line in the document. You may find that you have to edit a few things after dictating. For example, I dictated "item two" and got "item to" in one instance.

Focus Learning with Guided Access

1. Guided Access is a new feature of iOS 6. You can use it to limit a user's access on iPad to a single app and even limit access within that app to certain features. This is considered useful in several situations, ranging from a student with attention deficit disorder in a classroom to a public setting such as a kiosk where you don't want users to open other apps. To turn on Guided Access, tap Settings and then tap General.

2. Tap Accessibility and then tap Guided Access. On the screen that follows (see **Figure** 4-16) tap the Guided Access On/Off button to turn the feature on.

3. Tap Set Passcode to activate a passcode so those using an app cannot return to the Home screen to access other apps. In the Set Passcode dialog that appears (see **Figure** 4-17), enter a passcode using the number pad. Enter the number again when prompted.

Tap to turn on Guided Access

Figure 4-16

Figure 4-17

4. Press the Home button and tap an app to open it.

5. Triple-press the Home button. You are presented with three choices along the bottom of the screen; make your choices here and then tap the Start button in the top left corner of the screen to implement Guided Access:

- **Hardware Buttons:** Tap to turn this Always On or Always Off. If you don't want users to be able to adjust volume using the volume toggle on the side of the iPad, for example, use this setting.

- **Touch:** If you don't want users to be able to use the touchscreen, turn this off.

- **Motion:** Turn this setting off if you don't want users to move the iPad around, for example to play a race car–driving game.

6. You can also use your finger to circle areas of the screen you want to disable, such as the Store button in the Music app.

7. Triple-press the Home button and then enter your passcode, if you set one, to return to the Home screen.

Part II
Taking the Leap Online

The 5th Wave   By Rich Tennant

"Hold on Barbara. I'm pretty sure there's an app for this."

Browsing the Internet with Safari

Getting on the Internet with your iPad is easy using its Wi-Fi, 3G or 4G capabilities. After you're online, the pre-installed browser (software that helps you navigate the Internet's contents), *Safari*, is your ticket to a wide world of information, entertainment, education, and more. Safari will look familiar to you if you've used it on a PC or Mac device before, though the way you move around by using the iPad touchscreen might be new to you. If you've never used Safari, this chapter takes you by the hand and shows you all its ins and outs.

In this chapter, you discover how to connect your iPad to the Internet, navigate among web pages, and use iCloud tabs to share your browsing among devices. Along the way, you see how to place a bookmark for a favorite site or place a web clip on your Home screen. You can also view your browsing history, save online images to your Photo Library, post photos to certain sites from within Safari, or e-mail or tweet a hotlink to a friend. You explore the Safari Reader and Safari Reading List features and learn how to keep yourself safer while online using private browsing. Finally, you review the simple steps involved in printing what you find online.

Get ready to . . .

➡ Connect to the Internet

➡ Explore Safari

➡ Navigate among Web Pages

➡ Use Tabbed Browsing

➡ View Browsing History

➡ Search the Web

➡ Add and Use Bookmarks

➡ Save Links and Web Pages to Safari Reading List

➡ Use Safari Reader

➡ Add Web Clips to the Home Screen

➡ Save an Image to Your Photo Library

➡ Post Photos from Safari

➡ Send a Link

➡ Make Private Browsing and Cookie Settings

➡ Print a Web Page

➡ Understand iCloud Tabs

Connect to the Internet

How you connect to the Internet depends on which iPad model you own:

➡ The Wi-Fi–only iPad connects to the Internet only via a Wi-Fi network. You can set up this type of network in your own home using your computer and some equipment from your Internet provider. You can also connect over public Wi-Fi networks, referred to as *hotspots*. You'll probably be surprised to discover how many hotspots your town or city has: Look for Internet cafés, coffee shops, hotels, libraries, and transportation centers such as airports or bus stations, for example. Many of these businesses display signs alerting you to their free Wi-Fi.

➡ If you own a Wi-Fi + 3G or Wi-Fi + 4G–enabled iPad, you can still use a Wi-Fi connection (in fact when one is available iPad defaults to using Wi-Fi to save money), but you can also use the paid data network provided by AT&T, Verizon, or Sprint to connect from just about anywhere you can get cellphone coverage via a cellular network.

If you have a 3G or 4G model, you don't have to do anything; with a contract for coverage, the connection is made automatically wherever cellular service is available, just as it is on your cellphone. To connect to a Wi-Fi network, you have to complete a few steps.

1. When you're in range of a hotspot, if access to several nearby networks is available, you see a message asking you to tap a network name to select it. After you select one (or if only one network is available), you see a message similar to the one shown in **Figure 5-1**.

2. If you're required to enter a network password, do so.

3. Tap the Join button and you're connected.

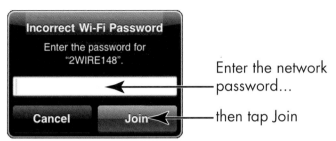

Enter the network
password...

then tap Join

Figure 5-1

 See Chapter 1 for more about the capabilities of different iPad models and the costs associated with 3G and 4G.

 Free public Wi-Fi networks typically don't require passwords, or the password is posted prominently for all to see. However, it's then possible for someone else to track your online activities over these *unsecured* networks. Avoid accessing financial accounts or sending e-mails with sensitive information when connected to a public hotspot.

Explore Safari

1. After you're connected to a network, tap the Safari icon on the Home screen. Safari opens, probably displaying the Apple iPad home page the first time you go online (see **Figure 5-2**).

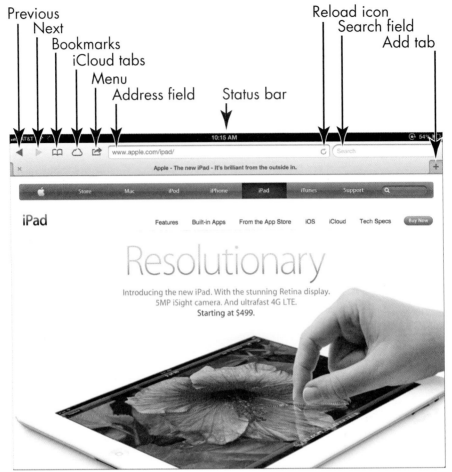

Figure 5-2

2. Put two fingers together on the screen and swipe them outward to enlarge the view, as shown in **Figure 5-3**. Double-tap the screen with a single finger to restore the default screen size.

3. Put your finger on the screen and flick upward to scroll the page contents and view additional contents lower on the page.

Figure 5-3

4. To return to the top of the web page, put your finger on the screen and drag downward or tap the Status bar at the top of the screen.

Using the pinch method to enlarge or reduce the size of a web page on your screen allows you to view what's displayed at various sizes, giving you more flexibility than the double-tap method.

When you enlarge the display, you gain more control using two fingers to drag from left to right or from top to bottom on the screen. On a reduced display, one finger works fine for making these gestures.

Navigate among Web Pages

1. Tap in the Address field. The onscreen keyboard appears (see **Figure 5-4**).

Delete key

Go key

Figure 5-4

2. To clear the field, press the Delete key on the keyboard. Enter a web address; for example, you can go to this book's companion website: www.ipadmadeclear.com.

3. Tap the Go key on the keyboard (refer to **Figure 5-4**). The website appears.

 • If, for some reason, a page doesn't appear, tap the Reload icon on the right end of the Address field.

 • If Safari is loading a web page and you change your mind about viewing the page, you can tap the Stop icon (the X), which appears on the right end of the Address field during this process, to stop loading the page.

 4. Tap the Previous arrow to go backward to the last page you displayed.

5.Tap the Next arrow to go forward to the page you just came from.

6. To follow a link to another web page (links are typically colored text or graphics), tap the link with your finger. To view the destination web address of the link before you tap it, just touch and hold the link; a menu appears that displays the address at the top, as shown in **Figure 5-5**.

←The link's web address

Figure 5-5

 By default, AutoFill is turned on, causing entries you make in fields such as the Address field to automatically display possible matching entries. You can turn off AutoFill by using iPad Settings for Safari.

Use Tabbed Browsing

1. Safari includes a feature called *tabbed browsing*, which allows you to have several websites open at once on separate tabs so you can move easily among those sites. To add a tab, tap the Add Tab button near the upper-right corner of the screen (refer to **Figure 5-2**).

2. The search field becomes active and the onscreen keyboard appears. Begin to type a search term or speak it using the Dictation feature, and possible matches appear (see **Figure 5-6**). You can tap an item from a recent search, or tap in the search field and enter the name of a site to open. The site opens on a new tab.

Figure 5-6

3. You can now switch among open sites by tapping
another tab.

 Using tabbed browsing, you can place not only a site
on a tab, but also a search results screen. If you
recently searched for something, those search results
are on your Recent Searches list. Also, if you are displaying a search results page when you tap the plus
sign to add a tab, the first ten suggested sites in the
results will be listed there for you to choose from.

View Browsing History

 1. As you move around the web, your browser keeps a
record of your browsing history. This record can be
handy when you want to visit a site that you viewed
previously but you've now forgotten its address. With
Safari open, tap the Bookmarks icon.

2. On the menu shown in **Figure 5-7,** tap the History tab in
the middle of the bottom of the menu.

History tab

Figure 5-7

3. In the History list that appears (see **Figure** 5-8), tap a date if available, and then tap a site to navigate to it.

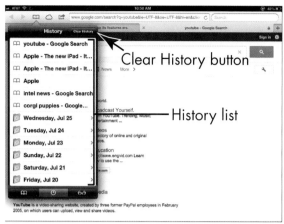

Figure 5-8

 To clear the history, tap the Clear History button (refer to **Figure 5-8**). This button is useful when you don't want your spouse or grandchildren to see where you've been browsing for birthday or holiday presents!

 You can tap and hold the Previous button to quickly display a list of your browsing history.

Search the Web

1. If you don't know the address of the site you want to visit (or you want to research a topic or find other information online), get acquainted with Safari's Search feature on iPad. By default, Safari uses the Google search engine. With Safari open, tap in the Search field. The onscreen keyboard appears.

2. You can tap on one of the suggested sites, or enter a search word or phrase, and tap the Search key (see **Figure 5-9**) on your keyboard.

Suggested sites   Search field

Figure 5-9

3. In the search results, tap a link to visit that site.

 To change your default search engine from Google to Yahoo! or Bing, in iPad Settings, tap Safari and then tap Search Engine. Tap Yahoo! or Bing, and your default search engine changes.

 You can browse for specific items such as images, videos, or maps by tapping the corresponding link at the top of the Google results screen. Also, tap the More button in this list to see even more options to narrow your results, such as searching for books or YouTube videos on the subject.

Add and Use Bookmarks

1. Bookmarks are a way to save favorite sites so you can easily visit them again. With a site you want to bookmark displayed, tap the Menu icon.

2. On the menu that appears (see **Figure 5-10**), tap Bookmark.

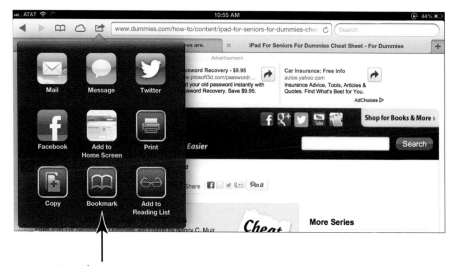

Tap this option

Figure 5-10

3. In the Add Bookmark dialog, shown in **Figure 5-11,** edit the name of the bookmark if you want. To do so, tap the name of the site and use the onscreen keyboard to edit its name.

4. Tap the Save button.

5. To go to the bookmark, tap the Bookmarks icon.

Edit name here

Figure 5-11

6. On the Bookmarks menu that appears (see **Figure 5-12**), tap the bookmarked site you want to visit.

Tap a bookmark site to visit it

Figure 5-12

 If you want to sync your bookmarks on your iPad browser to your computer, connect your iPad to your computer and make sure that the Sync Safari Bookmarks setting on the Info tab of iTunes is activated.

To create folders to organize your bookmarks, tap the Bookmarks icon and then tap Bookmarks Bar. On the Bookmarks Bar menu that appears, tap the Edit button, then tap the New Folder button and enter a name for the new folder. The next time you add a bookmark, you can then choose, from the dialog that appears, any folder to which you want to add the new bookmark.

Save Links and Web Pages to Safari Reading List

 1. The Safari Reading List provides a way to save web pages that contain content you want to read at a later time so you can easily visit them again. With iOS 6, you can save not only links to sites, but also the sites themselves, which allows you to read the content even when you're offline. With a site you want to add to your Reading List displayed, tap the Bookmarks icon.

2. On the menu that appears, tap the Reading List tab (it looks like a pair of reading glasses). Tap the + Symbol in the top right corner and the site is added to your list.

3. To view your Reading List, tap the Bookmarks icon and tap the Reading List tab.

4. On the Reading List that appears (see **Figure 5-13**), tap the content you want to revisit and resume reading.

If you want to see both Reading List material you've read and that material you haven't read, tap the All tab in the Reading List pane (refer to **Figure 5-13**). To see only the material you haven't read, use the Unread tab.

Tap an item to resume reading

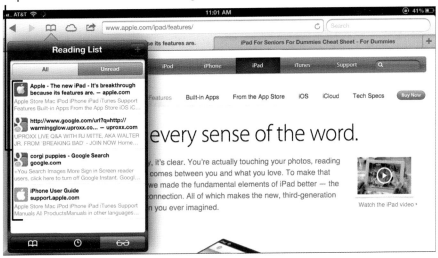

Figure 5-13

 To save an image to your Reading List, tap and hold the image until a menu appears, and then tap Add to Reading list. To delete an item, with the Reading List displayed, swipe left or right on an item and a Delete button appears. Tap this button to delete the item from Reading List.

Use Safari Reader

1. The Safari Reader feature gives you an e-reader type of experience right within your browser, removing other stories and links as well as those distracting advertisements. When you're on a site reading content such as an article, Safari displays a Reader button on the right side of the Address field (see **Figure 5-14**). Tap the Reader button. The content appears in a reader format (see **Figure 5-15**).

Reader button

Figure 5-14

Tap here to increase/decrease the text size

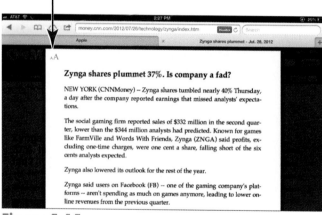

Figure 5-15

2. Scroll down the page. The entire content is contained in this one long page.

3. When you finish reading the material, just tap the Reader button in the Address field again to return to the material's source.

 To enlarge the text in the Reader, tap the large *A* in the top-left corner (refer to **Figure 5-15**).

If you're holding iPad in landscape orientation, the Reader window doesn't fill the screen, and you can tap either side of the Reader window to go back to the source material.

Add Web Clips to the Home Screen

 1. The *Web Clips* feature allows you to save a website as an icon on your Home screen so that you can go to the site at any time with one tap. With Safari open and displaying the site you want to add, tap the Menu icon.

2. On the menu that appears (refer to **Figure 5-10**), tap Add to Home Screen.

3. In the Add to Home dialog that appears (see **Figure 5-16**), you can edit the name of the site to be more descriptive, if you like. To do so, tap the name of the site and use the onscreen keyboard to edit its name.

Edit the name here

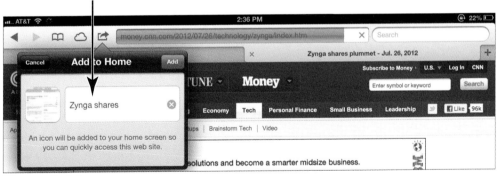

Figure 5-16

4. Tap the Add button. The site is added to your Home screen.

 Remember that you can have as many as 11 Home screens on your iPad to accommodate all the web clips and apps you download (though there is a limit to how many will fit). If you want to delete an item from your Home screen for any reason, press and hold the icon on the Home screen until all items on the screen start to jiggle and Delete icons appear on all items except the preinstalled apps. Tap the Delete icon on each item you want to delete, and it's gone. (To get rid of the jiggle, press the Home button.)

Save an Image to Your Photo Library

1. Display a web page that contains an image you want to copy.

2. Press and hold the image. The menu shown in **Figure 5-17** appears.

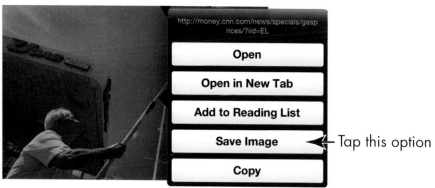

http://money.cnn.com/news/specials/gasp rices/?iid=EL

Open

Open in New Tab

Add to Reading List

Save Image ←— Tap this option

Copy

Figure 5-17

3. Tap the Save Image option (refer to **Figure 5-17**). The image is saved to your library.

Be careful about copying images from the Internet and using them for business or promotional activities. Most images are copyrighted, and you may violate the copyright even if you simply use an image in (say) a brochure for your association or a flyer for your community group. Note that some search engines' advanced search settings offer the option of browsing only for images that aren't copyrighted.

Post Photos from Safari

1. Before iOS 6, you had to post photos from within apps such as Photos. Now you can post photos to sites such as eBay, craigslist, or Facebook from within Safari, rather than going through Photos or Videos. In this example, go to Facebook and sign in.

2. Tap an Add Photo/Video or similar link, like the one shown in **Figure 5-18.**

Tap the Add Photo/Video link

Figure 5-18

3. Tap Choose File.

4. Tap Choose Existing to get a photo on your iPad (if you'd rather take a picture or record a video at this point, tap Take Photo or Video; see **Figure 5-19**).

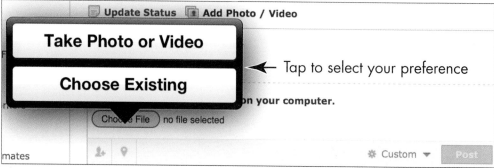

Figure 5-19

5. Tap on a photo source such as Camera Roll or My Photo Stream and then tap the photo or video you want to post. Tap Post to post the photo or video.

Send a Link

 1. If you find a great site that you want to share, you can do so easily by sending a link in an e-mail. With Safari open and the site you want to share displayed, tap the Menu icon.

2. On the menu that appears (refer to **Figure 5-10),** tap Mail.

3. On the message form that appears (see **Figure 5-20**), enter a recipient's e-mail address, a subject, and your message.

Figure 5-20

4. Tap Send, and the e-mail goes on its way.

 The e-mail is sent from the default e-mail account you have set up on iPad. For more about setting up an e-mail account, see Chapter 6.

 To tweet the link using your Twitter account, in Step 2 of this task, choose Tweet, enter your tweet message in the form that appears, and then tap Send. For more about using Twitter with iPad, see Chapter 7.

Make Private Browsing and Cookie Settings

Apple has provided some privacy settings for Safari that you should consider using. *Private Browsing* automatically removes items from the download list, stops Safari from letting AutoFill save information used to complete your entries in the search or address fields as you type, and doesn't save some browsing history information. These features can keep your online activities more private. The *Accept Cookies* setting allows you to stop the downloading of *cookies* (small files that document your browsing history so you can be recognized the next time you go to or move within a site) to your iPad.

You can control both settings by choosing Safari in the Settings window. Tap to turn Private Browsing on or off (see **Figure 5-21**). Tap the arrow on Accept Cookies and choose to never save cookies, always save cookies, or save only cookies from visited sites.

Tap to turn on Private Browsing

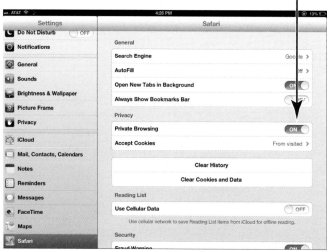

Figure 5-21

 You can also use those two settings to clear your browsing history, saved cookies, and other data manually (refer to **Figure 5-21**).

Print a Web Page

 1. If you have a wireless printer that supports Apple's AirPrint technology (a few manufacturers such as Canon, Epson, and Hewlett-Packard include AirPrint printers in their product lines), you can print web content using a wireless connection. With Safari open and the site you want to print displayed, tap the Menu icon.

 The apps Printopia and AirPrint Activator 2 make any shared or network printer on your home network visible to your iPad. Printopia has more features, but is more expensive, whereas AirPrint Activator is free.

2. On the menu that appears (refer to **Figure 5-10**), tap Print.

3. In the Printer Options dialog that appears (see **Figure 5-22**), tap Select Printer. In the list of printers that appears, tap the name of your wireless printer.

Tap Select Printer

Figure 5-22

4. Tap either the plus or minus button in the Copy field to adjust the number of copies to print.

5. Tap Print to print the displayed page.

 If you don't have an AirPrint–compatible wireless printer or don't wish to use an app to help you print wirelessly, just e-mail a link to the web page to yourself, open the link on your computer, and print from there.

Understand iCloud Tabs

 1. iCloud Tabs are new with iOS 6. What this feature allows you to do is to access all browsing history among your different devices that use iCloud compatible browsers from any device. iCloud Tabs could come in handy; for example, say you begin to research a project on your iPad before you leave home. Then, as you sit in a waiting room with your iPhone, just pick up where you left off.

First, check to make sure both devices are using the same iCloud account by tapping Settings, then iCloud and checking the account name.

2. Open Safari on your iPad and tap the iCloud Tabs button shown in **Figure 5-23**. All items in your other devices' browsing history are displayed (in the case of **Figure 5-23**, the history is for my iPhone).

Tap the iCloud Tabs button

Figure 5-23

Working with E-mail in Mail

*S*taying in touch with others by using e-mail is a great way to use your iPad. You can access an existing account using the handy Mail app supplied with your iPad or sign in to your e-mail account using the Safari browser. Using Mail involves adding one or more existing e-mail accounts by way of iPad Settings. Then you can use Mail to write, format, retrieve, and forward messages from one or more accounts.

Mail offers the capability to mark the messages you've read, delete messages, organize your messages in folders, and use the handy search feature. New with iOS 6 comes the ability to create a VIP list so you're notified when that special person sends you an e-mail. In this chapter, you read all about Mail and its various features.

Get ready to . . .

→ Add an iCloud, Gmail, Yahoo!, AOL, or Microsoft Hotmail Account

→ Set Up a POP3 E-mail Account

→ Open Mail and Read Messages

→ Reply to or Forward E-mail

→ Create and Send a New Message

→ Format E-mail

→ Search E-mail

→ Delete E-mail

→ Organize E-mail

→ Create a VIP List

Add an iCloud, Gmail, Yahoo!, AOL, or Microsoft Hotmail Account

1. You can add one or more e-mail accounts, including the e-mail account associated with your iCloud account, using iPad Settings. If you have an iCloud, Gmail, Yahoo!, AOL, or Microsoft Hotmail account, iPad pretty much automates the setup. To set up iPad to retrieve messages from your e-mail account at one of these popular providers, first tap the Settings icon on the Home screen.

2. In the Settings dialog, tap Mail, Contacts, Calendars. The settings shown in **Figure 6-1** appear.

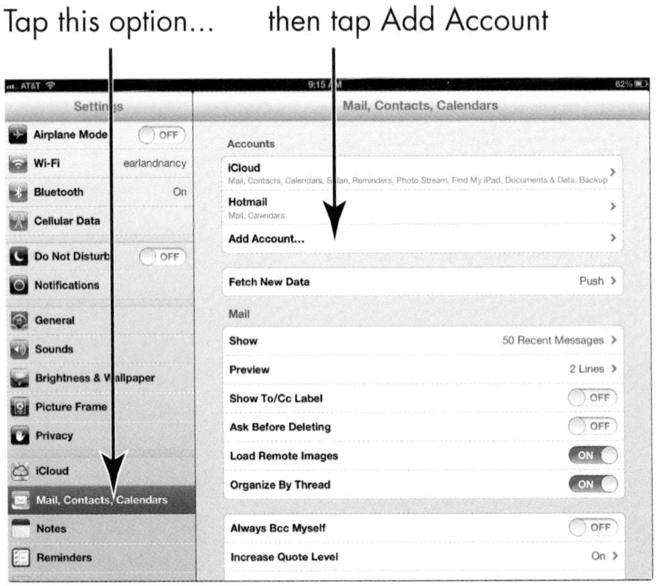

Tap this option...   then tap Add Account

Figure 6-1

3. Tap Add Account. The options shown in **Figure 6-2** appear.

Tap to select your e-mail provider

Figure 6-2

4. Tap iCloud, Gmail, Yahoo!, AOL, or Microsoft Hotmail. Enter your account information in the form that appears (see **Figure 6-3**).

Enter your account info

Figure 6-3

5. After iPad takes a moment to verify your account information, you can tap any on/off button to have Mail, Contacts, Calendars, or Reminders from that account synced with iPad.

6. When you're done, tap Save. The account is saved, and you can now open it using Mail.

Set Up a POP3 E-mail Account

1. You can also set up most popular e-mail accounts, such as those available through EarthLink or a cable provider's service, by obtaining the host name from the provider. To set up an existing account with a provider other than iCloud, Gmail, Microsoft Hotmail, Yahoo!, or AOL, you have to enter the account settings yourself. First, tap the Settings icon on the Home screen.

2. In Settings, tap Mail, Contacts, Calendars, and then tap the Add Account button at the top right.

3. On the screen that appears (refer to **Figure 6-2**), tap Other.

4. On the screen shown in **Figure 6-4**, tap Add Mail Account.

Tap this option

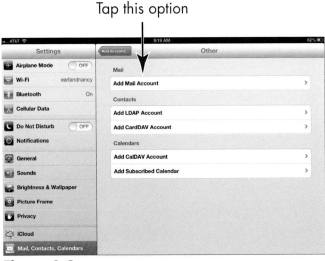

Figure 6-4

5. In the form that appears (refer to **Figure 6-3**), enter your name and an account address, password, and description, and then tap Next. iPad takes a moment to verify your account and then returns you to the Mail, Contacts, Calendars page, with your new account displayed.

 If you have a less mainstream e-mail service, you may have to enter the mail server protocol (POP3 or IMAP — ask your e-mail provider for this information) and your password. iPad will probably add the outgoing mail server (SMTP) information for you, but if it doesn't, you may have to enter it yourself. Your Internet service provider (ISP) can provide this information, as well.

6. To make sure that the Account field is set to On for receiving e-mail, tap the account name on the Mail, Contacts, Calendars page of Settings. In the dialog that appears, tap the On/Off button for the Mail field and then tap Done to save the setting. You can now access the account through Mail.

 If you turn on Calendars in the Mail account settings, any information you've put into your calendar in that e-mail account will be brought over into the Calendar app on your iPad and reflected in the Notification Center (discussed in more detail in Chapter 17).

Open Mail and Read Messages

1. Tap the Mail app icon, located on the Dock on the Home screen (see **Figure 6-5**). A red circled number on the icon indicates the number of unread e-mails in your Inbox.

Tap this icon

Figure 6-5

2. In the Mail app, if the Inbox you want isn't displayed, tap the arrow shaped-button to the left of the word *Inbox* (see **Figure 6-6**) to display your list of inboxes. Tap the inbox whose contents you want to display.

Tap this button

Figure 6-6

3. Tap a message to read it. It opens (see **Figure 6-7**).

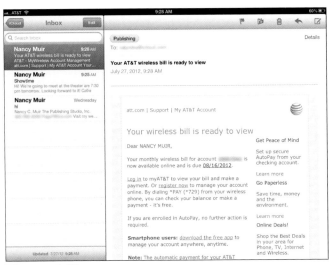

Figure 6-7

4. If you need to scroll to see the entire message, just place your finger on the screen and flick upward to scroll down.

You can swipe right while reading a message in portrait orientation to open the Inbox list of messages, and then swipe left to hide the list.

 You can tap the Hide button (top-right corner of the message) to hide the address details (the To field) so that more of the message appears on your screen. To reveal the field again, tap the Details button (which becomes the Hide button when details are displayed).

 E-mail messages you haven't read are marked with a blue circle in your Inbox. After you read a message, the blue circle disappears. You can mark a read message as unread to help remind you to read it again later. With a message open, tap the Flag button in the toolbar above a message and then tap Mark as Unread. To flag a message — which places a little flag next to it in your inbox, helping you to spot items of more importance or to read again — tap the Flag button and then tap Flag.

 To escape your e-mail now and then (or to avoid having messages retrieved while you're at a public Wi-Fi hotspot), you can stop retrieval of e-mail by using the Fetch New Data control in the Mail, Contacts, Calendars section of iPad Settings.

 To refresh your inbox so you can view new e-mails, simply swipe downward on the Mail screen. This handy feature arrived with iOS 6.

Reply To or Forward E-mail

1. With an e-mail message open (see the previous task), tap the Reply/Forward button, shown in **Figure 6-8**.

Reply/Forward button

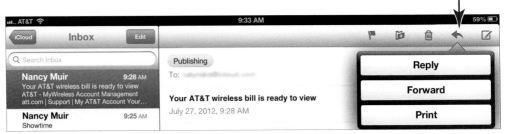

Figure 6-8

2. Take one of the following actions:

- Tap Reply to respond to the sender of the message or, in a message that had other recipients, tap Reply All to respond to the sender and all recipients. The Reply Message form, shown in **Figure 6-9,** appears. Tap in the message body and enter a message.

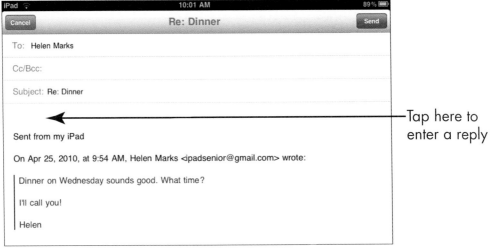

Tap here to enter a reply

Figure 6-9

- Tap Forward to send the message to somebody else. The form shown in **Figure 6-10** appears. Enter a recipient in the To field and then tap in the message body and enter a message.

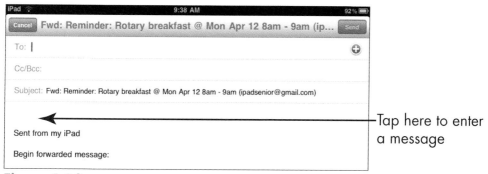

Figure 6-10

3. Tap Send. The message goes on its way.

 If you want to copy an address from the To field to the Cc or Bcc field, tap and hold the address and drag it to the other field.

Create and Send a New Message

 1. With Mail open, tap the New Message icon. A blank message form appears (see **Figure 6-11**).

Figure 6-11

 2. Enter a recipient's address in the To field either by typing or by tapping the Dictation key on the onscreen keyboard and speaking the address. If you have saved addresses in Contacts, tap the plus sign (+) in the Address field to choose an addressee from the Contacts list that appears.

3. If you want to send a copy of the message to other people, enter their addresses in the Cc/Bcc field. If you want to send both carbon copies and *blind* carbon copies (copies you don't want other recipients to be aware of), note that when you tap the Cc/Bcc field, two fields are displayed; use the Bcc field to specify recipients of blind carbon copies.

4. Enter the subject of the message in the Subject field.

5. Tap in the message body and type your message.

6. Tap Send.

 Mail keeps a copy of all deleted messages for a time in the Trash folder. To view deleted messages, tap the Inbox button and then, in the dialog that appears, tap the Mailboxes button to show all mailboxes. If you have more than one mail account (therefore more than one mailbox), tap the account name in the Accounts list in the Mailboxes pane and a list of folders opens. Tap the Trash folder and all deleted messages are displayed.

Format E-mail

1. A feature that arrived with iOS 5 was the capability to apply formatting to e-mail text. You can use bold, underline, and italic formats, and indent text using the Quote Level feature.

2. Tap the text in a message and choose Select or Select All to select a single word or all the words in the e-mail. Note that if you select a single word, handles appear that you can drag to add adjacent words to your selection.

3. To apply bold, italic, or underline formatting, tap the B/U button (see **Figure 6-12**).

Tap this button

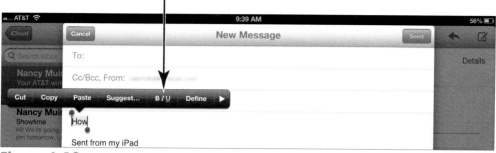

Figure 6-12

4. In the toolbar that appears (see **Figure 6-13**) tap Bold, Italics, or Underline to apply the respective formatting.

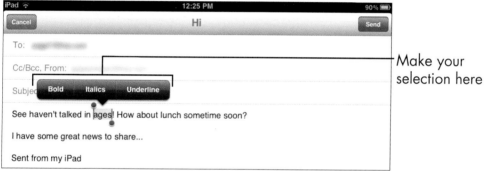

Make your selection here

Figure 6-13

5. To change the indent level, tap at the beginning of a line and then tap the arrow at the far end of the toolbar (refer to **Figure 6-12**). In the toolbar that appears, tap Quote Level.

6. Tap Increase to indent the text or Decrease to move indented text further toward the left margin.

 To use the Quote Level feature, make sure it's on using the iPad Settings. Tap Mail, Contacts, Calendars, and then tap the Increase Quote Level On/Off button.

Search E-mail

1. What if you want to find all messages from a certain person or that contain a certain word in the Subject field? You can use Mail's handy Search feature to find these e-mails. With Mail open, tap an account to display its inbox.

2. In the Inbox, tap in the Search field. The onscreen keyboard appears.

3. Enter a search term or name as shown in **Figure 6-14**.

Enter a search term here

Search results

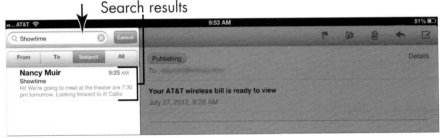

Figure 6-14

4. Tap the From, To, or Subject tab to view messages that contain the search term in one of those fields, or tap the All tab to see messages in which any of these three fields contains the term. Matching e-mails are listed in the results (refer to **Figure 6-14**).

 You can also use the Spotlight Search feature covered in Chapter 2 to search for terms in the To, From, or Subject lines of mail messages.

 To start a new search or go back to the full Inbox, tap the Delete key in the top-right corner of the onscreen keyboard to delete the term or just tap the Cancel button.

Delete E-mail

1. When you no longer want an e-mail cluttering your Inbox, you can delete it. With the Inbox displayed, tap the Edit button. Circular check boxes are displayed to the left of each message (see **Figure 6-15**).

Tap to select a message   Check marks indicate selected messages

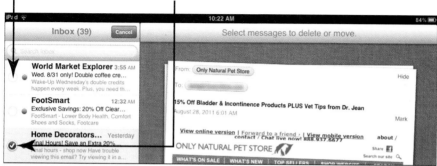

Figure 6-15

2. Tap the circle next to the message you want to delete. (You can tap multiple items if you have several e-mails to delete.) A message marked for deletion shows a check mark in the circular check box (refer to **Figure 6-15**).

3. Tap the Delete button at the bottom of the Inbox dialog. The message is moved to the Trash folder.

 You can also delete an open e-mail by tapping the Trashcan icon on the toolbar that runs across the top of Mail or swiping left or right on a message displayed in an inbox and tapping the Delete button that appears.

Organize E-mail

1. You can move messages into any of several predefined folders in Mail. (These will vary depending on your e-mail provider and the folders you've created on their server.) After displaying the folder containing the message you want to move (for example, an Archive, Trash, or Inbox), tap the Edit button. Circular check boxes are displayed to the left of each message (refer to **Figure 6-15**).

2. Tap the circle next to the message you want to move.

3. Tap the Move button.

4. In the Mailboxes list that appears on the left (see **Figure 6-16**), tap the folder where you want to store the message. The message is moved.

Figure 6-16

 If you receive a junk e-mail, you might want to move it to the Spam or Junk folder if your e-mail account provides one. Then any future mail from the same sender is automatically placed in the Spam or Junk folder.

 If you have an e-mail open, you can move it to a folder by tapping the Folder icon on the toolbar along the top. The Mailboxes list appears; tap a folder to move the message.

Create a VIP List

 1. iOS 6 brings a new feature to Mail called VIP List. This is a way to create a list of senders; when any of these senders send you an e-mail, you are notified through the Notifications feature of iPad. In the Mailboxes list of Mail, tap the arrow to the right of VIP (see **Figure 6-17**).

Tap this arrow

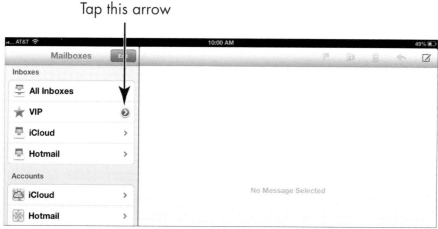

Figure 6-17

2. Tap Add VIP and your Contacts list appears (see **Figure 6-18**). Tap a contact to add that person to the VIP List.

Tap a contact to add them to the VIP List

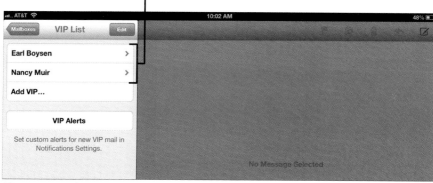

Figure 6-18

3. Press the Home button and then tap Settings.

4. Tap Notifications and then tap Mail. In the settings that appear, shown in **Figure 6-19,** tap VIP.

Tap this option

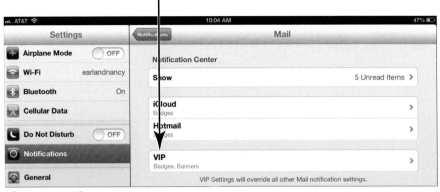

Figure 6-19

5. Tap the Notification Center On/Off button to turn on notifications for VIP mail.

6. Tap an alert style and choose whether a badge icon, sound, or preview should occur. You can also choose to display the notification on your Lock Screen (see **Figure 6-20**).

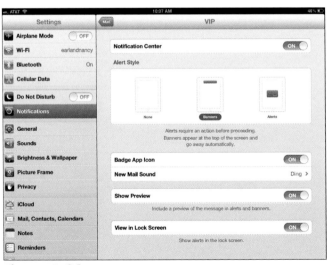

Figure 6-20

7. Press the Home button to close Settings. New mail from your VIPs should now appear in Notifications when you swipe down from the top of the screen, and depending on the settings you chose, may cause a sound to play or a note to appear on your Lock Screen, or a blue star icon to appear to the left of these messages in Mail inbox.

Getting Social with FaceTime, Twitter, and iMessage

FaceTime is an excellent video-calling app that's been available on the iPhone since the release of iPhone 4 in mid-2010; it then came to the iPad line and the Mac. The app lets you call people who have FaceTime on their devices using either a phone number or an e-mail address. You and your friend or family member can see each other as you talk, which makes for a much more personal calling experience.

Twitter is a social networking service referred to as a *microblog* because it involves only short posted messages. Twitter has been incorporated into iOS 5 and later so you can "tweet" people from within the Safari, Photos, Camera, YouTube, Maps, and many other apps. You can also download the free Twitter app and use it to post tweets whenever you like.

Finally, iMessage is an instant messaging (IM) feature available through the preinstalled Messages app. IM involves sending a text message to somebody's iPhone (using their phone

Get ready to . . .

- ➡ Understand Who Can Use FaceTime
- ➡ Get an Overview of FaceTime
- ➡ Make a FaceTime Call with Wi-Fi or 3G/4G
- ➡ Accept and End a FaceTime Call
- ➡ Switch Views
- ➡ Experience Twitter on iPad
- ➡ Set Up an iMessage Account
- ➡ Use iMessage to Address, Create, and Send Messages
- ➡ Clear a Conversation

number) or iPod touch or iPad (using their e-mail address) to carry on an instant conversation.

In this chapter, I introduce you to FaceTime, Twitter, and iMessage and review their simple controls. In no time, you'll be socializing with all and sundry.

Understand Who Can Use FaceTime

Here's a quick rundown of what device and what information you need for using FaceTime's various features:

⟹ FaceTime is available on the iPad 2 and third-generation iPad.

⟹ You can use FaceTime to call people who have iPhone 4 or later, iPad 2, third-generation iPad, fourth-generation iPod touch, or Mac (running Mac OS X 10.6.6 or later).

⟹ You can use a phone number to connect with iPhone 4 or later.

⟹ You can connect using an e-mail address with a Mac, iPod touch, iPad 2, or third-generation iPad.

Get an Overview of FaceTime

The FaceTime app works with the cameras built into the iPad 2 and third-generation iPad and lets you call other folks who have a device that supports FaceTime (see the previous task for compatibility). You can use FaceTime to chat while sharing video images with another person. This preinstalled app is useful for seniors who want to keep up with distant family members and friends and see (as well as hear) the latest-and-greatest news.

You can make and receive calls with FaceTime using a phone number (iPhone 4 or later) or an e-mail account (iPad 2, third-generation iPad, iPod touch, or Mac) and show the person on the other end what's going on around you. Just remember that you can't adjust audio volume from within the app or record a video call. Nevertheless, on the positive side, even though its features are limited, this app is straightforward to use.

You can use your Apple ID and e-mail address to access FaceTime, so it works pretty much right away after you install it. See Chapter 3 for more about getting an Apple ID.

 If you're having trouble using FaceTime, make sure the FaceTime feature is turned on. That's quick to do: Tap Settings on the Home screen, tap FaceTime, and then tap the On/Off button to turn it on, if necessary. On this Settings page, you can also select the e-mail account that others can use to call you.

Make a FaceTime Call with Wi-Fi or 3G/4G

1. If you know that the person you're calling has FaceTime on an iPhone 4 or later, an iPad 2 or later, or a Mac, first be sure you've added that person to your iPad Contacts. (See Chapter 18 for how to do this.)

2. Tap the FaceTime app icon on the Home screen; on the screen that appears, tap the Contacts button in the bottom-right corner of the screen.

3. Scroll to locate a contact and tap the contact's name to display his or her information (see **Figure 7-1**).

Figure 7-1

4. Tap the contact's stored phone number that is FaceTime-capable or e-mail address that's been associated with FaceTime by the contact. You've just placed a FaceTime call!

 You have to use the appropriate method for placing a FaceTime call depending on the kind of device the person you're calling has. If you're calling someone with an iPhone 4 or later, you should use a phone number the first time you call and thereafter you can use the phone number or e-mail address; if you're calling an iPad 2 or third-generation iPad, an iPod touch, or a FaceTime for Mac user, you have to make the call using that person's e-mail address.

 When you call somebody using an e-mail address, the person must be signed in to his or her Apple ID account and have verified that the address can be used for FaceTime calls. iPad 2 and third-generation iPad and iPod touch (fourth-generation and later) users can make this setting by tapping Settings and then FaceTime; FaceTime for Mac users make this setting by clicking FaceTime⇨Preferences.

5. When the person accepts the call, you see the recipient's image and a small draggable box containing your image (see **Figure** 7-2).

Figure 7-2

 You can also simply go to the Contacts app, find a contact, and tap the FaceTime icon in that person's record and then tap their phone number or e-mail address in the pop-up that appears to make a FaceTime call. You can also open the Messages app and tap the FaceTime button to initiate a call.

 To view recent calls, tap the Recents button in Step 2. Tap a recent call, and iPad displays that person's information. You can tap the contact to call the person back.

 If you have iOS 6, you can use FaceTime over both a Wi-Fi network and your iPad 3G or 4G connection. However, remember that if you use FaceTime over a phone connection, you may incur costly data usage fees.

Accept and End a FaceTime Call

1. If you're on the receiving end of a FaceTime call, accepting the call is about as easy as it gets. When the call comes in, tap the Accept button to take the call, or tap the Decline button to reject it (see **Figure 7-3**).

Figure 7-3

2. Chat away with your friend, swapping video images. To end the call, tap the End button (see **Figure 7-4**).

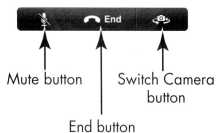

Mute button   Switch Camera button

End button

Figure 7-4

To mute sound during a call, tap the Mute button (refer to **Figure** 7-4). Tap the button again to unmute your iPad or iPhone.

 To add a caller to your Favorites list, with FaceTime open, tap the Favorites button and then tap the plus sign (+) and select a name from the contact list. You can then locate the person to make a call to him by tapping Favorites and choosing that person from a short list rather than scrolling through all your Contacts.

 If you'd rather not be available for calls you can go to Settings and turn on the Do Not Disturb feature. This stops any incoming calls or notifications. After you turn on Do Not Disturb you can schedule when its active, allow calls from certain people, or allow a second call from the same person in a three minute interval to go through by using the Do Not Disturb settings under Notifications.

Switch Views

1. When you're on a FaceTime call, you might want to use iPad's built-in camera to show the person you're talking to what's going on around you. Tap the Switch Camera button (refer to **Figure** 7-4) to switch from the front-facing camera that's displaying your image to the back-facing camera that captures whatever you're looking at (see **Figure** 7-5).

Figure 7-5

2. Tap the Switch Camera button again to switch back to the front camera displaying your image.

Experience Twitter on iPad

Twitter is a social networking service for *microblogging,* which involves posting very short messages (limited to 140 characters) online so your friends can see what you're up to. You can go to www.twitter.com to sign up with the service; you can also download and use a free Twitter app for iPad to manage your Twitter account. After you have an account, you can post "tweets," have people follow your tweets, and follow the tweets that other people post.

With iOS 5 for iPad, the ability to tweet became integrated into several apps. You can post tweets using the Menu button within Safari, Photos, Camera, YouTube, and Maps. First, go to iPad Settings and tap Twitter. Then tap the Install button and add your account information.

Now when you're using Safari, Photos, Camera, YouTube, or Maps, you can choose Twitter from any Menu button. You'll see a Tweet form like that shown in **Figure 7-6.** Just write your message in the form and then tap Send.

Enter your message here...   then tap Send

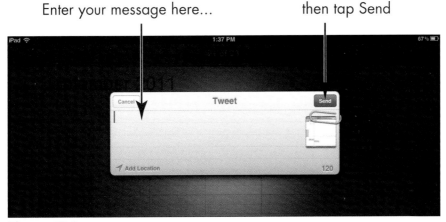

Figure 7-6

See Chapters 5, 12, or 13 for more about tweeting from the Safari, Photos, or YouTube apps.

Set Up an iMessage Account

1. iMessage is a feature that was new in iOS 5 (available through the preinstalled Messages app) that allows you to send and receive instant messages (IM) to others using an Apple iOS device or suitably configured Macs. Instant messaging differs from e-mail or tweeting in an important way. Whereas you might e-mail somebody and wait days or weeks before that person responds, or you might post a tweet that could sit there awhile before anybody views it, with instant messaging, communication happens immediately. You send an IM, and it appears on somebody's Apple device right away, and assuming the person wants to participate, a live conversation begins immediately, allowing a back and forth dialog in real time. To set up iMessage, tap Settings on the Home screen.

2. Tap Messages, and the settings shown in **Figure 7-7** appear.

Make sure this is set to On

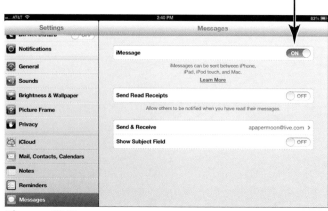

Figure 7-7

3. If iMessage isn't set to On (refer to **Figure** 7-7), tap the On/Off button to turn it on.

4. Check the Send & Receive setting to be sure the e-mail account associated with your iPad is correct (this should be set up automatically based on your Apple ID).

5. To allow a notice to be sent when you've read somebody's messages, tap the On/Off button for Send Read Receipts. You can also choose to show a subject field in your messages.

6. Press the Home button to leave the settings.

 To change the e-mail account that iMessage uses, tap Send & Receive, tap Add Another Email, and then follow the directions to add another e-mail account.

Use iMessage to Address, Create, and Send Messages

1. Now you're ready to use iMessage. From the Home screen, tap the Messages icon. In the screen that appears (see **Figure** 7-8), you tap the New Message button to begin a conversation.

New Message button   Address field   Plus icon

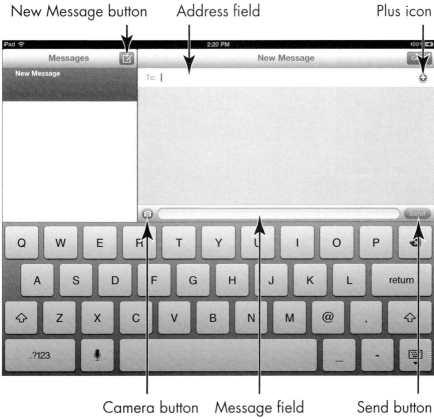

Camera button   Message field   Send button

Figure 7-8

2. You can address a message in a couple of ways:

- Begin to type an address in the To: field, and a list of matching contacts appears. Or tap the Dictation key on the onscreen keyboard and speak the address.

- Tap the plus icon on the right of the address field, and the All Contacts list is displayed, as shown in **Figure 7-9.**

Figure 7-9

3. Tap a contact on the list you choose from in Step 2. If the contact has both an e-mail address and phone number stored, the Info dialog appears, allowing you to tap one or the other, which addresses the message.

4. To create a message, simply tap in the message field near the bottom of the screen and type or dictate your message.

5. To send the message, tap the Send button (refer to **Figure 7-8**). When your recipient(s) responds, you'll see the conversation displayed on the right side of the screen, as shown in **Figure 7-10**.

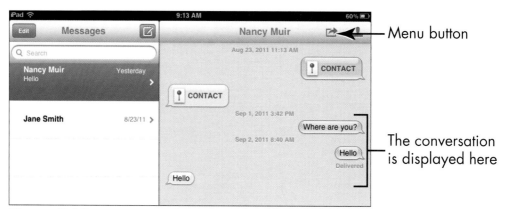

Figure 7-10

You can address a message to more than one person by simply choosing more recipients in Step 2 in the preceding steps.

 If you want to include a photo or video with your message, tap the Camera button to the left of the message field (refer to **Figure 7-8**). Tap Take Photo or Video or Choose Existing and then tap Use to attach a photo or video. When you send your message, the photo or video will go along with your text.

Clear a Conversation

1. When you're done chatting, you might want to clear a conversation to remove the clutter before you start a new one. With Messages open, tap the Menu button (refer to **Figure 7-10**).

2. Tap the Clear All button (see **Figure 7-11**).

Clear All button

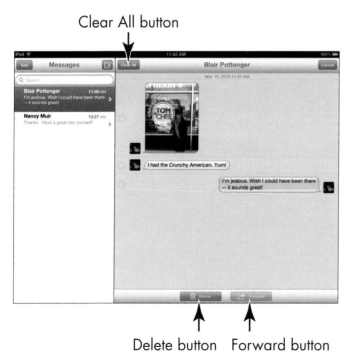

Delete button   Forward button

Figure 7-11

3. Tap Clear Conversation.

 You can also tap the Menu button, then tap the text of a particular conversation, and then tap the Delete or Forward button on the bottom of the screen (refer to **Figure 7-11**) to delete that one conversation or forward its contents to somebody. One final option is to tap on text and then tap the Edit button and tap the Delete button to the left of a comment to delete it.

Shopping the iTunes Store

*T*he iTunes app that comes preinstalled in iPad lets you easily shop for music, movies, TV shows, and audiobooks at Apple's iTunes Store.

In this chapter, you discover how to find content on the iTunes website. The content can be downloaded directly to your iPad, or to another device and then synced to your iPad. In addition, I cover a few options for buying content from other online stores.

Note that I cover opening an iTunes account and downloading iTunes software to your computer in Chapter 3. If you need to, refer to Chapter 3 to see how to handle these two tasks before digging in to this chapter.

Get ready to . . .

→ Explore the iTunes Store

→ Find a Selection

→ Preview Music, a Movie, or an Audiobook

→ Buy a Selection

→ Rent Movies

→ Shop Anywhere Else

→ Enable Auto Downloads of Purchases from Other Devices

Explore the iTunes Store

1. Visiting the iTunes Store from your iPad is easy with the built-in iTunes app. Tap the iTunes icon on the Home screen.

2. If you're not already signed in to iTunes, the dialog shown in **Figure 8-1** appears, asking for your iTunes password. Enter your password and tap OK.

Tap here and enter your password

Figure 8-1

3. Tap the Music button in the row of buttons at the bottom of the screen, if it's not already selected, to view selections as shown in **Figure 8-2**.

4. Tap the See All link to display more music selections (refer to **Figure 8-2**).

See All link

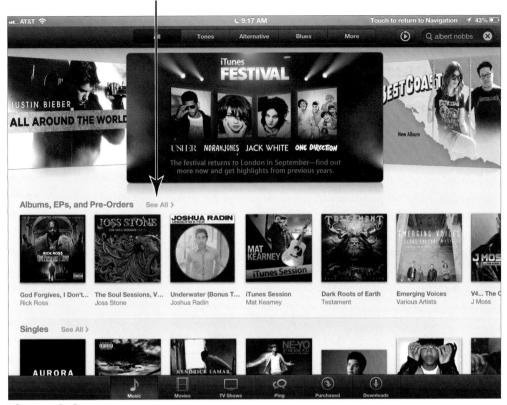

Figure 8-2

5. Tap the button in the top-left corner labeled Music to go back to the featured Music selections, and then tap the More button at the top of the screen. This step displays a list of music categories you can choose from; click one. Items in the category are organized by criteria such as New and Noteworthy Albums and Top Songs.

6. Tap any listed item to see more details about it, as shown in **Figure** 8-3.

Figure 8-3

 The navigation techniques in these steps work essentially the same in any of the content categories (the buttons at the bottom of the screen), which include Music, Movies, and TV Shows. Just tap one to explore it.

 Podcasts and iTunes U (courses) used to be accessible through the iTunes Store, but now you have to install separate apps for them. Go to the App Store on your iPad and search for Podcasts or iTunes U and install these free apps to get access to this additional content.

Find a Selection

You can look for a selection in the iTunes Store several ways. You can use the Search feature, search by genre or category, or view artists' pages. Here's how these work:

⟶ Tap in the Search field shown in **Figure 8-4** and enter a search term using the onscreen keyboard. Tap the Search button on the keyboard or, if a suggestion in the list of search results appeals to you, just tap it.

Enter a search term

Figure 8-4

⟶ Tap a category button at the top of the screen, or tap the More button. A list of genres or categories like the one shown in **Figure 8-5** appears.

More button

Figure 8-5

⟶ On a description page that appears when you tap a selection, you can find more offerings by people involved. For example, for a music selection, tap the artist's name to follow a link to a page showing all of that artist's selections. For a movie, tap the name of someone in the movie credits to see more of that person's work, as shown for Robert Downey Jr. in **Figure 8-6**.

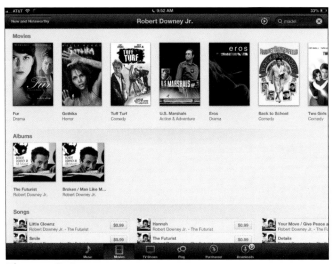

Figure 8-6

 If you find a selection you like, tap the Menu button on its description page to share your discovery with a friend via e-mail, Message, Twitter, or Facebook. A message appears with a link your friend can click to view the selection. Enter an address in the To field and tap Send or Post. Your friend is now in the know.

 When displaying items on the home page for any type of content, tap the See All link to see all featured selections rather than only the top New and Noteworthy selections.

Preview Music, a Movie, or an Audiobook

1. Because you've already set up an iTunes account (if you haven't done so yet, see Chapter 3), when you choose to buy an item, it's automatically charged to the credit card or PayPal account you have on record or against any allowance you have outstanding from an iTunes gift card. You might want to preview an item before you buy it. If you like it, buying and downloading are then easy and quick. Open iTunes and use any method outlined in earlier tasks to locate a selection you might want to buy.

2. Tap the item to see detailed information about it, as shown in **Figure 8-7**.

Tap here to watch the trailer

Figure 8-7

3. For a movie selection, tap the Play button (refer to **Figure 8-7**) to view the theatrical trailer if one's available (for audiobooks, tap the Preview button to play a preview). If you're looking at a music selection, tap the track number or name of a selection, as shown in **Figure 8-8**.

Tap a track name or number to listen to a preview

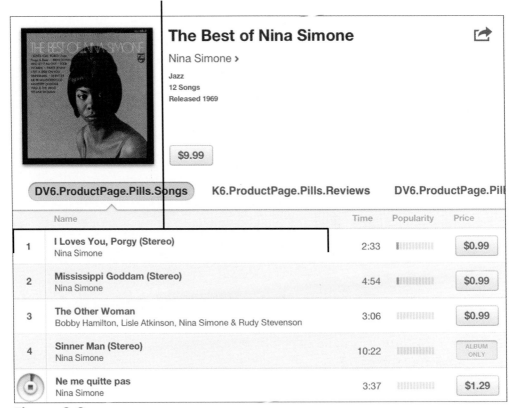

Figure 8-8

Buy a Selection

1. When you find an item you want to buy, tap the button that shows either the price (if it's a selection available for purchase; see **Figure 8-9**) or the button with the word *Free* on it (if it's a selection available for free).

2. The button label changes to Buy X, where X is the type of content you're buying such as a song or album (refer to **Figure 8-9**).

Tap the price button

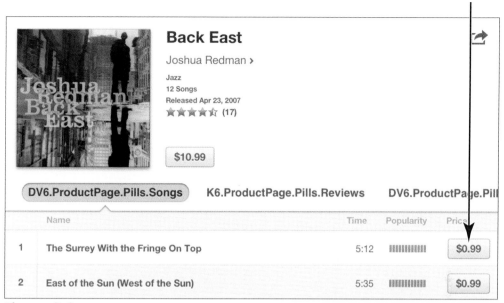

Figure 8-9

3. Tap the Buy *X* button. The iTunes Password dialog appears (refer to **Figure 8-1**).

4. Enter your password and tap OK. The item begins downloading (see **Figure 8-10** to see a movie download in progress), and the cost is automatically charged against your account. When the download finishes, you can view the content using the Music or Video app, depending on the type of content.

The selection is being downloaded

Figure 8-10

If you want to buy music, you can open the description page for an album and click the album price, or buy individual songs rather than the entire album. Tap the price for a song, and then proceed to purchase it.

 Note the Redeem button on many iTunes screens. Tap this button to redeem any iTunes gift certificates you might have received from your generous friends, or from yourself.

 If you don't want to allow purchases from within apps (for example Music or Videos) but rather want to allow purchases only through the iTunes store, you can go to Settings, General, tap Restrictions, then tap Enable Restrictions, and enter a passcode. After you've set a passcode, you can tap individual apps to turn on restrictions for them, as well as for actions such as deleting apps or using Siri.

 If you have a 3G or 4G iPad model, you can allow content to be downloaded over your 3G cellular network. Be aware, however, that this could incur hefty data charges with your provider. However, if you aren't near a Wi-Fi hotspot, it might be your only option. Go to Settings, Store and tap the On/Off button for the Cellular setting.

Rent Movies

1. In the case of movies, you can either rent or buy content. If you rent, which is less expensive, you have 30 days from the time you rent the item to begin to watch it. After you've begun to watch it, you have 24 hours remaining from that time to watch it on the same device as many times as you like. With iTunes open, tap the Movies button.

2. Locate the movie you want to rent and tap the Rent button, shown in **Figure 8-11**.

Figure 8-11

3. The gray Rent button changes to a green Rent Movie button (see **Figure 8-12**); tap it to confirm the rental. The movie begins to download to your iPad immediately, and your account is charged the rental fee.

Figure 8-12

4. To check the status of your download, tap the Downloads button. The progress of your download is displayed. After the download is complete, you can use either the Music or Videos app to watch it. (See Chapters 11 and 13 to read about how these apps work.)

Some movies are offered in high-definition versions. These *HD* movies look great on that crisp, colorful iPad screen, especially if you have a third-generation iPad with Retina display.

 You can also download content to your computer and sync it to your iPad. See Chapter 3 for more about this process.

Shop Anywhere Else

One feature that's missing from the iPad is support for *Flash*, a format of video playback that many online video-on-demand services use. Many online stores that sell content such as movies and music are hurriedly adding iPad-friendly videos to their collections, so you do have alternatives to iTunes for your choice of movies and TV shows. You can also shop for music from sources other than iTunes such as Amazon.com.

You can open accounts at one of these stores by using your computer or your iPad's Safari browser and then following the store's instructions for purchasing and downloading content.

These sources offer iPad-compatible video content, and more are opening all the time:

➡ **ABC:** http://abc.go.com

➡ **CBS News:** www.cbsnews.com

➡ **Clicker:** www.clicker.com

➡ **Netflix:** www.netflix.com

➡ **Ustream:** www.ustream.tv

For non–iPad-friendly formats, you can download the content on your computer and stream it to your iPad using Air Video ($2.99) on the iPad and Air Video Server (which is free) using your Mac or Windows computer. For more information, go to www.inmethod.com/air-video/index.html. Another free utility for Mac and Windows that converts most video to an iPad-friendly format is HandBrake. Go to http://handbrake.fr for more information.

Enable Auto Downloads of Purchases from Other Devices

1. With iCloud, you can make a purchase or download free content on any of your Apple devices and have those purchases automatically copied onto all your Apple devices. To enable this auto download feature on iPad, start by tapping Settings on the Home screen.

 To use iCloud, first set up an iCloud account. See Chapter 3 for detailed coverage of iCloud, including setting up your account.

2. Tap iTunes & App Stores.

3. In the options that appear, tap the On/Off button to turn on any category of purchases you want to auto download to your iPad from other Apple devices: Music, Apps, or Books (see **Figure 8-13**).

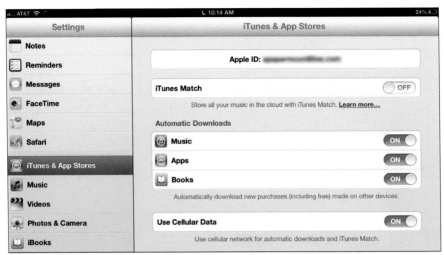

Figure 8-13

 At this point, Apple doesn't offer an option of auto-downloading video content using these settings, probably because video is such a memory hog. You can always download video directly to your iPad through the iTunes or iTunes U (for educational content) apps or sync to your computer using iTunes to get the content.

Expanding Your iPad Horizons with Apps

*S*ome *apps* (short for *applications*) come pre-installed on your iPad, such *as* Contacts and Videos. But there's a world of other apps out there that you can get for your iPad, some for free (such as iBooks) and some for a price (typically, from $0.99 to about $10, though some can top out at $90 or more).

Apps range from games to financial tools and productivity applications, such as the iPad version of Pages, the Apple software for word processing and page layout.

In this chapter, I suggest some apps you might want to check out and explain how to use the App Store feature of iPad to find, purchase, and download apps.

Get ready to . . .

➦ Explore Senior-Recommended Apps

➦ Search the App Store

➦ Get Applications from the App Store

➦ Organize Your Applications on Home Screens

➦ Organize Apps in Folders

➦ Delete Applications You No Longer Need

➦ Update Apps

Explore Senior-Recommended Apps

As I write this book, apps are being furiously created for iPad, so many more apps that could fit your needs will be available by the time you have this book in your hands. Still, to get you exploring what's available, I want to provide a quick list of apps that might whet your appetite.

Access the App Store by tapping the App Store icon on the Home screen. Then check out an app by typing its name in the Search Store box and tapping the Search key on the onscreen keyboard. Here are some interesting apps to explore:

⟹ **Sudoku Daily (Free):** If you like this mental logic puzzle in print, try it out on your iPad (see **Figure 9-1**). It has three lessons and several levels ranging from easiest to nightmare, making it a great way to make time fly by in the doctor's or dentist's waiting room.

Figure 9-1

➟ **Real-Time Stocks (Free):** Keep track of your investments with this app on your iPad. You can use the app to create a watch list and record your stock performance.

➟ **DealCatcher iPad Edition (Free):** Use this app to find low prices on just about everything local to your area. Read product reviews and compare list prices.

➟ **Flickr + (Free):** If you use the Flickr photo-sharing service on your computer, why not bring the same features to your iPad? This app is useful for sharing images with family and friends.

➟ **Paint Studio ($3.99):** Get creative! You can use this powerful app to draw, add color, and even create special effects. If you prefer a free paint program, try iPaint Studio.

➟ **GarageBand ($4.99):** If you love to make music, you'll love this app, which has been part of the Mac stable for several years. Play piano, guitar, or a variety of other virtual musical instruments.

➟ **Mediquations Medical Calculator ($4.99):** Use this handy utility to help calculate medications with built-in formulas and read scores for various medications. Check with your physician before using!

➟ **iPhoto ($4.99):** This is an Apple app that provides all kinds of tools for editing those great photos you can grab with the third-generation iPad's cool iSight rear-facing camera.

 iBooks is the outstanding, free e-reader app that opens up a world of reading on your iPad. See Chapter 10 for details about using iBooks.

Most iPhone apps work on your iPad, so if you own the mobile phone and have favorite apps on it, sync them to your iPad!

 Be aware that apps that haven't been optimized for the third-generation iPad's 2048 x 1536 Retina display won't look super crisp — in fact, they may look worse than they did on an iPad 2. When the third-generation iPad came out only a few apps were optimized, but developers the world over have been furiously producing optimized apps. Check to see if an app has been optimized for Retina display before you buy. Apple offers a list of some of these apps at `www.apple.com/ipad/from-the-app-store`.

Search the App Store

1. Tap the App Store icon on the Home screen. The site shown in **Figure 9-2** appears.

2. At this point, you have several options for finding apps:

- Tap in the Search Store field, enter a search term, and tap the Search button on the onscreen keyboard to see results.

- Swipe the screen downward to scroll down or swipe to the right to see more selections.

- Tap the All Categories, Books, Business, Catalogs, or More tab at the top of the screen to see that category of apps.

Search Store field

All Categories, Books, Business, Catalogs, and More tabs

Charts button

Purchased button

Figure 9-2

- Tap the Charts button at the bottom of the screen to see which free and paid apps other people are downloading most.

- Tap the Purchased button to view apps you've already purchased, as shown in **Figure 9-3**.

Figure 9-3

Get Applications from the App Store

1. Getting free apps or buying apps requires that you have
an iTunes account, which I cover in Chapter 3. After you
have an account, you can use the saved payment information there to buy apps or download free apps in a few
simple steps. I strongly recommend that you install the
free iBooks app (which I walk you through using in
Chapter 10), so in this task I give you the steps for getting it. With the App Store open, tap in the Search Store
field, enter iBooks and then tap the Search button on the
onscreen keyboard.

2. Tap the Install button for iBooks in the results that
appear, as shown in **Figure 9-4.** (To get a *paid* app, you
tap the same button, which would be labeled with a
price.)

3. The Install button changes to read *Installing* (or, in the
case of a paid app, the button changes to read *Buy App*).
Tap the button; you may be asked to enter your iTunes
password, and tap the OK button to proceed.

Tap this button

Figure 9-4

4. The app downloads; if you purchase an app that isn't free, at this point, your credit card or gift card allowance is charged for the purchase price.

Out of the box, only preinstalled apps are located on the first iPad Home screen. Apps you download are placed on additional Home screens, and you have to scroll to view and use them. See the next task for help in finding your newly downloaded apps using multiple Home screens.

If you've opened an iCloud account, anything you purchase on your iPad can be set up to be automatically pushed to other Apple iOS devices. See Chapter 3 for more about iCloud.

Organize Your Applications on Home Screens

1. iPad can display up to 11 Home screens. By default, the first contains preinstalled apps; other screens are created to contain any apps you download or sync to your iPad.

At the bottom of any iPad Home screen (just above the Dock), a magnifying-glass icon represents the Search screen to the left of the primary Home screen; dots that appear to the right of the magnifying-glass icon indicate the number of Home screens; and a solid dot specifies which Home screen you're on now, as shown in **Figure 9-5**. Press the Home button to open the last displayed Home screen.

The screen you're currently on

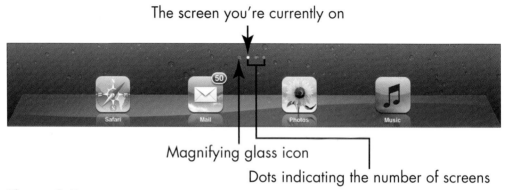

Magnifying glass icon

Dots indicating the number of screens

Figure 9-5

2. Flick your finger from right to left to move to the next Home screen. To move back, flick from left to right.

3. To reorganize apps on a Home screen, press and hold any app on that page. The app icons begin to jiggle (see **Figure 9-6**) and any apps you installed will sport a Delete button (a black circle with a white X on it).

Figure 9-6

4. Press, hold, and drag an app icon to another location on the screen to move it.

5. Press the Home button to stop all those icons from jiggling!

 To move an app from one page to another, while the apps are jiggling, you can press, hold, and drag an app to the left or right to move it to the next Home screen. You can also manage what app resides on what Home screen and in which folder from iTunes when you've connected iPad to iTunes via a cable or wireless sync, which may be easier for some.

Organize Apps in Folders

As with iPhone, iPad lets you organize apps in folders. The process is simple:

1. Tap and hold an app until all apps do their jiggle dance.

2. Drag an app on top of another app. A bar appears across the screen, showing the two apps and a file with a place-holder name (see **Figure 9-7**).

Placeholder name

Figure 9-7

3. To change the folder name, tap in the field at the end of the placeholder name, and the keyboard appears.

4. Press the Delete key to delete the placeholder name and type one of your own.

5. Tap anywhere outside the bar to save the name.

6. Press the Home button to stop the icons from dancing around and you see your folder appear on the Home screen where you began this process.

Delete Applications You No Longer Need

1. When you no longer need an app you have installed, it's time to get rid of it. (You can't delete apps that are preinstalled on the iPad, such as Notes, Calendar, or Photos.) If you use iCloud to push content across all Apple iOS devices, note that deleting an app on your iPad won't affect that app on other devices. Display the Home screen that contains the app you want to delete.

2. Press and hold the app until all apps begin to jiggle.

3. Tap the Delete button for the app you want to delete (see **Figure 9-8**).

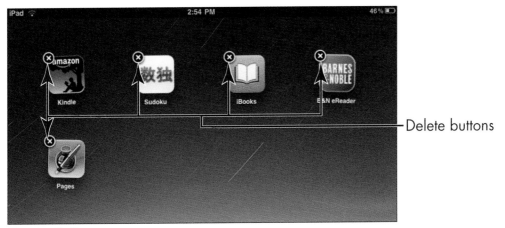

Delete buttons

Figure 9-8

4. A confirmation like the one shown in **Figure** 9-9 appears. Tap Delete to proceed with the deletion.

Figure 9-9

5. A dialog appears asking you to rate an app before deleting it; you can tap the Rate button to rate it or tap No Thanks to opt out of the survey.

 Don't worry about wiping out several apps at once by deleting a folder. When you delete a folder, the apps that were contained within the folder are placed back on Home screens.

If you have several apps to delete, you can delete
them by using iTunes connected to your iPad, making the process a bit more streamlined.

Update Apps

1. App developers update their apps all the time to fix problems or add new features, so you might want to check for
those updates. The App Store icon on the Home screen will
display the number of available updates in a red circle.
Tap the App Store icon.

2. Tap the Updates button to access the Updates screen (see
Figure 9-10) and then tap any item you want to update.
To update all, tap the Update All button.

Updates button

Figure 9-10

3. On the app screen that appears, tap Update. You may be asked to confirm that you want to update, or to enter your Apple ID Password; tap OK to proceed. You may also be asked to confirm that you're over a certain age or agree to terms and conditions; if so, scroll down the terms dialog (reading the terms as you go, of course) and, at the bottom, tap Agree.

 In iOS 5, Apple introduced the capability to download multiple apps at once. If you choose more than one app to update instead of downloading them sequentially, all items will download simultaneously.

 If you have an iCloud account which you have made active on various devices and update an app on your iPad, it will also be updated on any other Apple iOS devices automatically and vice versa.

Part III

Having Fun and Consuming Media

The 5th Wave   By Rich Tennant

Accessories

iPadPad

"It's a docking system for the iPad that comes with 3 bedrooms, 2 baths, and a car port."

Using Your iPad as an E-Reader

A traditional *e-reader* is a device that's used to read the electronic version of books, magazines, and newspapers. Apple has touted iPad as a great e-reader, so although it isn't a traditional e-reader device like the Barnes & Noble Nook, you won't want to miss out on this cool functionality.

Apple's free, downloadable app that turns your iPad into an e-reader is *iBooks*, which enables you to buy and download books from Apple's iBookstore. You can also use one of several other free e-reader apps — such as Kindle, Stanza, or Nook — to download books to your iPad from a variety of online sources such as Amazon and Google so you can read to your heart's content.

An app that arrived with iOS 5 was Newsstand. It has a similar look and feel to iBooks, but its focus is on subscribing to and reading magazines, newspapers, and other periodicals.

In this chapter, you discover the options available for reading material and how to buy books and subscribe to publications. You also learn how to get around electronic publications: how to navigate an e-book, interactive books, or periodicals and adjust the brightness and type, as well as how to search books and organize your iBooks and Newsstand libraries.

Get ready to . . .

- ➡ Discover How iPad Differs from Other E-Readers
- ➡ Find Books at iBooks
- ➡ Explore Other E-Book Sources
- ➡ Buy Books
- ➡ Navigate a Book
- ➡ Work with Interactive Books
- ➡ Adjust Brightness
- ➡ Change the Font Size and Type
- ➡ Search in Your Book
- ➡ Use Bookmarks and Highlights
- ➡ Use My Notes and Study Cards in Textbooks
- ➡ Check Words in the Dictionary
- ➡ Organize Your Library
- ➡ Organize Books in Collections
- ➡ Download Magazine Apps to Newsstand
- ➡ Buy Issues
- ➡ Read Periodicals

Discover How iPad Differs from Other E-Readers

An *e-reader* is any electronic device that enables you to download and read books, magazines, or newspapers. These devices are typically portable and dedicated only to reading the electronic version of published materials. Most e-readers use E Ink technology to create a paperlike reading experience.

The iPad is a bit different: It isn't only for reading books, and you have to download an app to enable it as an e-reader (although almost all the apps are free). Also, the iPad doesn't offer the paperlike reading experience — you read from a computer screen (though you can adjust the brightness and background color of the screen).

When you buy a book or magazine online (or get one of many free publications), it downloads to your iPad in a few seconds using a Wi-Fi or 3G/4G connection. The iPad offers several navigation tools to move around a book, which you explore in this chapter.

 iBooks version 2.0 introduced tools for reading and interacting with book content. You can even create and publish your own interactive books using a new free app called iBooks Author on a Macintosh. Read more about this feature in the later task, "Work with Interactive Books."

Find Books at iBooks

1. In Chapter 9, I walk you through the process of downloading the iBooks application in the "Get Applications from the App Store" task, so you should go do that first, if you haven't already. To shop using iBooks, tap the iBooks application icon to open it. (It's probably on your second Home screen, so you may have to swipe your finger to the left on the Home screen to locate it, or consider placing iBooks on the iPad Dock by pressing and holding it until it jiggles and then dragging it to the Dock.)

2. In the iBooks library that opens (see **Figure 10-1**), you see a bookshelf; yours probably has only one free book already downloaded to it. (If you don't see the bookshelf, tap the Library button to go there or, if no Library button is on the screen, tap the Bookshelf button in the top-right corner of the screen — it sports four small squares.) Tap the Store button, and the shelf pivots 180 degrees.

Tap the Store button

Figure 10-1

3. In the iBookstore, shown in **Figure 10-2**, featured titles are shown by default. Try any of the following to find a book:

- Tap the Search Store field and type a search word or phrase using the onscreen keyboard.

- Tap Purchased on the bottom of the screen to see any books you've bought on devices signed in with the same Apple ID. You can tap the All tab to show content from all devices (see **Figure 10-3**), or tap the Not on this iPad tab to just see content purchased on other devices.

- Tap the appropriate button at the bottom of the screen to view particular categories: Books to see featured books; NYTimes to display the *New York Times* bestseller list; Top Charts for books listed on top charts; Browse for browse-worthy lists of authors, categories, or paid or free items

If you go to an item by tapping a button at the bottom of the screen and you want to return to the original screen, just tap Books again.

• Tap a suggested selection or featured book to open more information about it.

Library button

Search Store field

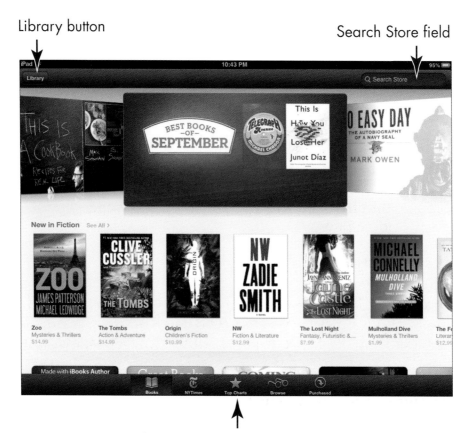

Books, NYTimes, Top Charts, Browse, and Purchased buttons

Figure 10-2

Tap the All tab

Figure 10-3

 Download free samples before you buy. You get to read several pages of the book to see whether it appeals to you, and it doesn't cost you a dime! Look for the Get Sample button when you view details about a book. If you like the book you can buy it from within iBooks app by tapping the sample and then tapping Buy.

Explore Other E-Book Sources

The iPad is capable of using other e-reader apps to read book content from other bookstores, so you can get books from sources other than iBookstore. To do so, first download another e-reader application such as Kindle from Amazon or the Barnes & Noble Nook reader from the iPad App Store. (See Chapter 9 for how to download apps.) Then use their features to search for, purchase, and download content.

The Kindle e-reader application is shown in **Figure 10-4.** Any content you have already bought from Amazon is archived online (tap the Cloud tab to see these titles) and can be downloaded to your iPad for you to read anytime you like. Tap the Device tab to see titles stored on iPad. To delete a book from this reader, press the title with your finger and the Remove from Device button appears.

Figure 10-4

 You can also get content from a variety of other sources: Project Gutenberg (www.gutenberg.org), Google, some publishers like Baen (www.baen.com), and so on. Get the content using your computer and then just add them to Books in iTunes and sync them to your iPad. Many public libraries allow you to "borrow" e-book versions of books and sync them to your iPad easily using their systems. Certain formats may need to be associated to the app for that format, such as as the mobi format for Kindle.

Buy Books

1. If you've set up an account with iTunes, you can buy books at the iBookstore using the iBooks app. (See Chapter 3 for more about iTunes.) Open iBooks and tap Store. When you find a book in the iBookstore that you want to buy, tap it and then tap the price button (see **Figure 10-5**). The button changes to the Buy Book button. (If the book is free, these buttons are labeled *Free* and *Get Book*, respectively.)

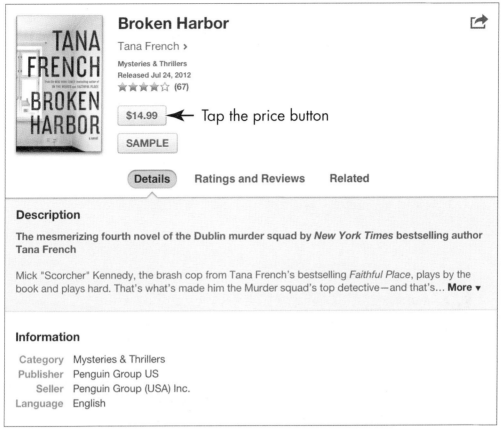

Broken Harbor

Tana French >

Mysteries & Thrillers
Released Jul 24, 2012
★★★★☆ (67)

$14.99 ◄— Tap the price button

SAMPLE

(Details)   Ratings and Reviews   Related

Description

The mesmerizing fourth novel of the Dublin murder squad by *New York Times* bestselling author Tana French

Mick "Scorcher" Kennedy, the brash cop from Tana French's bestselling *Faithful Place*, plays by the book and plays hard. That's what's made him the Murder squad's top detective—and that's... **More ▼**

Information

Category   Mysteries & Thrillers
Publisher   Penguin Group US
Seller   Penguin Group (USA) Inc.
Language   English

Figure 10-5

2. Tap the Buy Book or Get Book button. If you haven't already signed in, the iTunes Password dialog, shown in **Figure 10-6,** appears.

 If you have signed in, your purchase is accepted immediately — no returns are allowed, so tap carefully!

iTunes Password
ipadsenior@gmail.com

Password

Cancel   OK

Figure 10-6

3. Enter your password and tap OK. The book appears on your bookshelf, and the cost is charged to whichever credit card you specified when you opened your iTunes account.

You can also sync books you've downloaded to your computer to your iPad by using the data-connection cord and your iTunes account, or by setting up iCloud and choosing to automatically download books by tapping Settings⇨iTunes & App Stores. Using this method, you can find lots of free books from various sources online and drag them into your iTunes Book library; then simply sync them to your iPad. You can also sync wirelessly from your computer to your iPad. See Chapter 3 for more about syncing and iCloud.

Navigate a Book

1. Tap iBooks and, if your Library (the bookshelf) isn't already displayed, tap the Library button.

2. Tap a book to open it. The book opens, as shown in **Figure 10-7**. (If you hold your iPad in portrait orientation, it shows one page; in landscape orientation, it shows two.)

3. Take any of these actions to navigate the book:

- **To go to the book's table of contents:** Tap the Table of Contents button at the top of the page (it looks like a little bulleted list) and then tap the name of a chapter to go to it (see **Figure 10-8**).

Table of Contents button

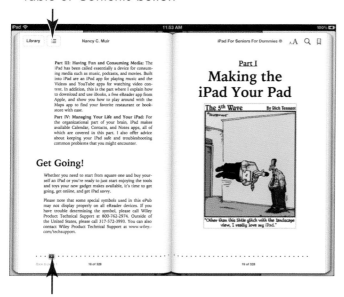

Slider to move to another page

Figure 10-7

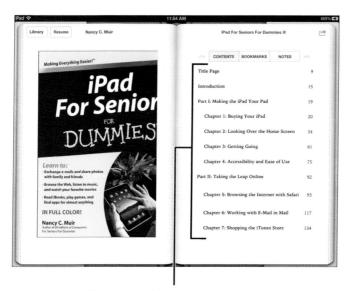

Tap any chapter to go to it

Figure 10-8

- **To turn to the next page:** Place your finger in the bottom-right or top-right corner or right edge of a page and flick to the left.

- **To turn to the preceding page:** Place your finger in the bottom-left or top-left corner or left edge of a page and flick to the right.

- **To move to another page in the book:** Tap and drag the slider at the bottom of the page to the right or left.

 To return to the Library to view another book at any time, tap the Library button. If the button isn't visible, tap anywhere on the page, and the tools appear.

Work with Interactive Books

With the introduction of iBooks version 2.0 came the ability to purchase books, especially textbooks, that have interactive features. For example, you might browse through a textbook and find a small image of a map; click the map, and it enlarges to display the full map. Or you might see an icon and a label indicating a movie clip; click that icon, and the movie plays.

Interactivity goes beyond displaying or playing objects. Such books can also include quizzes like the one shown in **Figure 10-9.** You might be asked to click a picture to select the right match, or click a button to complete a multiple-choice question. At the end of the series of questions, your score for the number of correct answers in the quiz appears.

Test your knowledge by taking a quiz

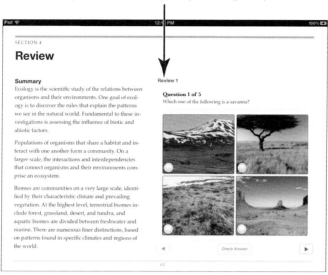

Figure 10-9

This textbook feature is bound to be a huge boon to students who will spend less money on the books and suffer less from the weight of carrying the books around campus or town. To explore some of these titles, go to the Store through iBooks, tap the More button on the top of the screen, and then tap Textbooks.

iBooks Author is a free app you can download and use to create your own interactive books on a Mac running Mac OS X Lion or later. It's a pretty nifty app that makes it easy to flow Word or Pages documents and pictures into handy templates. You can build in interactive elements such as multiple-choice quizzes and pictures that expand when clicked. When you're done, you can publish your e-book and sell it (or give it away for free) in the iBookstore. For more about working with iBooks Author, check out *iBooks Author For Dummies*, by Galen Gruman.

Adjust Brightness

1. iBooks offers an adjustable brightness setting that you can use to make your book pages comfortable to read. With a book open, tap the Font button, shown in **Figure 10-10.**

Tap the Font button...

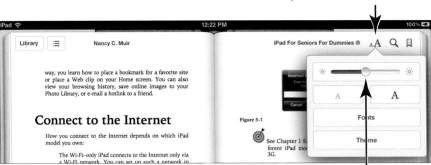

Figure 10-10

and adjust the screen brightness

2. In the Font dialog that appears (refer to **Figure 10-10**), tap and drag the Brightness slider to the right to make the screen brighter, or to the left to dim it.

3. Tap anywhere in the book to close the Brightness dialog.

 Try using the Themes button located in the Font dialog to choose Normal, Sepia, or Night (black background with white lettering), which is covered in the next task. Sepia mutes the background to a soft beige color that may work better for some.

Change the Font Size and Type

1. If the type on your screen is a bit small for your taste, you can change to a larger font size or choose a different font for readability. With a book open, tap the Font button (it sports a small letter *A* and a large *A*, as shown in **Figure 10-11**).

Tap the Font button to change font size and type

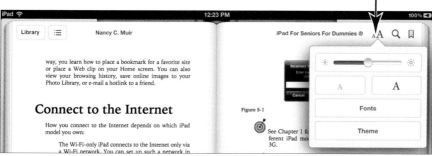

Figure 10-11

2. In the Font dialog that appears (refer to **Figure 10-11**), tap the button with a small *A* on the left to use smaller text, or the button with the large *A* on the right to use larger text.

3. Tap the Fonts button. The list of fonts shown in **Figure 10-12** appears.

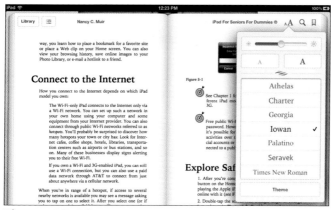

Figure 10-12

4. Tap a font name to select it. The font changes on the book page.

5. If you want a sepia tint on the pages, or to reverse black and white, which can be easier on the eyes, tap the Themes button and then tap Normal, Sepia, or Night to choose the theme you want to display.

6. Tap outside the Font dialog to return to your book.

 Some fonts appear a bit larger on your screen than others because of their design. If you want the largest fonts, use Cochin or Verdana.

 If you are reading a PDF file, you're reading a picture of a document rather than an electronic book, so be aware that zooming in and out and moving from page to page works a bit differently.

Search in Your Book

1. You may want to find a certain sentence or reference in your book. To do so, with the book displayed, tap the Search button shown in **Figure 10-13.** The onscreen keyboard appears.

Search button

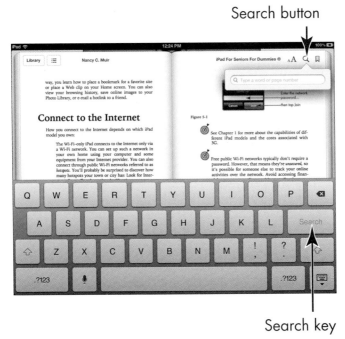

Search key

Figure 10-13

2. Enter a search term by typing or tapping the Dictation key on the onscreen keyboard and speaking the term and then tap the Search key on the keyboard. iBooks searches for any matching entries.

3. Use your finger to scroll down the entries (see **Figure 10-14**).

Scroll through the entries

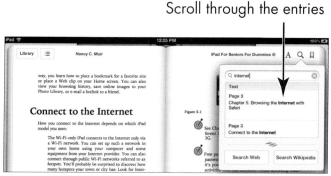

Figure 10-14

4. You can use either the Search Web or Search Wikipedia button at the bottom of the Search dialog if you want to search for information about the search term online.

 You can also search for other instances of a particular word while in the book pages by pressing your finger on the word and tapping Search on the toolbar that appears. If what you're looking for is a definition of the word, consider tapping Define rather than Search on this toolbar.

Use Bookmarks and Highlights

1. Bookmarks and highlights in your e-books are like favorite sites you save in your web browser: They enable you to revisit a favorite passage or refresh your memory about a character or plot point. To bookmark a page, with that page displayed, just tap the Bookmark button in the top-right corner (see **Figure 10-15**).

←Bookmark button

Figure 10-15

2. To highlight a word or phrase, press a word until the toolbar shown in **Figure 10-16** appears.

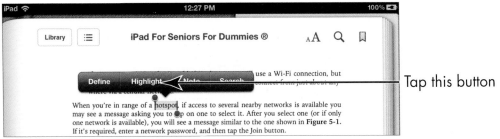

Tap this button

Figure 10-16

3. Tap the Highlight button. A colored highlight is placed on the word.

4. To change the color of the highlight or remove it, tap the highlighted word. The toolbar shown in **Figure 10-17** appears.

Figure 10-17

5. Tap one of these options:

- *The colors buttons:* Tap any colored circle to change the highlight color.

- *The Underline button:* Tap this button to add a red line under the selected text.

- *The Remove Highlight button:* Tapping the white circle with a red line through it removes the highlight (or underline).

- *The Note button:* Tap the Note icon to add a note to the item.

6. Tap outside the highlighted text to close the toolbar.

7. To go to a list of bookmarks and highlights, tap the Table of Contents button on a book page.

8. In the table of contents, tap the Bookmarks or Notes tab. As shown in **Figure 10-18,** all bookmarks or notes are displayed on their respective tabs.

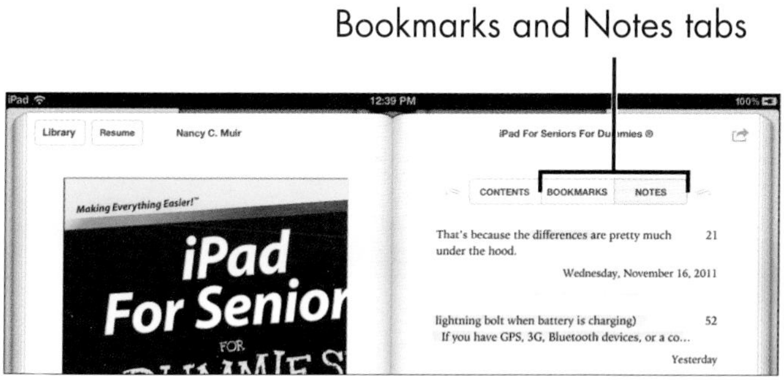

Bookmarks and Notes tabs

Figure 10-18

9. Tap a bookmark or highlight in this list to go there.

iPad automatically bookmarks where you left off reading in a book so you don't have to do it manually and, because that information is stored in the iTunes Store, you can even pick up where you left off on your iPhone, iPod touch, or another iPad.

You can also highlight illustrations in a book. Display the page and press the image until the Highlight button appears above it. Tap the button, and the illustration is highlighted in yellow. As with

highlighted text, you can tap a bookmarked illustration to change the highlight color or remove its
highlight.

Use My Notes and Study Cards in Textbooks

Textbooks, which you can explore using the free iTunes U app, work
slightly differently than other books when it comes to saving notes,
highlights, and bookmarks. When you're in a textbook, the toolbar
across the top of the book includes a new icon (it looks like a sheet of
notebook paper) to the right of the Table of Contents icon on the left
side of the screen. Tap this little white rectangle, and the My Notes
panel appears (see **Figure 10-19**). This is where the list of notes and
highlights in the currently selected chapter are displayed (rather than
in the table of contents as with other types of books).

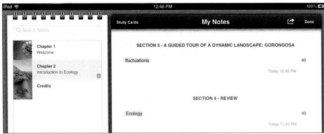

Figure 10-19

Tap the Study Cards button, and a stack of virtual index cards appears
with notes you've made, as well as cards for built-in topics that the
textbook publisher included, such as glossary terms with definitions
located on the back of the cards. You can flip through the stack of
cards with your finger, or reveal the back of a card by tapping those
that sport two arrows in the bottom-right corner. You can customize
study options for study cards. Tap the Study Options button in the
top-left corner. Here you have three options:

⇒ Tap the arrow on the right of the Highlights and Notes option and from the menu that appears, choose what you want included in the cards (all, only highlights of a certain color, or underlined items).

⇒ To stop displaying Glossary Terms, tap that option in the Study Options menu.

⇒ To randomly shuffle study cards rather than display the most recent on top, tap the Shuffle On/Off button.

When you've finished reviewing your study cards, tap the Done button to return to the My Notes panel.

Check Words in the Dictionary

1. As you read a book, you may come across unfamiliar words. Don't skip over them — take the opportunity to learn a new word! With a book open, press your finger on a word and hold it until the toolbar shown in **Figure 10-20** appears.

Tap this button

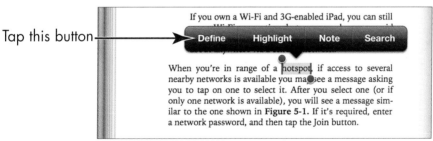

If you own a Wi-Fi and 3G-enabled iPad, you can still

Define   Highlight   Note   Search

When you're in range of a hotspot, if access to several nearby networks is available you may see a message asking you to tap on one to select it. After you select one (or if only one network is available), you will see a message similar to the one shown in **Figure 5-1.** If it's required, enter a network password, and then tap the Join button.

Figure 10-20

2. Tap the Define button. A definition dialog appears, as shown in **Figure 10-21.**

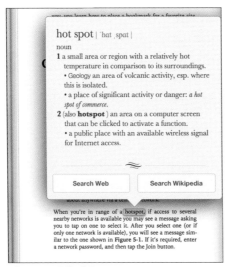

Figure 10-21

3. Tap the definition and scroll down to view more.

4. When you finish reviewing the definition, tap anywhere on the page, and the definition disappears.

Organize Your Library

1. Your iPad's library looks like a bookshelf with books stored on it, with the most recently downloaded title in the top-left corner. However, if you prefer, you can view your library in a few other ways. With the bookshelf version of the library displayed, tap the List button, shown in **Figure 10-22**.

Figure 10-22

2. Your books appear in a list, as shown in **Figure** 10-23. To organize the list alphabetically by title or author, tap the appropriate button on the bottom of the screen.

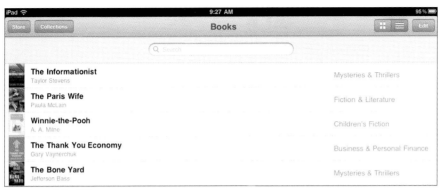

Figure 10-23

3. To organize by category, tap the Categories button on the bottom of the page. Your titles are divided by category titles such as Fiction, Mysteries & Thrillers, or Literary.

4. Press and hold a title and manually drag it to a new location on the shelf.

5. To return to Bookshelf view at any time, tap the Bookshelf view button.

Tap the Bookshelf button at the bottom of the list view to remove categories and list the most recently downloaded book first.

Use the Edit button in List view to display small circles to the left of all books in the list. Tap in any of the circles and then tap the Delete button at the top of the page to delete books, and then tap the Done button to exit the Edit function.

Organize Books in Collections

1. iBooks lets you create collections of books to help you organize them by your own logic, such as Tear Jerkers, Work-related, and Recipes Dave Likes. You can place a book in only one collection, however. To create a collection from the Library bookshelf, tap Collections.

2. In the dialog that appears, tap New. On the blank line that appears, type a name (see **Figure 10-24**) and tap Done.

Enter a name for the collection...

then tap Done

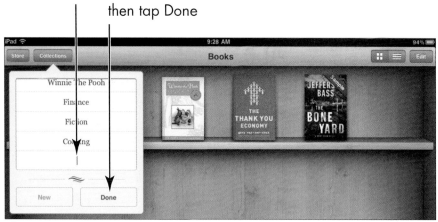

Figure 10-24

3. Tap Books, which closes the dialog and returns you to the Library. To add a book to a collection from the Library, tap Edit.

4. Tap a book and then tap the Move button that appears in the top-left corner of the screen. In the dialog that appears (see **Figure 10-25**), tap a Collection to move the book to.

Figure 10-25

5. To delete a book from a collection, with the collection displayed, tap Edit, tap the selection circle for the book, and then tap Delete.

 To delete a collection, with the Collections dialog displayed, tap Edit. Tap the minus sign to the left of any collection and then tap Delete to get rid of it. A message appears asking you to tap Remove to remove the contents of the Collection from your iPad or Don't Remove. Note that if you choose Don't Remove, all titles within a deleted collection are returned to their original collections in your library.

Download Magazine Apps to Newsstand

1. Newsstand is an app introduced with iOS 5 and allows you to subscribe to and read magazines, newspapers, and other periodicals rather than books. The app comes pre-installed on iPad and has a similar look and feel to iBooks. When you download a free publication, you're actually downloading an app to Newsstand. You can then tap that app to buy individual issues, as covered in the next task. Tap the Newsstand icon on the Home screen to open Newsstand (see **Figure 10-26**).

Figure 10-26

2. Tap the Store button. The store opens, offering Featured periodicals, Top Charts, Genius recommendations, and along the top of the screen, categories for your shopping pleasure (see **Figure 10-27**).

Figure 10-27

3. Tap any of the items displayed, tap the arrow buttons to move to other choices, or tap in the Search field at the top and enter a search term to locate a publication you're interested in.

If you tap other icons at the bottom of the screen, such as Top Charts or Purchased, you're taken to types of content other than periodicals. Also if you tap Featured again after tapping one of these icons, you're taken to apps other than periodicals. Your best bet: Stay on the Store screen that appears when you tap the Store button in Newsstand.

4. When you find an item, tap it to view a detailed description (see **Figure 10-28**).

Free button

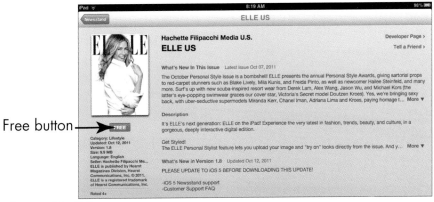

Figure 10-28

5. Tap the Free button and then tap Install App. The app downloads to Newsstand.

Buy Issues

1. Tap a periodical app in Newsstand. The message shown in **Figure 10-29** appears, asking if you'd like to be informed of new issues. Tap OK if you would.

Figure 10-29

2. Tap the Preview Issue button to take a look at a description of its content, or tap the Buy button.

3. In the purchase confirmation dialog that appears, tap Buy. The issue is charged to your iTunes account.

Read Periodicals

1. If you buy a periodical or download a free subscription preview, such as The New York Times Update shown in **Figure 10-30,** you can tap the publication in Newsstand to view it.

Figure 10-30

2. In the publication that appears, use your finger to swipe left, right, or up and down to view more of the pages.

3. For many publications, you can tap the Sections button shown in **Figure 10-31** to navigate to different sections of the publication.

Sections button   Subscribe button

Figure 10-31

4. To subscribe to a publication when viewing a free sample, tap the Subscribe button (refer to **Figure 10-31**).

 Note that different publications offer different options for subscribing, buying issues, and organizing issues. Think of Newsstand as a central collection point for apps that allow you to preview and buy content in each publication's store.

Playing with Music on iPad

*i*Pad includes an iTunes-like app called Music that allows you to take advantage of the iPad's amazing little sound system to play your favorite music or podcasts and audiobooks.

In this chapter, you get acquainted with the Music app and its features that allow you to sort and find music and control playback. You also get an overview of the Ping feature of iTunes, which you can use to share your musical preferences with others, as well as AirPlay features, which you can use to access and play your music over a home network.

Get ready to . . .

➡ View the Library Contents

➡ Create Playlists

➡ Search for Audio

➡ Play Music and Other Audio

➡ Shuffle Music

➡ Adjust the Volume

➡ Understand Ping

➡ Use AirPlay

View the Library Contents

1. Tap the Music app icon, located on the Dock on the Home screen. The Music library appears (the Albums view is shown in **Figure 11-1**).

Tap a criteria to use

Figure 11-1

2. Tap the Playlists, Songs, Artists, or Albums buttons at the bottom of the library to view your music according to these criteria (refer to **Figure 11-1**).

3. Tap the More button (see **Figure 11-2**) to view music by genre or composer, or to view any audiobooks or podcasts you've acquired.

Tap this button

Figure 11-2

 iTunes has several free items you can download and use to play around with the features in Music. You can also sync content stored on your computer or other Apple devices to your iPad and play that content using the Music app. (See Chapter 3 for more about syncing and Chapter 8 for more about getting content from iTunes.)

 You can tap the Store button to go to the iTunes Store to buy additional music.

 Apple offers a service called iTunes Match (www. apple.com/itunes/itunes-match). You pay $24.99 per year for the capability to match the music you've bought from other providers (and stored on your computer) to what's in the iTunes catalog. If there's a match (and there usually is), that content is added to your iTunes library. Then, using iCloud, you can sync the content among all your Apple devices.

Create Playlists

1. You can create your own playlists to put tracks from various sources into collections of your choosing. In the Music app, tap the Playlists button at the bottom of the iPad screen.

2. Tap New. In the dialog that appears, enter a name for the playlist and tap Save.

3. In the list of selections that appears (see **Figure 11-3**), tap the plus sign next to each item you want to include.

Tap the plus sign to add
the song to the playlist

Figure 11-3

4. Tap the Done button, and then tap Done again on the list of songs that appears.

5. Tap the Playlists button; your playlist appears in the list, and you can now play it by tapping the list name and then the Play button.

 To delete a song from the playlist, swipe left to right across the name of the song you want to delete and then tap the Delete button.

Search for Audio

1. You can search for an item in your Music library by using the Search feature. With Music open, tap in the Search field in the lower-right corner (see **Figure 11-4**) to open the onscreen keyboard.

Tap here to search for audio

Dictation button

Figure 11-4

2. Enter a search term in the Search field, or tap the Dictation key on the onscreen keyboard (refer to **Figure** 11-4) and speak the search term, and then tap the Search button on the onscreen keyboard. Results are displayed, narrowing as you type. Results of a search with the Songs tab selected are shown in **Figure 11-5.**

Results display as you type

Amazing Grace	Susan Boyle	I Dreamed a Dream	3:34
Boulevard Of Broken Dreams	Diana Krall	All For You: A Dedication To The Nat King...	6:28
Cry Me a River	Susan Boyle	I Dreamed a Dream	2:42
Daydream Believer	Susan Boyle	I Dreamed a Dream	3:19
The End of the World	Susan Boyle	I Dreamed a Dream	3:14
How Great Thou Art	Susan Boyle	I Dreamed a Dream	3:13
I Dreamed a Dream	Susan Boyle	I Dreamed a Dream	3:11

Figure 11-5

3. Tap an item to play it.

 You can enter (or speak) an artist's name, an author's or a composer's name, or a word from the item's title in the Search field to find what you're looking for.

Play Music and Other Audio

1. Locate the song or audiobook you want to play using the methods described in previous tasks in this chapter.

2. Tap the item you want to play. *Note:* If you're displaying the Songs tab, you don't have to tap an album to open a song; you need only tap a song to play it. If you're using any other tab, you have to tap items such as albums or multiple songs from one artist to find the song you want to hear. When you find it, tap it.

3. Tap the item you want to play from the list that appears (see **Figure 11-6**); it begins to play. Tap the musical note symbol to the right of the playback tools to display the album cover full screen.

Tap an item to play it

Musical note symbol

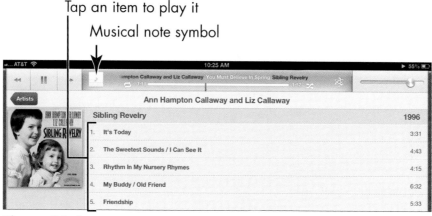

Figure 11-6

4. Use the Previous and Next buttons that display when you tap the top of the screen shown in **Figure 11-7** to navigate the audio file that's playing. The Previous button takes you back to the beginning of the item that's playing; the Next button takes you to the next item.

Previous
Pause
Next
Progress bar
Genius Playlist symbol
Volume slider

Back to Library arrow
Album List button

Figure 11-7

5. Tap the Pause button to pause playback.

6. Tap and drag the line that indicates the current playback location on the Progress bar to the left or right to "scrub" to another location in the song.

7. If you don't like what's playing, here's how to make
another selection: Tap the Back to Library arrow in the
bottom-left corner to return to Library view or tap the
Album List button in the bottom-right corner to show
other selections in the album that's playing.

 If you play a song on an album, the album cover displays full screen. To close the album cover and return to your Music library, place two fingers on the screen and pinch them inward.

 You can use Siri to play music hands-free. Just press and hold the Home button and when Siri appears, say something like "Play Take the A Train" or "Play The White Album."

 The Home Sharing feature of iTunes allows you to share music among up to five devices that have Home Sharing turned on (Apple TVs don't count against that limit). To use the feature, each device has to have the same Apple ID on your network. After you set up the feature via iTunes, you can retrieve music and videos from your iTunes shared library to any of the devices. For more about Home Sharing visit this site: www.apple.com/support/homesharing.

Shuffle Music

1. If you want to play a random selection of the music
you've purchased or synced to your iPad, you can use the
Shuffle feature. With Music open, tap either the Music,
Playlist, or Purchased button in the Source List and then
tap the Songs button at the bottom of the screen.

2. Tap the Shuffle button (see **Figure 11-8**). Your content
plays in random order.

Tap this button

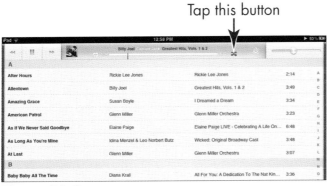

Figure 11-8

Adjust the Volume

1. Music offers its own volume control that you can adjust during playback. This volume is set relative to the system volume you control using iPad's Settings; if you set it to 50% it plays at 50% of the system volume setting. With Music open, tap a piece of music or an audiobook to play it.

2. In the controls that appear onscreen (see **Figure 11-9**), press and drag the button on the Volume slider to the right for more volume or to the left for less volume.

Use the Volume slider to adjust the volume

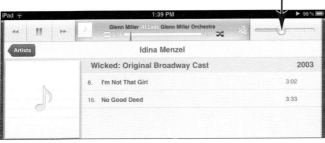

Figure 11-9

If the volume is set high and you're still having trouble hearing, consider getting a headset. It cuts out extraneous noises and may improve the sound quality of what you're listening to, as well as adding stereo to iPad's mono speaker. I recommend that you use a 3.5mm stereo headphone; insert it in the headphone jack at the top of your iPad.

Understand Ping

Ping is a social network for music lovers. If you think of Facebook or other social networking sites and imagine that they're focused around musical tastes, you have a good image of what Ping is all about.

After you join Ping, you can share the music you like with friends, take a look at the music your friends are purchasing, and follow certain artists (see **Figure 11-10**). You can also access short previews of the sounds your friends like.

Figure 11-10

If this sounds like something your grandchildren would do, you might be right. But if you have a few musical friends with whom you want to connect, Ping can be great fun.

To use Ping, you need to activate it using iTunes on a PC or Mac by clicking the Ping link in the Source List and entering your Apple ID and password to create an account. Then fill in profile information, such as your name, gender, town, and musical preferences (see **Figure 11-11**). After you save this information, you have a Ping home page and can start inviting friends to share musical inspirations with you.

 One cool Ping feature is the list on your Ping page of concerts happening near you. Even in my small town, Ping alerted me to several interesting events to check out.

Figure 11-11

Use AirPlay

The AirPlay streaming technology is built in to the iPhone, iPod touch, and iPad. *Streaming* technology allows you to send media files from one device to play on another. You can send (say) a movie you've purchased on your iPad or a slideshow of your photos to be played on your TV — and control the TV playback from your iPad. You can also send music to play over speakers.

You can take advantage of AirPlay in a few ways: Purchase Apple TV and stream video, photos, and music to the TV, or purchase AirPort Express and attach it to your speakers to play music. Finally, if you buy AirPort-enabled wireless speakers, you can stream audio directly to them. Because this combination of equipment varies, my advice — if you're interested in using AirPlay — is to visit your nearest Apple Store or certified Apple Reseller and find out which hardware combination will work best for you.

 If you get a bit antsy watching a long movie, one of the beauties of AirPlay is that you can still use your iPad to check e-mail, browse photos or the Internet, or check your calendar while the media file is playing.

Playing with Photos

*W*ith its gorgeous screen, the iPad is a natural for viewing photos. It supports most common photo formats, such as JPEG, TIFF, and PNG. You can shoot your photos by using the built-in cameras in iPad or sync photos from your computer, iPhone, or digital camera. You can also save images you find online, or receive by e-mail, to your iPad.

If you have the third-generation iPad, its rear-facing camera has a built-in iSight camera. This improvement on previous iPad cameras is a 5-megapixel beauty with an illumination sensor that adjusts for whatever lighting is available. Face detection balances focus across as many as ten faces in your pictures. The video camera option offers 1080p HD (high-definition video) with video stabilization that makes up for some shaking as you hold the device to take videos.

When you have photos to play with, the Photos app lets you organize photos from the Camera Roll, view photos in albums, one by one, or in a slideshow. You can also e-mail, message, post to Facebook, tweet a photo to a friend, print it, or use your expensive gadget as an electronic picture frame. The Photo Stream feature lets you share groups of photos with people using iCloud on an iOS 6 device or on

Get ready to . . .

➡ Take Pictures with the iPad Cameras

➡ Import Photos from an iPhone, iPod, iPod touch, or a Digital Camera

➡ Save Photos from the Web

➡ View an Album

➡ View Individual Photos

➡ Edit Photos

➡ Organize Photos in Camera Roll

➡ Share Photos with Mail, Twitter, and Facebook

➡ Share Photos Using Photo Stream

➡ Print Photos

➡ Run a Slideshow

➡ Display Picture Frame

➡ Delete Photos

➡ Play around with Photo Booth

a Mac computer with the Mountain Lion OS installed. And if you like to play around with photo effects, you'll enjoy the photo-editing features as well as the preinstalled Photo Booth app. You can read about all these features in this chapter.

Take Pictures with the iPad Cameras

1. The cameras in the iPad 2 or the third-generation iPad are just begging to be used, so let's get started! Tap the Camera app icon on the Home screen to open the app.

2. If the Camera/Video slider setting at the bottom-right corner of the screen (see **Figure 12-1**) is shifted to the right, slide it to the left to choose the still camera rather than video.

3. Tap the Options button, tap the On/Off button for Grid, and then tap Done. This turns on a grid that helps you position a subject within the grid and autofocus.

4. Move the camera around until you find a pleasing image. You can do a couple of things at this point to help you take your photo:

- Tap the area of the grid where you want the camera to autofocus.

- Pinch the screen to display a zoom control; drag the circle in the zoom bar to the right or left to zoom in or out on the image.

Capture button

Options button   Switch between front and rear cameras

Previously captured image or video   Camera/Video slider

Figure 12-1

5. Tap the Capture button at the right side of the screen in the center. You've just taken a picture (see **Figure 12-1**), and it has been stored in the Photos app automatically.

> You can also use the up switch on the volume rocker on the right side of your iPad to capture a picture or start or stop video camera recording.

6. Tap the icon in the bottom-right corner to switch between the front camera and rear camera. You can then take pictures of yourself, so go ahead and tap the Capture button to take another picture.

7. To view the last photo taken, swipe from left to right or tap the thumbnail of the latest image in the bottom-left corner of the screen; the Photos app opens and displays the photo.

8. Tap the Menu button to display a menu that allows you to e-mail, share with others as a Photo Stream, post to Facebook, tweet the photo, assign it to a contact, use it as iPad wallpaper, print it, or copy it (see **Figure 12-2**).

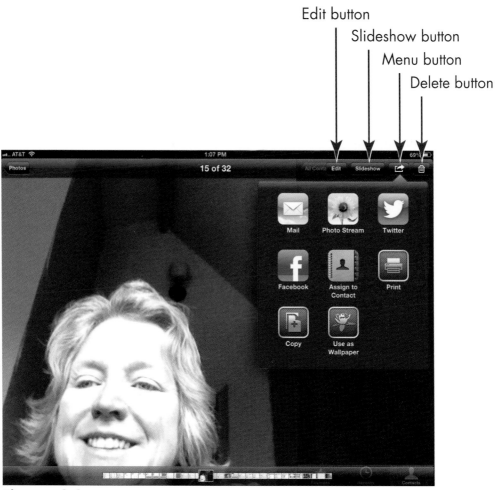

Edit button
Slideshow button
Menu button
Delete button

Figure 12-2

9. To delete the image, tap the Delete button.

10. Press the Home button to close Photos and return to the Home screen.

Import Photos from an iPhone, iPod, or a Digital Camera

1. You can find information in Chapter 3 about syncing your computer with your iPad through either iTunes or iCloud to import photos. However, your computer isn't the only photo source available to you. You can also import photos from a digital camera or an iPhone if you buy the iPad Camera Connection Kit from Apple. The kit contains two adapters (see **Figure 12-3**): a USB Camera Connector to import photos from a digital camera or an iPhone and an SD Card Reader to import image files from an SD card. Start the import process by putting your iPad to sleep.

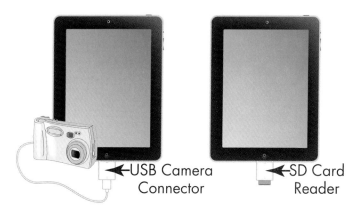

Figure 12-3

2. Insert the USB Camera Connector into the Dock connector slot of your iPad.

3. Connect the USB end of the cord that came with your digital camera or iPhone into the USB Camera Connector.

4. Connect the other end of the cord that came with your camera or iPhone into that device.

5. Wake your iPad. The Photos app opens and displays the photos on the digital camera or iPhone.

6. Tap Import All on your iPad; if you want to import only selected photos, tap individual photos and then tap Import. Finally, tap Import rather than Import All. The photos are saved to the Last Import album.

7. Disconnect the cord and the adapter and you're done!

 You can also import photos stored on a *secure digital (SD)* memory card, often used by digital cameras as a storage medium. Simply put the iPad to sleep, insert the SD Card Reader into the iPad, insert the SD card containing the photos, and then follow Steps 5 through 7 in this steps list.

Save Photos from the Web

1. The web offers a wealth of images you can download to your Photo Library. Open Safari and navigate to the web page containing the image you want.

2. Press and hold the image; a menu appears, as shown in **Figure 12-4.**

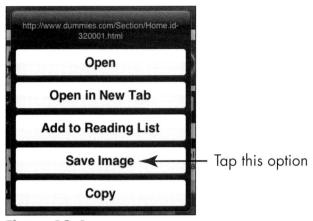

http://www.dummies.com/Section/Home.id-320001.html

Open

Open in New Tab

Add to Reading List

Save Image ——— Tap this option

Copy

Figure 12-4

3. Tap Save Image. The image is saved to your Camera Roll album in the Photos app, as shown in **Figure 12-5.**

The Camera Roll album

Figure 12-5

 For more about how to use Safari to navigate to or search for web content, see Chapter 5.

View an Album

1. The Photos app organizes your pictures into albums, using such criteria as the folder on your computer from which you synced the photos or photos captured using the iPad camera. You may also have albums for images you synced from devices such as your iPhone or digital camera. To view your albums, start by tapping the Photos app icon on the Home screen.

2. If the Photos tab is selected when the Photos app opens, tap the Albums tab, shown in **Figure 12-6**.

Tap this tab to view albums

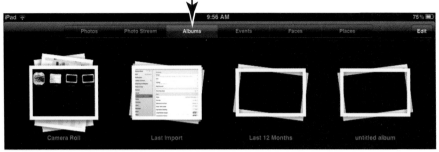

Figure 12-6

3. Tap an album. The photos in it are displayed.

View Individual Photos

1. Tap the Photos app icon on the Home screen.

2. Tap the Photos tab, shown in **Figure 12-7**.

Tap this tab

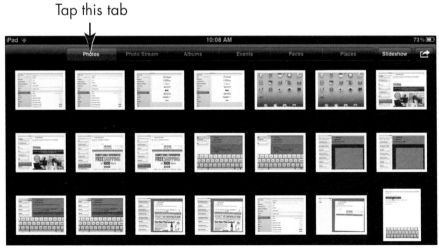

Figure 12-7

3. To view a photo, either tap the photo or pinch your fingers together, place them on the photo, and then spread your fingers apart. The picture expands, as shown in **Figure 12-8**.

Figure 12-8

4. Flick your finger to the left or right to scroll through the album to look at the individual photos in it.

5. To reduce the size of the individual photo and return to the multipicture view, place two fingers on the photo and then pinch them together. You can also tap the Albums button (which may display the open album's name) to view the album's entire contents.

 You can place a photo from Photos on a person's information page in Contacts. For more about how to do it, see Chapter 18.

Edit Photos

1. The Photos app also lets you edit photos. Tap the Photos app on the Home screen to open it.

2. Using methods previously described in this chapter, locate a photo you want to edit.

3. Tap the Edit button; the Edit Photo screen shown in **Figure 12-9** appears.

Figure 12-9

4. At this point, you can take four possible actions:

- *Rotate:* Tap the Rotate button to rotate the image 90 degrees at a time. Continue to tap the button to move another 90 degrees.

- *Enhance:* Tap Enhance to turn Auto-Enhance on or off. This feature optimizes the crispness of the image.

- *Red-Eye:* Tap Red-Eye if a person in a photo has that dreaded red-eye effect. When you activate this feature, simply tap each eye that needs clearing up.

- *Crop:* To crop the photo to a portion of its original area, tap the Crop button. You can then tap on any corner of the image and drag inward or outward to remove areas of the photo.

Each of the four editing features has a Cancel, an Undo, and a Revert to Original button. If you don't like the changes you made, use these to stop making changes or undo the changes you've already made.

Organize Photos in Camera Roll

1. If you want to create your own album, display the Camera Roll album (if you have an original iPad with no camera, this album is called Saved Photos).

2. Tap the Edit button in the top-right corner, and then tap individual photos to select them. Small check marks appear on the selected photos (see **Figure 12-10**).

Check marks indicate selected photos

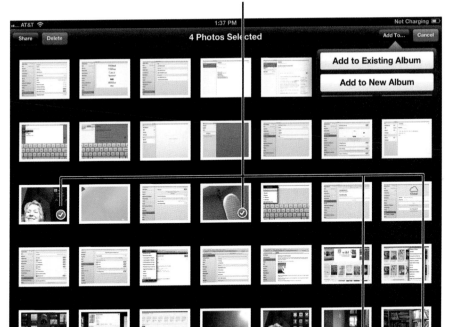

Figure 12-10

3. Tap the Add To button and tap Add to Existing Album (which appears only if you've previously created albums) or Add to New Album.

4. Tap an existing album or enter a name for a new album (depending on your previous selection) and tap Save. If you created a new album, it now appears in the Photos main screen with the Albums displayed.

 You can also choose the Copy or Delete button when you've selected photos in Step 2 of this task. This allows you to copy or delete multiple photos at a time.

Share Photos with Mail, Twitter, and Facebook

1. You can easily share photos stored on your iPad by sending them as e-mail attachments, posting them to Facebook, or tweeting them via Twitter. First, tap the Photos app icon on the Home screen.

2. Tap the Photos tab and locate the photo you want to share.

3. Tap the photo to select it and then tap the Menu button. (It looks like a box with an arrow jumping out of it.) The menu shown in **Figure 12-11** appears.

4. Tap the Mail, Twitter, or Facebook option (you have to install the Twitter and Facebook apps and link them to a Twitter or Facebook account in Settings before you can use this feature with these services).

Tap the menu button...

then tap one of these options

Figure 12-11

5. In the message form that appears, make any modifications you want in the To, Cc/Bcc, or Subject field and then type a message for e-mail or enter your Facebook post or tweet text.

6. Tap the Send button, and the message and photo go on their way.

 You can also copy and paste a photo into documents such as those created in the available Pages word processor application. To do this, press and hold a photo in Photos until the Copy command appears. Tap Copy and then, in the destination application, press and hold the screen and tap Paste.

Share Photos Using Photo Stream

1. Photo Stream allows you to automatically send copies of any new photos to any iCloud devices and to share photo streams with others. You can also subscribe to another person's photo stream if they share it with you. To set up Photo Stream, tap Settings⇨Photos & Camera and tap the On/Off button for My Photo Stream to share among your devices and Shared Photo Streams to share with others.

2. To share a photo stream with somebody else, return to the Home screen and tap Photos. Locate a photo you want to share, tap the Menu button, and then tap Photo Stream.

3. In the form that appears (see **Figure 12-12**) enter a recipient, photo stream name, and then if you like, tap the On/Off button to allow anybody to view the photo stream on iCloud.com.

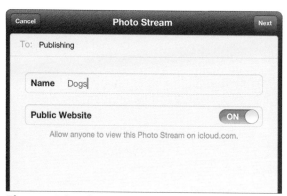

| Cancel | Photo Stream | Next |

To: Publishing

Name   Dogs

Public Website   ON

Allow anyone to view this Photo Stream on icloud.com.

Figure 12-12

4. Tap Next and enter a comment in the following dialog if you wish. Tap Post, and the photo is posted.

 When you have photos stored on your iPad you can use the Picture Frame feature to play your photos in a continuous slideshow. Check out the Picture Frame item under Settings to see how to set this up including the type of dissolve effect to use between photos, then tap the Picture Frame icon in the bottom-right of the lock screen to activate Picture Frame.

Print Photos

1. If you have a wireless printer that's compatible with Apple AirPrint technology, you can print photos. With Photos open, locate the photo you want to print and tap it to maximize it.

2. Tap the Menu button (refer to **Figure 12-11**) and then tap Print.

3. In the Printer Options dialog that appears (see **Figure 12-13**), tap Select Printer. iPad searches for any compatible wireless printers on your local network.

Figure 12-13

4. Tap the plus or minus symbols in the Copy field to set the number of copies to print.

5. Tap the Print button, and your photo is on its way to the printer.

Run a Slideshow

1. You can run a slideshow of your images in Photos and even play music and choose transition effects for the show. Tap the Photos app icon to open the application.

2. Tap the Photos tab (refer to **Figure 12-7**).

3. Tap the Slideshow button to see the Slideshow Options menu, shown in **Figure 12-14.**

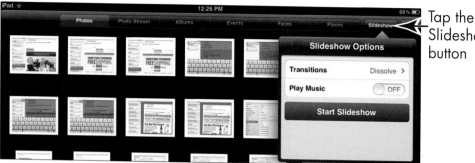

Tap the Slideshow button

Figure 12-14

4. If you want to play music along with the slideshow, tap the On/Off button on the Play Music field.

5. To choose music to play along with the slideshow, tap Music and, in the list that appears (see **Figure 12-15**), tap any selection from your Music library.

6. In the Slideshow Options dialog, tap Transitions and then tap the transition effect you want to use for your slideshow.

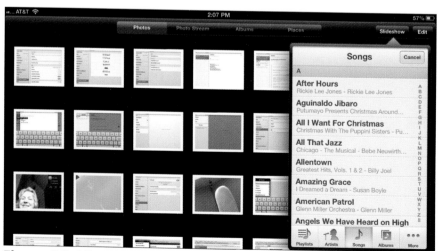

Figure 12-15

7. Tap the Start Slideshow button. The slideshow begins.

 To run a slideshow that includes only the photos contained in a particular album, tap the Albums tab instead of the Photos tab in Step 2, tap an album to open it, and then tap the Slideshow button to make settings and run a slideshow.

Display Picture Frame

1. You can use the slideshow settings you created in the previous task to run your slideshow while your iPad screen is locked so that you can view a continuous display of your pictures. Tap the Sleep/Wake button to lock iPad and then press the Home button to go to the unlock screen; the bottom of this screen looks like **Figure 12-16.**

The Picture Frame button

Figure 12-16

2. Tap the Picture Frame button (refer to **Figure 12-16**). The slideshow begins. To end the show, press the Home button.

 If you don't like the effects used on the picture frame, go back to Photos and use the Slideshow button to change your slideshow's settings.

Delete Photos

1. You might find that it's time to get rid of some of those old photos of the family reunion or the last community center project. If the photos weren't transferred from your computer but instead were downloaded or captured as screenshots on the iPad, you can delete them. Tap the Photos app icon on the Home screen.

2. Tap the Albums or Photos tab and then tap an album to open it.

3. Tap the Menu button.

4. Tap each photo you want to get rid of (a blue check mark appears; see **Figure 12-17**), and then tap the Delete button. Tap the Delete Photo/Selected Photos button that appears to finish the deletion.

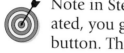 Note in Step 4 that if you're using an album you created, you get a Remove button rather than a Delete button. That's because you may remove a photo from that album, but it remains in the Camera Roll.

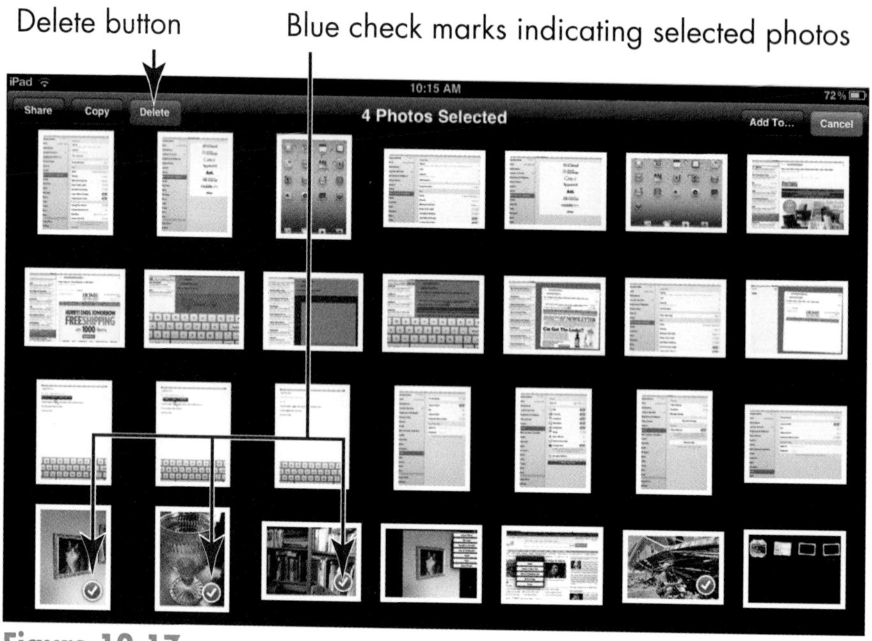

Delete button   Blue check marks indicating selected photos

Figure 12-17

Play around with Photo Booth

1. Photo Booth is a photo-manipulation app that's provided with every iPad from iPad 2 on and works with the iPad cameras. You can use this app to capture photos using various fun effects. To open Photo Booth, tap its icon on the Home screen.

2. The different possible effects that can be used in the current view of the camera appear (see **Figure 12-18**).

Figure 12-18

3. Tap an effect and then tap the Capture button (see **Figure 12-19**) to capture an image using that effect. To return to the various effects, tap the Effects button in the bottom-left corner of the screen.

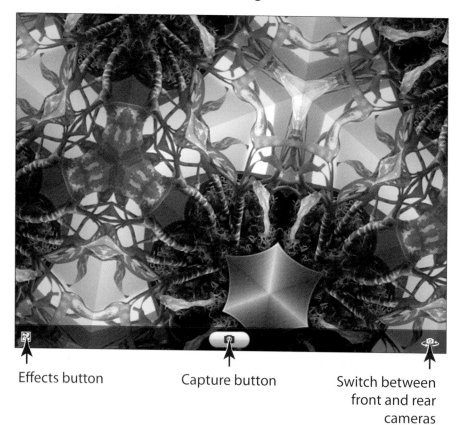

Effects button   Capture button   Switch between front and rear cameras

Figure 12-19

4. The image appears along with a filmstrip of all images you've captured using Photo Booth. If you want to delete one, tap the photo, tap the X that appears, and then tap Delete Photo.

5. Press the Home button to return to the Home screen. Your photos are now available in the Camera Roll album of the Photos app.

Getting the Most Out of Video Features

*U*sing the Videos app, you can watch down-loaded movies or TV shows, as well as media you've synced from iCloud or your Mac or PC.

In addition, iPad 2 and third-generation iPad sport two video cameras you can use to capture your own videos. If you own a third-generation iPad, you can take advantage of the improved rear-facing iSight camera with the ability to record video in 1080p HD (high definition) and video stabilization to prevent those wobbly video moments. You can also benefit from the new Retina display to watch videos with super high resolution, which simply means they'll look very, very good.

By purchasing the iMovie app (a more limited version of the longtime mainstay on Mac computers), you can add the capability to edit those videos.

In this chapter, I explain all about shooting and watching video content from a variety of sources. For practice, you might want to refer to Chapter 8 first to purchase or download one of many available free TV shows or movies.

Get ready to . . .

→ Capture Your Own Videos with the Built-in Cameras

→ Play Movies, Podcasts, or TV Shows with Videos

→ Turn on Closed Captioning

→ Go to a Movie Chapter

→ Delete Video Content from the iPad

Capture Your Own Videos with the Built-in Cameras

1. To capture a video, tap the Camera app on the Home screen.

In iPad 2 and the third-generation iPad, two video cameras can capture video from either the front or back of the device and make it possible for you to then edit the videos with third-party video apps or share them with others. (See more about this topic in the next task.)

2. The Camera app opens. Use the Camera/Video slider to switch from the still camera to the video camera (see **Figure 13-1**).

Record button

Previously captured image or video

Switch between front and rear cameras

Camera/Video slider

Figure 13-1

3. If you want to switch between the front and back cameras, tap the icon near the bottom-right corner of the screen (refer to **Figure 13-1**).

4. Tap the Record button to begin recording the video. (This button flashes when the camera is recording.) When you're finished, tap the Record button again. Your new video is now listed in the bottom-left corner of the screen.

 Before you start recording, remember that the camera lens is in the top-right corner of the back when holding iPad in a portrait orientation — you can easily put your fingers directly over the lens!

Play Movies, Podcasts, or TV Shows with Videos

1. When you first open the Videos app, you may see relatively blank screens with a note that you don't own any videos and a link to the iTunes Store. After you've purchased TV shows and movies or rented movies from the iTunes Store or other sources, you'll see tabs of the different kind of content you own. Tap the Videos app icon on the Home screen to open the application.

2. On a screen like the one shown in **Figure 13-2**, tap Rentals or TV Shows, depending on which one you want to watch.

Tap a tab

Figure 13-2

3. Tap an item to open it. A description appears, as shown in **Figure 13-3**.

Play button

Figure 13-3

4. Tap the Play button. The movie or TV show opens and begins playing. Note that the progress of the playback is displayed on the Progress bar (see **Figure 13-4**), showing how many minutes you've viewed and how many remain. If you don't see the bar, tap the screen once to display it briefly, along with a set of playback tools at the bottom of the screen.

5. With the playback tools displayed, take any of these actions:

- Tap the Pause button to pause playback.

- Tap either Go to Previous Chapter or Go to Next Chapter to move to a different location in the video playback.

- Tap the circular button on the Volume slider and drag the button left or right to decrease or increase the volume, respectively.

Done button   Progress bar

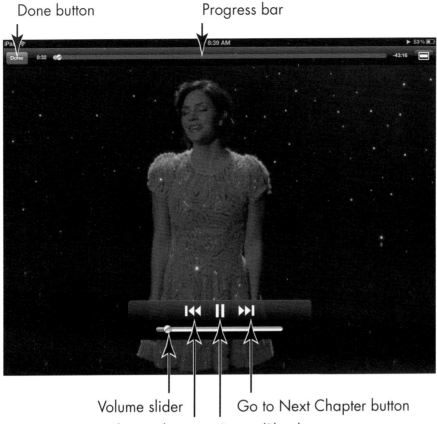

Volume slider   Go to Next Chapter button
Go to Previous Chapter button   Pause/Play button

Figure 13-4

6. To stop the video and return to the information screen, tap the Done button on the Progress bar.

Note that if you've watched a video and stopped it partway, it opens by default to the last spot you were viewing. To start a video from the beginning, tap and drag the circular button on the Progress bar all the way to the left.

If your controls disappear during playback, just tap the screen and they reappear.

If you like to view things on a bigger screen, you can even use iPad's AirPlay feature to send your iPad movies and photos to your TV by using the Apple Digital AV Connector, a $39.95 accessory, or Apple TV, a device that will cost you $99. Depending upon your TV, model, you might need the Composite (virtually any analog set) or Component (some analog and almost any digital set) connector, rather than the Digital AV Connector which is used for HDTV-only.

Turn on Closed-Captioning

1. iTunes and iPad offer support for closed-captioning and subtitles. If a movie you purchased or rented has either closed-captioning or subtitles, you can turn on the feature in iPad. Look for the "CC" logo on media you download to use this feature; be aware that video you record won't have this capability. Begin by tapping the Settings icon on the Home screen.

2. On the screen that appears (see **Figure 13-5**), scroll down and tap Videos in the Settings section on the left side of the screen.

 3. On the menu that appears on the right side of the screen (refer to **Figure 13-5**), tap the Closed Captioning On/Off button to turn on the feature. Now when you play a movie with closed-captioning, you can tap the Audio and Subtitles button to the left of the playback controls to manage this feature.

Tap videos...   then tap here to turn on Closed Captioning

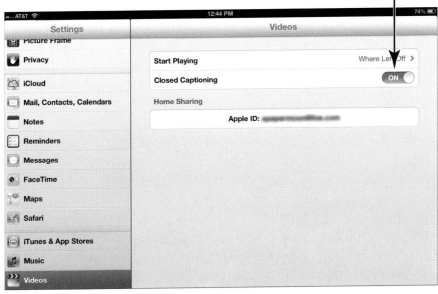

Figure 13-5

Go to a Movie Chapter

1. Tap the Videos app icon on the Home screen.

2. Tap the Movies tab, if it isn't already displayed.

3. Tap the title of the movie you want to watch. Information about the movie is displayed (refer to **Figure 13-3**).

4. Tap the Chapters tab. A list of chapters is displayed, as shown in **Figure 13-6.**

5. Tap a chapter to play it.

 You can also use the playback tools to go back one chapter or forward one chapter. See the "Play Movies, Podcasts, or TV Shows with Videos" task, earlier in this chapter, for more information.

Chapters tab

Figure 13-6

Delete Video Content from the iPad

1. Videos take up lots of space so it's a good idea to delete them from your iPad after you've watched them. Tap the Videos app icon on the Home screen.

2. Locate the item you want to delete on the Movies, Podcasts, or TV Shows tab.

3. Press and hold the item; the Delete button appears, as shown in **Figure 13-7**. (To delete multiple items, tap the Edit key instead at this point.)

The Delete button

Figure 13-7

4. Tap the Delete button. The item is deleted.

 If you buy a video using iTunes, sync to download it to your iPad, and then delete it from your iPad, it's still saved in your iTunes library. You can sync your computer and iPad again to download the video once more at no additional charge. Remember, however, that rented movies, after deleted, are gone with the wind.

 iPad has much smaller storage capacity than your typical computer, so downloading lots of TV shows or movies can fill its storage area quickly. If you don't want to view an item again, delete it to free up space.

Playing Games

The iPad is super for playing games, with its bright screen (especially bright if you're using the Retina display on the third-generation iPad), great sound system, as well as the ability to rotate the screen as you play and track your motions. You can download game apps from the App Store and play them on your device. You can also use the preinstalled Game Center app to help you find and buy games, add friends to play against, and track and share scores.

In this chapter, you get an overview of game playing on your iPad, including opening a Game Center account, adding a friend, purchasing and downloading games, and playing basic games solo or against friends.

 Of course, you can also download games from the App Store and play them on your iPad without having to use Game Center. What Game Center provides is a place where you can create a gaming profile, add a list of gaming friends, keep track of and share your scores and perks, and shop for games (and only games) in the App Store, along with listings of top-rated games and game categories to choose from.

Get ready to . . .

➡ Open an Account in Game Center

➡ Create a Profile

➡ Add Friends

➡ Purchase and Download Games

➡ Master iPad Game-Playing Basics

➡ Play against Yourself

➡ Play Games with Friends in Game Center

➡ Share High Scores with Friends

Open an Account in Game Center

1. From the Home screen, tap the Game Center icon. If you've never used Game Center, you're asked whether to allow *push* notifications: If you want to receive these notices alerting you that your friends want to play a game with you, tap OK. You should, however, be aware that push notifications can drain your iPad's battery more quickly.

2. On the Game Center opening screen (see **Figure 14-1**), if you want to use Game Center with a new Apple ID, tap Create New Apple ID.

Tap this button

Figure 14-1

3. If the correct country isn't listed in the New Account dialog, tap in the Location field and select another location. If the correct location is already showing, tap Next to confirm it.

4. In the next dialog you see, tap the Month, Day, and Year fields, enter your date of birth, and then tap Next.

5. In the Game Center Terms & Conditions dialog, swipe to scroll down (and read) the conditions, and then tap Agree if you want to continue creating your account. A confirmation dialog appears; tap Agree once more to accept for real!

6. In the next dialog that opens, tap each field or the Next button at the top of the onscreen keyboard and enter your name, e-mail address, and password information. Tap the Question field to select a security question to identify yourself, and tap the Answer field and type in an answer to the question. Be sure to scroll to the bottom of this dialog and choose to turn off the e-mail notification subscription if you don't want to have Game Center send you messages. Tap Next to proceed. See the following task, "Create a Profile," to create your Game Center profile in subsequent dialogs.

 When you first register for Game Center, if you use an e-mail address other than the one associated with your Apple ID, you may have to create a new Apple ID and verify it by responding to an e-mail message that's sent to your e-mail address. See Chapter 3 for more about creating an Apple ID when opening an iTunes account.

Create a Profile

1. When you reach the last dialog in Step 6 of the previous task, you're ready to create your profile and specify some account settings. You can also make most of these settings after you've created your account by tapping your Account name on the Game Center home screen and then tapping View Account. In the dialog that appears (see **Figure 14-2**), in the Nickname field, enter the "handle" you want to be known by when playing games.

Figure 14-2

2. If you don't want other players to be able to invite you to play games when Game Center is open, tap the Game Invites On/Off slider to turn off the feature.

3. If you don't want other players to be able to see your real name, tap the Public Profile On/Off slider to turn this feature off.

4. If you want your friends to be able to send you requests for playing games via e-mail, check to see if the e-mail address listed in this dialog is the one you want them to use. If not, tap Add Another Email and enter another e-mail address.

5. Tap Done when you're finished with the settings. You return to the Game Center home screen, already signed in to your account with information displayed about friends, games, and gaming achievements (all at zero initially).

6. To add a picture to your profile, tap Change Photo. You might see a message that your photo will be shared with all other Game Center players. Tap OK.

7. The two options of Take Photo (on iPad 2 and third-generation iPad only) and Choose Photo appear. Tap Choose Photo to select a photo from your Camera Roll or a photo library. Tap the library you want to use and scroll to locate the photo.

8. Tap the photo, and it appears in a Choose Photo dialog. You can use your finger to move the photo around or scale it, and then tap Use. The photo now appears on your Game Center home screen (see **Figure** 14-3).

Your photo appears here

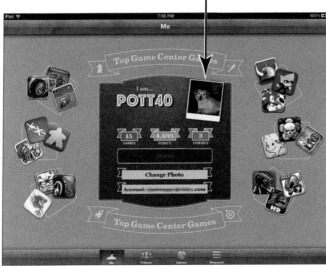

Figure 14-3

After you create an account and a profile, whenever you go to the Game Center, you log in by entering your e-mail address and password and then tapping Sign In.

 You can change account settings from the Game Center home screen: Tap your account name and then tap View Account. Make changes to your settings and then tap Done.

Add Friends

1. If you want to play Game Center games with others who have an Apple ID and an iPhone, iPod touch, or iPad, add them as friends so that you can invite them to play. (Game Center is also available on Macs with the Mountain Lion OS, but few cross-platform games are available for it.) From the Game Center home screen, tap the Friends button at the bottom of the screen.

2. On the Friends page, tap Add Friends.

3. Enter an e-mail address in the To field and edit the invitation, if you'd like.

4. Tap the Send button. A confirmation message tells you that your invitation has been sent. Tap OK. After your friend accepts your invitation, his or her name is listed on the Friends screen.

 With iOS 5, Game Center gained a Friend Recommendations feature. Tap the Friends tab, and then tap the A-Z button in the top-left corner. A Recommendations section appears above the list of your current friends. These are people who play the same or similar games, so if you'd like, try adding one or two as friends. You can also tap Use My Contacts to find recommendations of friends from your Contacts app and add them.

You will probably also receive requests from friends who know you're on Game Center. When you get these e-mail invitations, be sure that you know the person sending it before you accept it — especially if you've allowed e-mail access in your account settings. If you don't double-check, you could be allowing a stranger into your gaming world.

Purchase and Download Games

1. Time to get some games to play! Remember that you can buy any game app from the App Store or other sources and simply play it by tapping to open it on your iPad. But if you want to use Game Center to buy games, here are the steps involved. Open Game Center and sign in to your account.

2. Tap the Games button at the bottom of the screen, and then tap Find Game Center Games (see **Figure** 14-4).

Tap here to find more games

Figure 14-4

3. Scroll through the list of featured games that appears. To view different games, tap either the Top Charts or Categories button at the bottom of the screen. *Note:* Accessing these from the Game Center displays only game apps, as opposed to accessing apps from the App Store, which shows you all categories of apps.

4. To search for a particular title, tap the Search field in the top-right corner and enter the name by using the onscreen keyboard.

5. Tap a game title to view information about it. To buy a game, tap the button labeled with either the word *free* or the price (such as $1.99). Then tap the button again, which is now labeled *Install App.* A dialog appears, asking for your Apple ID and password. Enter these and then tap OK. Another verification dialog appears, asking you to sign in. Follow the instructions on the next couple of screens to enter your password and verify your payment information if this is the first time you've signed in to your account from this device.

6. When the verification dialog appears, tap Buy. The game downloads.

 If you've added friends to your account, you can go to the Friends page and view games your friends have downloaded. To purchase one of these games, just tap it in your friend's list.

 You may see buttons labeled Buy It Now or Available at the App Store while you're exploring game recommendations in the Games section of Game Center. Tapping these buttons takes you from Game Center directly to the App Store to buy the game.

Master iPad Game-Playing Basics

It's almost time to start playing games, but first let me give you an idea of iPad's gaming strengths. For many reasons, iPad may be the ultimate gaming device because of the following strengths:

➡ **Fantastic-looking screen:** First, the high-resolution, 9.7-inch screen has a backlit LED display that Apple describes as "remarkably crisp and vivid." The third-generation iPad with its Retina display takes this crisp screen to the max. Apple's claims about the iPad Retina display are no lie: See the *Haunted Manor* game in **Figure 14-5,** for example. In-plane switching (IPS) technology lets you hold your iPad at almost any angle (it has a 178-degree viewing angle) and still see good color and contrast.

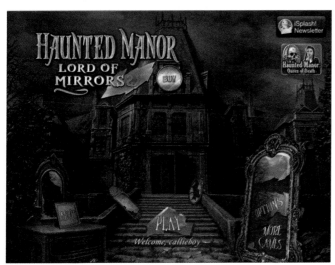

Figure 14-5

➡ **Faster processor:** The superfast A5 processor chip in your iPad 2 and A5X processor in the third-generation iPad can run rings around your iPhone, (but if you have the A6 processor in iPhone 5 you can give your iPad a run for its money) making the iPad ideal for gaming.

⇢ **Game play in full-screen mode:** Rather than play on a small iPhone screen, you can play most games designed for the iPad in full-screen mode. Seeing the full screen brings the gaming experience to you in an even more engaging way than a small screen ever could.

⇢ **Ability to drag elements onscreen:** Though the Multi-Touch screen in the iPad may be based on the same technology that's in the iPhone, it has been redone from the ground up for the iPad. The newer screen is responsive — and when you're about to be zapped by virtual aliens in a fight to the death, responsiveness counts.

⇢ **Ten-hour battery life:** A device's long battery life means that you can tap energy from it for many hours of gaming fun. Even with the extra power required for the third-generation iPad's Retina display, Apple managed to maintain this excellent battery life.

⇢ **Specialized game-playing features:** Some newer games have features that take full advantage of the iPad's capabilities. For example, N.O.V.A. (from Gameloft) features Multiple Target Acquisition, which lets you target multiple bad guys in a single move to blow them out of the water with one shot. In Real Racing 3 (Firemint), for example, you can look in your rearview mirror as you're racing to see what's coming up behind you, a feature made possible by the iPad's larger screen.

⇢ **Stellar sound:** The built-in iPad speaker is a powerful little item, but if you want an experience that's even more up-close and personal, you can plug in a headphone, some speaker systems, or a microphone using the built-in jack.

The iPad has a built-in motion sensor — the *three-axis accelerometer* — as well as a gyroscope. These features provide lots of fun for people developing apps for the iPad because they use the automatically rotating screen to become part of the gaming experience. For example, a built-in compass device reorients itself automatically as you switch your iPad from landscape to portrait orientation. In some racing games, you can grab the iPad as though it were a steering wheel and rotate the device to simulate the driving experience.

Play against Yourself

Many games allow you to play a game all on your own. Each has different rules and goals — so study a game's instructions and help to learn how to play it — but here's some general information about these types of games:

⟫ Often a game can be played in two modes: with others or in a solitaire version, where you play yourself or the computer.

⟫ Many games you may be familiar with in the offline world, such as Carcassonne or Scrabble, have online versions. For these, you already know the rules of play, so you simply need to figure out the execution. For example, in the online Carcassonne solitaire game, you tap to place a tile on the board, tap the placed tile to rotate it, and tap the check mark to complete your turn and reveal another tile.

⟫ All the games you play on your own record your scores in Game Center so you can track your progress.

Play Games with Friends in Game Center

1. After you've added a friend and both of you have down-loaded the same games, you're ready to play. The rules of play are different for each game, but here are the basic steps for getting a game going. Tap the Game Center app icon on the Home screen and sign in, if necessary.

2. Tap Friends. The Friends page (see **Figure** 14-6) appears.

Figure 14-6

3. Tap the name of the friend you want to play and then tap the name of a game you have in common. At this point, some games offer you an invitation to send to your friend — if so, wait for your friend to respond, which she can do by tapping Accept or Decline on her device.

4. The game appears, and you can tap Play to start playing according to whatever rules the game has. Your scores mount up as you play.

5. When you're done playing, tap either the Friends or Games button on the bottom of the Friends screen in Game Center to see your score and your friend's score listed. Game Center tracks your achievements, including points and perks that you've earned along the way. You can also compare your gaming achievements with those of top-ranking players across the Internet — and check your friends' scores by displaying the Friends page with the Points portion showing (refer to **Figure** 14-6).

 If your friends aren't available, you can play a game by tapping its title on the Games page and then tapping Play. You can then compare your scores with others around the world who have also played the game recently.

Share High Scores with Friends

1. It's fun to share your best scores with friends. Tap Game Center on the Home screen and then tap Me.

2. Tap a game score in the list on the left (see **Figure** 14-7) and then tap Share.

Tap Share

Figure 14-7

3. In the dialog that appears (see **Figure 14-8**) tap Mail, Message, or Twitter, or tap the second dot at the bottom of the dialog to scroll over to other options, and tap Facebook.

Tap a sharing method...

or tap this dot for more options

Figure 14-8

4. Depending on what method you chose for sharing, enter an e-mail address and message or enter account information and follow directions to forward your score.

Finding Your Way with Maps

*Y*ou may have used a maps app on a smart-phone before. The big difference with iPad is its large screen, on which you can view all the beautiful map visuals, traffic flow, and maps in 3D as long as you have an Internet connection. You can also display the map and written directions simultaneously or have Maps speak your directions, guiding you as you drive.

If you're new to the Maps app, you'll find it has lots of useful functions. You can find directions with suggested alternate routes from one place to another. You can bookmark locations to return to them again, and the Maps app makes it possible to get information about locations, such as the phone numbers and web links to businesses. You can even add a location to your Contacts list, or share a location with your buddy using Mail, Messages, Twitter, or Facebook.

Be prepared: This application is seriously cool, and you're about to have lots of fun exploring it in this chapter.

Get ready to . . .

⇒ Go to Your Current Location

⇒ Change Views

⇒ Zoom In and Out

⇒ Go to Another Location

⇒ Drop a Pin

⇒ Add and View a Bookmark

⇒ Delete a Bookmark

⇒ Find Directions

⇒ View Information about a Location

⇒ Add a Location to a Contact

⇒ Share Location Information

⇒ Get Turn-by-Turn Navigation Help

Go to Your Current Location

1. iPad can figure out where you are at any time and display
your current location as long as you have an Internet
connection. From the Home screen, tap the Maps icon.
Tap the Current Location icon (the small arrow in the
bottom-left corner; see **Figure 15-1**).

Current Location icon
Figure 15-1

2. Your current location is displayed with a pin in it and a
blue circle around it (refer to **Figure 15-1**). The circle
indicates how accurate the location is — it can be anywhere within the area of the circle.

3. Double-tap the screen to zoom in on your location.
(Additional methods of zooming in and out are covered
in the "Zoom In and Out" task, later in this chapter.)

If you don't have a 3G or 4G version of iPad, your current location is a rough estimate based on a triangulation method. Only 3G- and 4G-enabled iPads with the global positioning system (GPS) can pinpoint where you are. Still, if you type a starting location and an ending location to get directions, you can get pretty accurate results even with a Wi-Fi–only iPad.

Change Views

1. The Maps app offers three views: Standard, Satellite, and Hybrid. iPad displays the Standard view (see the top-left image in **Figure 15-2**) by default the first time you open Maps. To change views, with Maps open, swipe the bottom-right corner of the screen to the left to turn the "page" and reveal the Maps menu, shown in **Figure 15-3**.

Figure 15-2

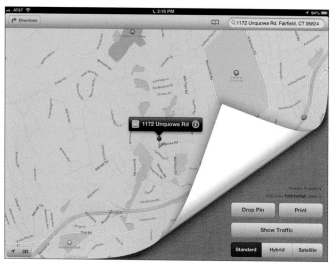

Figure 15-3

2. Tap the Satellite option. The Satellite view (refer to the top-right image in **Figure** 15-2) appears.

3. Swipe to reveal the menu again and then tap Hybrid. Satellite view is displayed with street names superimposed (refer to the bottom-left image in **Figure** 15-2).

4. Finally, you can display a 3D effect on any view by tapping the 3D button in the lower-left corner of the screen.

 On the Maps menu, there's also a traffic overlay feature. If you live in a larger metropolitan area (this feature doesn't really work in small towns or rural settings), turn on this feature by tapping the Show Traffic button. The traffic overlay shows red dashes on roads indicating accidents or road closures to help you navigate your rush hour commute or trip to the mall.

 You can drop a pin to mark a location on a map that you can return to. See the task "Drop a Pin," later in this chapter, for more about this topic.

To print any displayed map to an AirPrint-compatible wireless printer, just tap the Print button on the Maps menu.

Zoom In and Out

1. You'll appreciate the Zoom feature because it gives you the capability to zoom in and out to see more or less detailed maps and move around a displayed map. With a map displayed, double-tap with a single finger to zoom in (see **Figure** 15-4).

Figure 15-4

2. Double-tap with two fingers to zoom out, revealing less detail.

3. Place two fingers positioned together on the screen and move them apart to zoom in.

4. Place two fingers apart on the screen and then pinch them together to zoom out.

5. Press your finger to the screen and drag the map in any
direction to move to an adjacent area.

 It can take a few moments for the map to redraw
itself when you enlarge, reduce, or move around it,
so have a little patience. Areas that are being redrawn
look like blank grids that fill in eventually. Also, if
you're in Satellite or Hybrid view, zooming in may
take some time; wait it out because the blurred image
resolves itself.

Go to Another Location

1. With Maps open, tap in the Search field (see **Figure** 15-5);
the keyboard opens. If you have displayed directions for
a route you won't see the Search field in the upper-right
corner; tap the Clear button on a directions screen to get
back to the Search field.

Search field

Dictation key

Figure 15-5

2. Type a location, using a street address with city and state, a stored contact name, or a destination such as *Empire State Building* or *Detroit airport*. Maps may make suggestions as you type if it finds any logical matches. Tap the Search key on the keyboard, and the location appears with a pin inserted in it and a label with the location and an Information icon (see **Figure 15-6**). Note that if several locations match your search term, several pins may be displayed in a suggestions list.

 You can tap the Dictation key on the onscreen keyboard (refer to **Figure 15-5**) and speak a location to iPad if you prefer. Tap in the Search field, and then tap the Dictation key and say the location; tap the Dictation key or in the Search field again and what you've spoken appears there. Next, tap the Search button on the keyboard to display the location.

 Try double-pressing the Home button and asking Siri for a type of business or location by zip code. For example, if you crave something with pepperoni, say "Find pizza in 99208 zip code." The results typically display a small map you can tap to open the Maps app to find your way there. See Chapter 19 for more about using Siri.

3. You can also tap the screen and drag in any direction to move to a nearby location.

Bookmark icon

The information bar

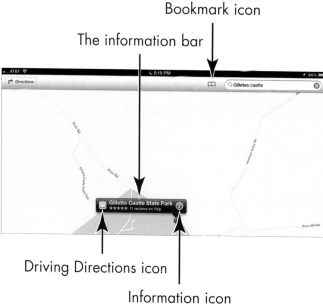

Driving Directions icon

Information icon

Figure 15-6

4. Tap the Bookmark icon (the little book symbol to the left of the Search field; refer to **Figure 15-6**), and then tap the Recents tab to reveal recently visited sites. Tap a bookmark to go there.

 As you discover later in this chapter, in the "Add and View a Bookmark" task, you can also quickly go to any location you've previously visited and saved using the Bookmarks feature.

 If you enter a destination such as *Bronx Zoo*, you might want to also enter its city and state. Entering *Bronx Zoo* landed me in the Woodland Park Zoo in Tacoma because Maps looks for the closest match to your geographical location in a given category.

Drop a Pin

1. *Pins* are markers: A green pin marks a start location, a red pin marks a search result, and a blue pin (referred to as the *blue marker*) marks your iPad's current location. If you drop a pin yourself, it appears in a lovely purple. Display a map that contains a spot where you want to drop a pin to help you find directions to or from that site.

2. If you need to, you can zoom in to a more detailed map to see a better view of the location you want to pin.

3. Press and hold your finger on the screen at the location where you want to place the pin. The pin appears, together with an information bar (refer to **Figure 15-6**).

4. Tap the Information icon (refer to **Figure 15-6**) on the information bar to display details about the pin location (see **Figure 15-7**).

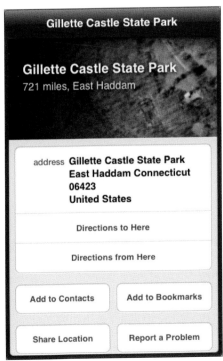

Gillette Castle State Park

Gillette Castle State Park
721 miles, East Haddam

address **Gillette Castle State Park
East Haddam Connecticut
06423
United States**

Directions to Here

Directions from Here

Add to Contacts   Add to Bookmarks

Share Location   Report a Problem

Figure 15-7

If a site has associated reviews on the restaurant review site Yelp (www.yelp.com), you can tap the More Info on Yelp button in its Information dialog to install the Yelp app and read them.

Add and View a Bookmark

1. A *bookmark* provides a way to save a destination so you can display a map or directions to it quickly. To add a bookmark to a location, first place a pin on it, as described in the preceding task.

2. Tap the Information icon to display the Information dialog.

3. Tap the Add to Bookmarks button (refer to **Figure 15-7**).

4. The Add Bookmark dialog (see **Figure 15-8**) and the keyboard appear. If you like, you can modify the name of the bookmark.

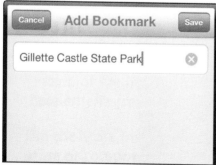

Figure 15-8

5. Tap Save.

6. To view your bookmarks, tap the Bookmark icon (it looks like a little open book; refer to **Figure 15-6**) at the top of the Maps screen. Be sure that the Bookmarks tab is selected; a list of bookmarks is displayed.

7. Tap on a bookmark to go to the location in Maps.

 You can also view recently viewed locations, even if you haven't bookmarked them. Tap the Bookmark icon and then, at the bottom of the Bookmarks dialog that appears, tap Recents. Locations you've visited recently are listed there. Tap one to return to it in Maps.

Delete a Bookmark

1. Tap the Bookmark icon and then tap the Bookmarks tab at the bottom of the dialog that appears, to be sure you're viewing Bookmarks.

2. Tap the Edit button. A red minus icon appears to the left of each bookmark, as shown in **Figure 15-9**.

Red minus icons

Figure 15-9

3. Tap a red minus icon.

4. Tap Delete. The bookmark is removed.

 You can also use a touchscreen shortcut after you've displayed the bookmarks in Step 1 above. Simply swipe across a bookmark and then tap the Delete button.

You can also clear out all recent locations stored by Maps to give yourself a clean slate. Tap the Bookmark icon and then tap the Recents tab. Tap Clear and then confirm by tapping Clear All Recents.

Find Directions

1. You can get directions in a couple of different ways. With at least one pin on your map in addition to your current location, tap the Directions button and then tap Route. A line appears, showing the route between your current location and the closest pin for the currently selected transportation method: by car, on foot, or by using public transit (see **Figure 15-10**).

Line indicating your route

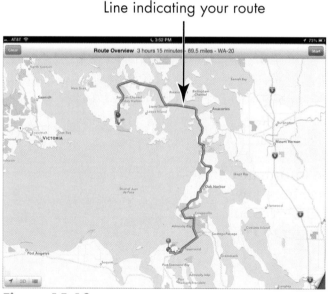

Figure 15-10

2. To show directions from your current location to another pin, tap the other pin, and in the dialog that appears, tap Route; the route is redrawn.

3. You can also enter two locations to get directions from one to the other. Tap the Directions button in Maps and then tap in the Start field (see **Figure 15-11**). The keyboard appears.

End field

Start field

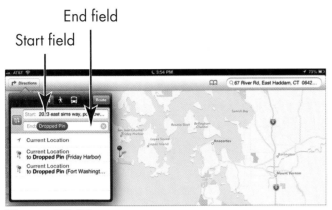

Figure 15-11

4. Enter a different starting location.

5. Tap in the End field and enter a destination location. If you like, you can tap the driving, walking, or public transit button and then press the Route button on the keyboard. The route between the two locations is displayed.

6. You can also tap the Information icon on the information bar that appears above any selected pin and use the Directions To Here or Directions From Here button to generate directions (refer to **Figure 15-7**).

7. When a route is displayed, an information bar appears along the top of the Maps screen (refer to **Figure 15-10**) telling you the distance and time it takes to travel between the two locations. Here's what you can do at this point:

• Tap the Directions button (it's the last icon on the right of the toolbar in the bottom-left corner) to display written directions (see **Figure 15-12**).

• Tap Start to begin turn-by-turn narration.

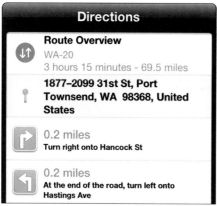

Figure 15-12

8. If there are alternate routes, Maps notes the number of alternate routes in the informational display and shows the routes on the map. Tap a route number to make it the active route (see **Figure 15-13**).

Tap a route number to select it

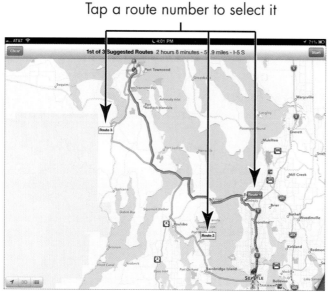

Figure 15-13

View Information about a Location

1. You've displayed the Information dialog for locations to add a bookmark or get directions in previous tasks. Now you focus on the useful information displayed there. Go to a location and tap the pin.

2. On the information bar that appears above the pinned location, tap the Information icon (refer to **Figure 15-6**).

3. In the Information dialog (see **Figure 15-14**), tap the web address listed in the Home Page field to be taken to the location's web page, if it has one associated with it.

4. You can also press and hold either the Phone or Address field (refer to **Figure 15-14**) and use the Copy button to copy the phone number, for example, so that you can place it in a Notes document for future reference.

5. Tap outside the Information dialog to close it.

 Rather than copy and paste information, you can easily save all information about a location in your Contacts address book. See the "Add a Location to a Contact" task, later in this chapter, to find out how it's done.

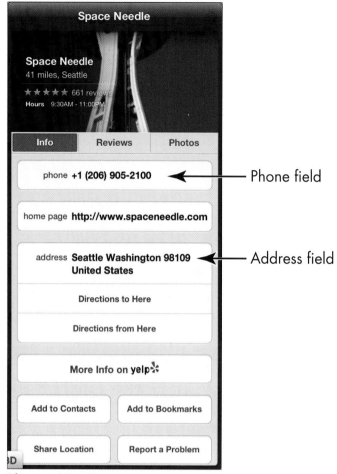

Phone field

Address field

Figure 15-14

Add a Location to a Contact

1. Tap a pin to display the information bar.

2. Tap the Information icon.

3. In the Information dialog that appears (refer to **Figure 15-14**), tap Add to Contacts.

4. In the resulting dialog, tap Create New Contact. The New Contact dialog appears (see **Figure 15-15**).

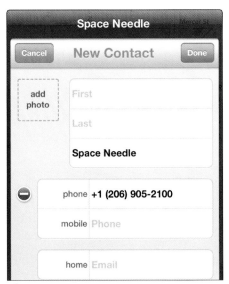

Figure 15-15

5. Whatever information was available about the location has already been entered. Enter any additional information you need, such as name, phone, or e-mail address.

6. Tap Done. The information is stored in your Contacts address book.

 You can choose a distinct ringtone or text tone for a new contact. Just tap the Ringtone or Text Tone field in the New Contact form to see a list of options. When that person calls via FaceTime or texts you via iMessage, you will recognize him or her from the tone that plays.

Share Location Information

1. Tap a pin to display the information bar.

2. Tap the Information icon.

3. In the Information dialog that appears, tap Share Location. In that dialog (see **Figure 15-16**), you can choose to share via text message, Twitter, Facebook, or e-mail. Tap Mail to see how this option works.

Tap this option

Figure 15-16

4. On the form that appears, use the onscreen keyboard to enter a recipient's information (if you're using Facebook or Twitter you'd enter recipient information as appropriate to the service you chose to use) and tap Send to share the map.

 You may have to install and set up the Twitter or Facebook app before sharing Maps content using those services. You also must have an account with these services to use them to share content.

Get Turn-by-Turn Navigation Help

1. When you've entered directions for a route and display that route, you can then begin listening to turn-by-turn navigation instructions that can be helpful as you're driving. Tap the Start button in the upper-right corner.

2. The narration begins and large text instructions are displayed, as shown in **Figure 15-17**. Continue driving according to the route until the next instruction is spoken.

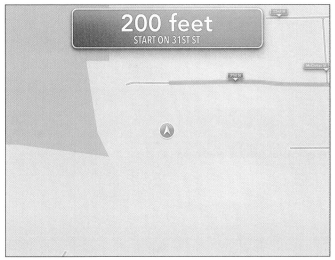

Figure 15-17

3. For an overview of your route, at any time you can tap the screen and then the Overview button that appears in the upper-right corner.

 To adjust the volume of the spoken navigation aid go to Settings➪Maps and then adjust the Navigation Voice Volume settings to No Voice, Low, Normal, or Loud.

Part IV

Managing Your Life and Your iPad

The 5th Wave — By Rich Tennant

@RICHTENNANT

iPad

"In fact it does come with a compass."

Keeping On Schedule with Calendar

Whether you're retired or still working, you have a busy life full of activities (even busier if you're retired, for some unfathomable reason). You may need a way to keep on top of all those activities and appointments. The Calendar app on your iPad is a simple, elegant, electronic daybook that helps you do just that.

In addition to being able to enter events and view them by the day, week, month, or year, you can set up Calendar to send alerts to remind you of your obligations and search for events by keywords. You can even set up repeating events, such as weekly poker games, monthly get-togethers with the girls or guys, or weekly babysitting appointments with your grandchild. To help you coordinate calendars on multiple devices, you can also sync events with other calendar accounts or use iCloud to sync calendars between supported devices.

A preinstalled app new to the iPad with iOS 6 is Clock. Though simple to use, Clock helps you view the time in multiple locations, set alarms, and use a timer.

Get ready to . . .

➡ View Your Calendar

➡ Add Calendar Events

➡ Add Events Using Siri

➡ Create Repeating Events

➡ Add Alerts

➡ Search Calendars

➡ Subscribe to and Share Calendars

➡ Delete an Event

➡ Display Clock

➡ Add or Delete a Clock

➡ Set an Alarm

➡ Use Stopwatch and Timer

In this chapter, you master the simple procedures for getting around your calendar, entering and editing events, setting up alerts, syncing, and searching. You also learn the simple ins and outs of using Clock.

View Your Calendar

1. Calendar offers several ways to view your schedule. Start by tapping the Calendar app icon on the Home screen to open it.

2. Tap the Day button at the top of the screen to display Day view (if it's not already displayed). This view, shown in **Figure 16-1,** displays your daily appointments with times listed on the left page, along with a calendar for the month, and an hourly breakdown of the day on the right page. Tap a day on the monthly calendar displayed in the top-right corner of the left page to change days in this view.

List of the day's appointments

Calendar for the month

Day button   Hourly breakdown of the day

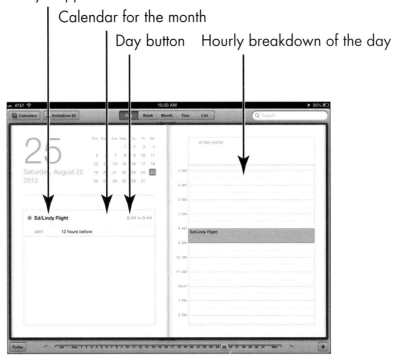

Figure 16-1

3. Tap the Week button to view all events for the current week, as shown in **Figure 16-2**. In this view, appointments appear with times listed along the left side of the screen.

Week button

Figure 16-2

4. Tap the Month button to get an overview of your busy month (see **Figure 16-3**). In this view, you see the name and timing of each event.

5. Tap the Year button to see your entire year of commitments, as shown in **Figure 16-4**.

Month button

Figure 16-3

Year button

Figure 16-4

6. Tap the List button to see List view, which displays your daily calendar with a list of all commitments for the month to the left of it, as shown in **Figure 16-5**.

List button   Search field

Today button
Backward button   Timeline   Forward button
                                  Add button

Figure 16-5

7. To move from one day, week, month, or year to another, use the Timeline displayed along the bottom of every view. Tap a day to move to it, or press the Forward or Backward button to move forward or backward one increment at a time: a day at a time in Day view, a week at a time in Week view, and so on.

8. To jump back to today, tap the Today button in the bottom-left corner of Calendar.

 For the feel of a paper calendar book, rotate your screen to landscape orientation when in the Calendar app. This orientation provides a nice book-like experience, especially in Day view.

Add Calendar Events

1. With any view displayed, tap the Add button (refer to **Figure 16-5**) to add an event. The Add Event dialog, shown in **Figure 16-6,** appears.

Figure 16-6

2. Enter a title for the event and, if you want, a location.

3. Tap the Starts/Ends field; the Start & End dialog, shown in **Figure 16-7,** is displayed.

Figure 16-7

4. Place your fingertip on the date, hour, minute, or AM/PM column and move your finger to scroll up or down. If you want to change the Time Zone, tap that field, begin to enter a new location, and then tap the location in the suggestions that appear. When each item is set correctly, tap Done. (Note that, if the event will last all day, you can simply tap the All-Day On/Off button and forget about setting start and end times.)

5. If you want to add notes, use your finger to scroll down in the Add Event dialog and tap in the Notes field. Type your note, and then tap the Done button to save the event.

 You can edit any event at any time by simply tapping it in any view of your calendar. The Edit Event dialog appears, offering the same settings as the Add Event dialog (shown earlier, in **Figure 16-6**). Tap the Done button to save your changes.

Add Events Using Siri

1. Press and hold the Home button.

2. Say "Create Meeting October 3rd at 2:30 p.m."

3. When Siri asks you if you're ready to schedule the event, say "Yes."

 You can schedule an event with Siri several ways because the feature is pretty flexible. You can say "Create event," and then Siri asks you first for a date, then for a time. Or you can say "I have a meeting with John on April 1st," and Siri might respond by saying "I don't find a meeting with John on April 1st; shall I create it?" You can say "Yes" to have Siri create it. Play around with this feature and Calendar; it's a lot of fun!

Create Repeating Events

1. If you want an event to repeat, such as a weekly or monthly appointment, you can set a repeating event. With any view displayed, tap the Add button to add an event. The Add Event dialog (refer to **Figure 16-6**) appears.

2. Enter a title and location for the event and set the start and end dates and times, as shown in the earlier task "Add Calendar Events."

3. Tap the Repeat field; the Repeat Event dialog, shown in **Figure 16-8,** is displayed.

Figure 16-8

4. Tap a preset time interval: Every Day, Week, 2 Weeks, Month, or Year.

5. Tap Done. You return to the Add Event dialog.

6. Tap Done again to save your repeating event.

 Other calendar programs might give you more control over repeating events; for example, you might be able to make a setting to repeat an event every Tuesday or the 1st and 3rd Sunday of the month. If you want a more robust calendar feature, you might consider setting up your appointments in iCal/Calendar or Outlook and syncing them to iPad. But if you want to create a simple repeating event in iPad's Calendar app, simply add the first event on a Tuesday and make it repeat every week. Easy, huh?

Add Alerts

1. If you want your iPad to alert you when an event is coming up, you can use the Alert feature. First tap the Settings icon on the Home screen and choose General, and then choose Sounds.

2. Tap Calendar Alerts and then tap any Alert Tone, which plays the tone for you. When you've chosen the alert tone you want, tap Sounds to return to Sounds settings.

3. Press the Home button and then tap Calendar and create an event in your calendar or open an existing one for editing, as covered in earlier tasks in this chapter.

4. In the Add Event (refer to **Figure 16-6**) or Edit dialog, tap the Alert field. The Event Alert dialog appears, as shown in **Figure 16-9**. Note that if you want two alerts — say, one the day before and one an hour before — you can repeat this procedure using Second Alert instead.

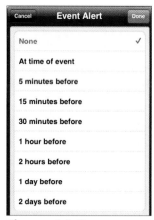

Figure 16-9

5. Tap any preset interval, from 5 Minutes to 2 Days Before or at the time of the event. (Remember that you can scroll down in the dialog to see more options.)

6. Tap Done to save the alert and then tap Done in the Add Event dialog to save all settings.

7. Tap the Day button to display Day view of the date of your event; note that the alert and time frame are listed under the event in that view, as shown in **Figure 16-10**.

An event's alert and time frame

Figure 16-10

 If you work for an organization that uses a Microsoft Exchange server, you can set up your iPad to receive and respond to invitations from colleagues in your company. When somebody sends an invitation that you accept, it appears on your calendar. Check with your company network administrator (who will jump at the chance to get her hands on your iPad) or the *iPad User Guide* to set up this feature if it sounds useful to you. Or you can check into using iCloud — which pretty much does the same thing minus the IT person.

Search Calendars

1. With Calendar open in any view, tap the Search field in the top-right corner (refer to **Figure 16-5**). The onscreen keyboard appears.

2. Type a word or words to search by and then tap the Search key on the onscreen keyboard. As you type, the Results dialog appears, as shown in **Figure 16-11**.

Figure 16-11

3. Tap any result to display it in the view you were in when you started the search. The Edit dialog appears; there you can edit the event if you want.

Subscribe to and Share Calendars

1. If you use a calendar available from an online service such as Yahoo! or Google, you can subscribe to that calendar to read events saved there on your iPad. Note that you can only read, not edit, these events. Tap the Settings icon on the Home screen to get started.

2. Tap the Mail, Contacts, Calendars option on the left.

3. Tap Add Account. The Add Account options, shown in **Figure 16-12,** appear.

4. Tap an e-mail choice, such as Gmail or Yahoo!.

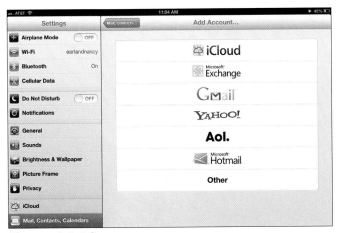

Figure 16-12

5. In the dialog that appears (see **Figure 16-13**), enter your name, e-mail address, and e-mail account password.

Figure 16-13

6. Tap Save. iPad verifies your address.

7. Your iPad retrieves data from your calendar at the interval you have set to fetch data. To review these settings, tap the Fetch New Data option in the Mail, Contacts, Calendars dialog.

8. In the Fetch New Data pane that appears (see **Figure 16-14**), be sure that the Push option's On/Off button reads *On*, and then choose the option you prefer for how frequently data is pushed to your iPad.

Make sure this is set to On

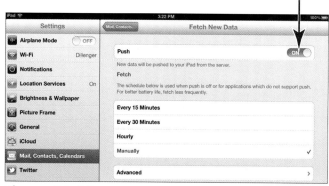

Figure 16-14

 If you use Microsoft Outlook's calendar or iCal/ Calendar on your main computer, you can sync it to your iPad calendar to avoid having to re-enter event information. To do this, use iCloud settings to sync automatically (see Chapter 3), sync wirelessly from iPad, or connect your iPad to your computer with the Dock Connector to USB Cable and use settings in your iTunes account to sync with calendars. Click the Sync button, and your calendar settings will be shared between your computer and iPad (in both directions). Read more in Chapter 3 about working with iTunes to manage your iPad content.

 If you store your contacts' birthdays in the Contacts app, the Calendar app then displays each one when the day comes around so you won't forget to pass on your congratulations . . . or condolences.

 You can also have calendar events sent if you sub- scribe to a push service. This can sync calendars from multiple e-mail accounts with your iPad calendar. Be aware that if you choose to have data pushed to your iPad, your battery may drain faster.

Delete an Event

1. When an upcoming luncheon or meeting is canceled, you may want to delete the appointment. With Calendar open, tap an event. Then tap the Edit button on the information bar that appears (see **Figure 16-15**). The Edit dialog opens.

 Tap this button

Figure 16-15

2. In the Edit dialog, tap the Delete Event button (see **Figure 16-16**).

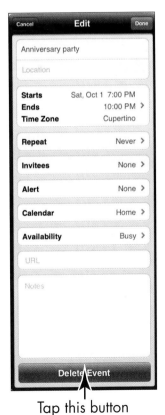

Tap this button

Figure 16-16

3. Confirming options appear, including a Delete Event button. If this is a repeating event, you have two buttons that offer the option to delete this instance of the event or this and all future instances of the event (see **Figure 16-17**). Tap the button for the option you prefer. The event is deleted, and you return to Calendar view.

Figure 16-17

 If an event is moved but not canceled, you don't have to delete the old one and create a new one: Simply edit the event to change the day and time in the Edit dialog.

Display Clock

1. Clock is a new, preinstalled app that comes with iOS 6. You can access it from the Home screen that contains all the other preinstalled apps such as Videos and Camera. Tap the Clock app to open it. Preset clocks are displayed along the top, and the location of these clocks on the world map are displayed below.

2. Tap a clock along the top of the screen to display it full screen (see **Figure 16-18**).

World Clock button

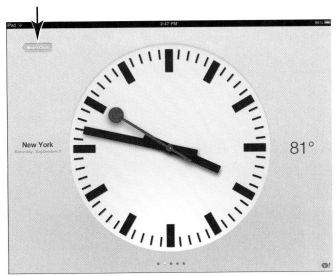

Figure 16-18

3. Tap the World Clock button to return to the Clock World Clock screen. (If the World Clock button isn't visible, tap the screen once and it appears.)

 Clocks for cities that are currently in nighttime are displayed in black. Clocks for cities that are currently in daytime are displayed in white.

Add or Delete a Clock

1. You can add a clock for many (but not all) locations around the world. With Clock open, tap Add on the clock on the far right.

2. Tap a city on the list, or tap a letter on the right side to display locations that begin with that letter. The clock appears in the last spot on the right, and the location is displayed on the world map.

3. To remove a location, tap the Edit button in the top-left corner of the World Clock screen.

4. Tap the minus symbol next to a location and then tap the Delete button (see **Figure 16-19**).

Delete button

Figure 16-19

Set an Alarm

1. With the Clock app open, tap the Alarm tab on the bottom of the screen.

2. Tap the Add button (a button with a plus symbol on it in the upper-right corner). In the Add Alarm dialog shown in **Figure 16-20,** take any of the following actions, tapping the Back button after you make each setting to return to the Add Alarm dialog:

- Tap Repeat if you want the alarm to repeat at a regular interval, such as every Monday or every Sunday.

- Tap Sound to choose the tone the alarm will play.

- Tap the On/Off button for Snooze if you want to use the Snooze feature.

- Tap Label if you want the alarm to have a name such as "Take Pill" or "Call Mom."

Add button

Figure 16-20

3. Place your finger on the three sliders at the bottom of the dialog and scroll to set the time when you want the alarm to occur and tap Save. The alarm appears on the calendar on the Alarm tab.

 To delete an alarm, tap the Alarm tab and tap Edit. All alarms appear. Tap the red circle with a minus in it and then tap the Delete button.

Use Stopwatch and Timer

Sometimes life seems like a countdown or a ticking clock counting the minutes you've spent on a certain activity. You can use the Stopwatch and Timer tabs of the Clock app to count down to a specific time, such as the moment when your chocolate chip cookies are done, or to time a walk.

These two work very similarly: Tap the Stopwatch or Timer tab and tap the Start button. When you set the Timer, iPad uses a sound to notify you when time's up. When you start the Stopwatch, you have to tap the Stop button when the activity is done (see **Figure 16-21**).

Stop button

Figure 16-21

Working with Reminders and Notifications

*W*ith the arrival of iOS 5, the Reminders app and the Notification Center feature appeared, warming the hearts of those of us who occasionally have a "senior" moment.

Reminders is a kind of to-do list that lets you create tasks and set reminders so you don't forget them.

Notifications allows you to review all the things you should be aware of in one place, such as new mail messages, text messages, calendar appointments, reminders, and alerts. You can also display weather and stock reports in the Notification Center.

If you occasionally need to escape all your obligations, try the Do Not Disturb feature, new with iOS 6. Turn this feature on and you won't be bothered with alerts until you turn it off again.

In this chapter, you discover how to set up and view tasks in Reminders and how the Notification Center can centralize all your alerts in one easy-to-find place.

Get ready to . . .

➡ Create a Task in Reminders

➡ Edit Task Details

➡ Schedule a Reminder

➡ Create a List

➡ Sync with Other Devices and Calendars

➡ Mark as Complete or Delete a Reminder

➡ Set Notification Types

➡ View Notification Center

➡ Go to an App from Notification Center

➡ Clear Notifications

➡ Get Some Rest with Do Not Disturb

Create a Task in Reminders

1. Creating a task in Reminders is pretty darn simple. Tap Reminders on the Home screen.

2. In the screen that appears (see **Figure 17-1**) tap the Add button to add a task. The onscreen keyboard appears.

3. Enter a task name or description using the onscreen keyboard and tap the Return button. The new task is added to the Reminders list.

 You can't add details about a task when you enter it, only a descriptive name. To add details about timing and so forth, see the next task.

Add button

Figure 17-1

Note that when you first begin to use Reminders, you will have only the Reminders list to add tasks to. However, you can create your own list categories. See the task "Create a List" later in this chapter to find out how to do this.

Edit Task Details

1. Tap a task to open the Details dialog. To see all the available options, tap Show More to display the choices shown in **Figure 17-2**. (Note that I explain reminder settings in the following task.)

2. Tap Priority, choose None, Low, Medium, or High from the choices that appear, and then tap Done.

3. Tap List and then, from the options displayed (see **Figure 17-3**), choose any list name to access the tasks from that list; then tap Done.

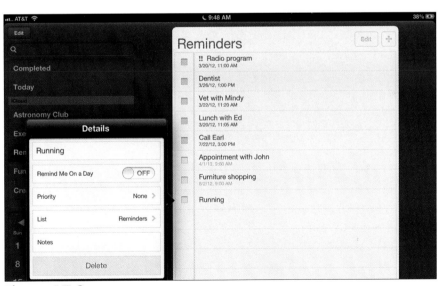

Figure 17-2

Tap any list to access its tasks

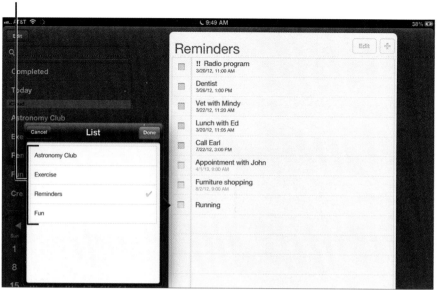

Figure 17-3

4. Tap Notes and then, using the onscreen keyboard, enter a
note about the task.

With this version of the app, priority settings don't
do much: They don't set a flag of any kind on a task
in a list, nor do they reorder tasks to show priority
tasks first. You can only see the priority of a task by
displaying its details.

Schedule a Reminder

1. One of the major features of Reminders is to remind you
of upcoming tasks. To set a reminder, tap a task.

2. In the dialog that appears, tap Remind Me On a Day to
turn the feature on.

3. Tap the date that appears below this setting and the
settings shown in **Figure 17-4** appear.

Make date settings here

Figure 17-4

4. Tap and flick the day, hour, and minutes fields to scroll to the date and time for the reminder.

5. Tap Done to save the settings for the reminder.

If you want a task to repeat with associated reminders, tap the Repeat field in the Details dialog, and from the dialog that appears, tap Every Day, Week, 2 Weeks, Month, or Year (for those annual meetings, or so you remember to buy your spouse an anniversary gift). Tap Done twice to save the setting.

You can scroll the monthly calendar display to show months in the past or future by tapping the forward or backward arrows, and tap any date to show its tasks in the daily list on the right.

Create a List

1. You can create your own lists of tasks to help you keep different parts of your life organized. Tap Reminders on the Home screen to open it.

2. Tap Create New List (see **Figure 17-5**) and enter the name of the list using the onscreen keyboard, and then tap Done on the keyboard.

Tap this option

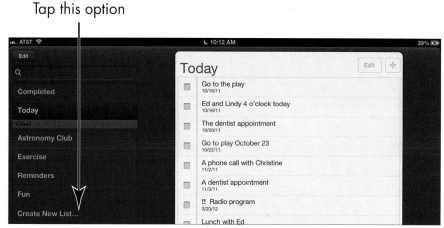

Figure 17-5

3. If you tap the list name in the List view, a new blank sheet appears on the right with that title. Tap the Add button to add new tasks to the list (see **Figure 17-6**).

Add button

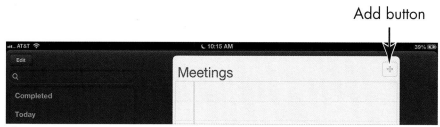

Figure 17-6

Sync with Other Devices and Calendars

Note that to make all these settings work, you should set up your default Calendar and set up your iCloud account under Accounts in the Mail, Contacts, Calendar settings.

1. To determine which tasks are brought over from other devices or calendars such as Outlook or iCal/Calendar, tap the Settings icon on the Home screen.

2. Tap iCloud and be sure that, in the list that appears in the right pane, Reminders is set to On (see **Figure 17-7**).

Make sure this is set to On

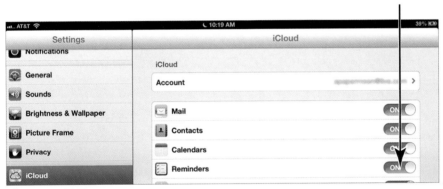

Figure 17-7

3. Also in the right pane, make sure that Calendars is set to On.

4. Tap Mail, Contacts, Calendars and scroll down to the Calendars category of settings.

5. Tap the Sync field and then choose how far back to sync Reminders (see **Figure 17-8**).

Tap this option

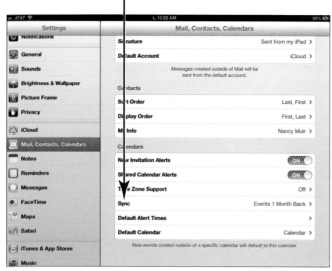

Figure 17-8

Mark as Complete or Delete a Reminder

1. You may want to mark a task as completed or just delete it entirely so you don't continue to get notifications about it. With Reminders open, tap a task to display the Details dialog shown in **Figure 17-9**.

2. Tap Delete. In the confirming dialog, tap Delete again.

3. To mark a task as complete, tap the check box to the left of the task in List view, and then tap the Completed category. The task moves to Completed and is removed from its previous category.

Figure 17-9

Set Notification Types

1. Notification Center is a list of various alerts and appointments you can display by swiping down from the top of any iPad screen. Notification Center is on by default, but you can make settings to control what types of notifications are displayed. Tap Settings and then tap Notifications.

2. In the settings that appear (see **Figure 17-10**), note that there is a list of items included in Notification Center and a list of items not included. For example, Messages and Reminders may be included, but alerts in game apps may not.

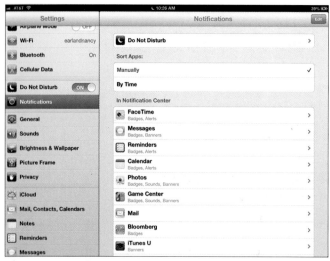

Figure 17-10

3. Tap any item and, in the settings that appear (see **Figure 17-11**), tap the On/Off button to include or exclude that item from Notification Center.

Include or exclude from Notification Center

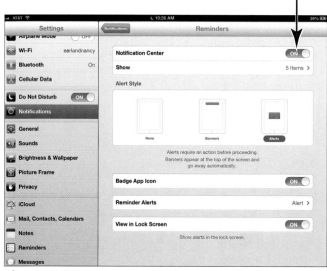

Figure 17-11

4. Tap an Alert Style to have no alert, a banner across the top of the screen, or a boxed alert appear. If you choose Banner, it will appear and then disappear automatically. If you choose Alerts, you have to take an action to dismiss the alert when it appears.

5. Badge App Icon is a feature that places a red circle and number on icons on your Home screens representing alerts associated with those apps. For example, with this feature turned on you would see an indication of how many new e-mails you have waiting for you. To turn this feature off, tap the On/Off button for Badge App Icon.

6. If you want to be able to view alerts such as alerts about new messages when the Lock Screen is displayed, turn on the View in Lock Screen setting. When you've finished making settings for an individual app, tap the Notifications button to go back to the Notifications settings, or press the Home button.

View Notification Center

1. After you've made settings for what should appear in Notification Center, you'll regularly want to take a look at those alerts and reminders. From any screen, tap the black Status bar on top and drag down to display Notification Center (see **Figure 17-12**).

Notification Center

Figure 17-12

2. Note that items are divided into lists by type, for example, Reminders, Mail, Calendar, and so on.

3. To close Notification Center, tap the three lines in the bottom center of the notification area and drag up toward the Status bar.

 To determine what is displayed in Notification Center, see the previous task.

Go to an App from Notification Center

1. You can easily jump from Notification Center to any app that caused an alert or reminder to appear. Tap the Status bar and drag down to display Notification Center.

2. Tap any item; it opens in its originating app. If you've tapped a message such as an e-mail, you can then reply to the message using the procedure described in Chapter 6.

Clear Notifications

1. To get rid of old notifications for an app, tap the Status bar and drag down to display Notification Center.

2. Tap the pale-gray X to the right of a notification category such as Mail. The button changes to read Clear (see Figure 17-13).

Tap this option

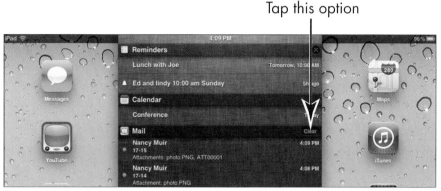

Figure 17-13

3. Tap the Clear button, and all items for that category are removed.

 If you change your mind about clearing all items in a group after you tap the Clear button, just close Notification Center.

Get Some Rest with Do Not Disturb

 1. Do Not Disturb is a simple but useful setting you can use to stop any alerts and FaceTime calls from appearing or making a sound. You can make settings to allow calls from certain people through, or to allow several repeat calls from the same person in a short time period to come through. (Apple is assuming such repeat calls may signal an emergency situation or urgent need to get through to you.) Tap Settings.

2. Tap Do Not Disturb to turn the feature on.

3. Tap Notifications and then tap Do Not Disturb.

4. In the settings shown in **Figure 17-14,** do any of the following:

- Tap Scheduled to allow alerts you scheduled using the Reminder app to appear.

- Tap Allow Calls From and then select Everyone, No One, Favorites, or All Contacts from the next screen.

- Tap Repeated Calls to allow a second call over FaceTime in a three minute time period to come through.

5. Press the Home button to return to the Home screen.

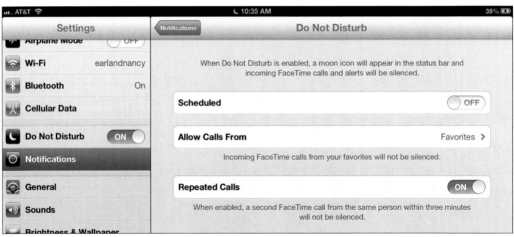

Figure 17-14

Managing Contacts

*C*ontacts is the iPad equivalent of the dog-eared address book that sits by your phone. The Contacts app is simple to set up and use, and it has some powerful features beyond simply storing names, addresses, and phone numbers.

For example, you can pinpoint a contact's address in iPad's Maps application. You can use your contacts to address e-mails, Facebook messages, and tweets quickly. If you store a contact record that includes a website, you can use a link in Contacts to view that website instantly. And, of course, you can easily search for a contact by a variety of criteria, including people related to you by family ties or mutual friends.

In this chapter, you discover the various features of Contacts, including how you can save yourself time by syncing many e-mail contacts lists to your iPad instantly.

Get ready to . . .

⟶ Add a Contact

⟶ Sync Contacts with iCloud

⟶ Assign a Photo to a Contact

⟶ Add Twitter or Facebook Information

⟶ Designate Related People

⟶ Set Ringtones

⟶ Search for a Contact

⟶ Go to a Contact's Website

⟶ Address E-mail Using Contacts

⟶ Share a Contact

⟶ View a Contact's Location in Maps

⟶ Delete a Contact

Add a Contact

1. Tap the Contacts app icon on the Home screen to open the application. If you haven't entered any contacts yet, you see a blank address book (except for your own contact information that may have been added in setting up your iPad), like the one shown in **Figure 18-1.**

Add button

Figure 18-1

2. Tap the Add button; it has a small plus sign (+) on it. A blank Info page opens (see **Figure 18-2**), and the onscreen keyboard is displayed.

3. Enter any contact information you want. (You only have to enter first name, last name, or company to create a contact.)

4. To scroll down the contact page and see more fields, flick up on the page with your finger.

5. If you want to add a mailing or street address, you can tap Add New Address, which opens additional entry fields.

Figure 18-2

6. To add another information field such as Nickname or
Job Title, tap Add Field. In the Add Field dialog that
appears (see **Figure 18-3**), choose a field to add. (You
may have to flick the page up with your finger to view all
the fields.)

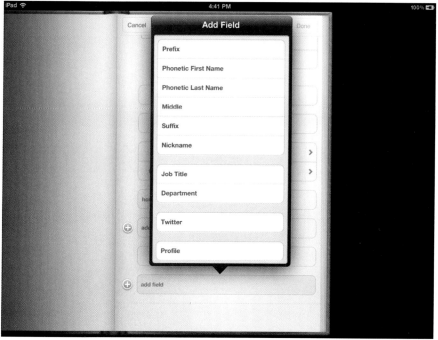

Figure 18-3

7. Tap the Done button when you finish making entries. The new contact appears in your address book. (**Figure 18-4** shows an address book with several entries added.)

Figure 18-4

 If your contact has a name that's difficult for you to pronounce, consider adding the Phonetic First Name or Phonetic Last Name field, or both, to that person's record (refer to Step 6).

 If you want to add multiple e-mail addresses to a contact so you can easily send e-mail to all of that contact's e-mail addresses, enter a work e-mail address in the steps above and another e-mail field opens up titled Other. Tap the pop-up and enter an appropriate title, and then enter another e-mail address there and another Other field opens up, and so on. Simply enter all e-mail addresses you want included for that contact and then tap Done.

Sync Contacts with iCloud

1. You can use your iCloud account to sync contacts from your iPad to back them up. These also become available to your iCloud e-mail account, if you set one up. Tap Settings on the Home screen and then tap iCloud.

2. In the iCloud settings shown in **Figure 18-5**, make sure the On/Off button for Contacts is set to On in order to sync contacts.

Make sure this is set to On

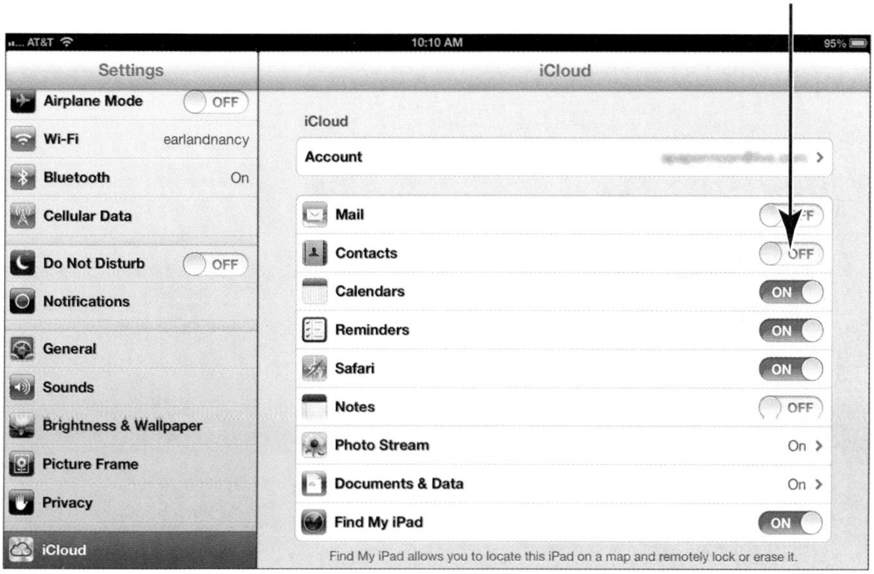

Figure 18-5

3. On the Merge Contacts dialog that appears, tap Merge (see **Figure 18-6**) to merge your iPad Contacts with iCloud.

Tap this option

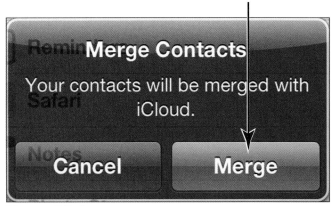

Figure 18-6

 You can also use iTunes to sync contacts among all your Apple devices and even a Windows PC. See Chapter 3 for more about making iTunes settings.

Assign a Photo to a Contact

1. With Contacts open, tap a contact to whose record you want to add a photo.

2. Tap the Edit button.

3. On the Info page that appears (see **Figure** 18-7), tap Add Photo.

Tap here...   then select a photo option

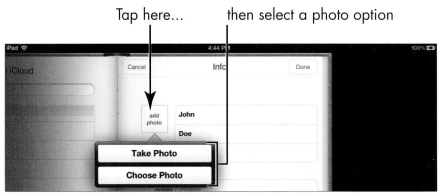

Figure 18-7

4. In the dialog that appears (refer to **Figure 18-7**), tap Choose Photo to choose an existing photo in the Photos app's Camera Roll (called the Saved Photos album on the original iPad), an album, or Photo Stream. You can also choose Take Photo to take that contact's photo on the spot.

5. In the Photo Albums dialog that appears, choose a source for your photo (such as Camera Roll, Photo Library, or Photo Stream) or categories such as Last Import, Last 12 Months, or Flags.

6. In the photo album that appears, tap a photo to select it. The Choose Photo dialog, shown in **Figure 18-8,** appears.

Figure 18-8

7. Tap the Use button to use the photo for this contact. The photo appears on the contact's Info page (see **Figure 18-9**).

Figure 18-9

8. Tap Done to save changes to the contact.

> While in the Choose Photo dialog in Step 6, you can modify the photo before saving it to the contact information. You can unpinch to expand the photo and move it around the space with your finger to focus on a particular section and then tap the Use button to use the modified version.

Add Twitter or Facebook Information

1. You can add Twitter information to a contact so you can quickly tweet (send a short message) others using Twitter or enter Facebook account information so you can post a message to your contact's Facebook account. With Contacts open, tap a contact.

2. Tap the Edit button.

3. Scroll down and tap Add Fields.

4. In the list that appears (refer to **Figure 18-3**) tap Twitter.

5. A Twitter field opens (see **Figure 18-10**). If you want to create a different social networking field, tap the Twitter label and a list of other options appears, including Sina Weibo (a Chinese social networking site), Facebook, Flickr, LinkedIn, and Myspace. You can also tap Add Custom Service to enter another service's information.

Tap in the field and enter the contact's username information for an account.

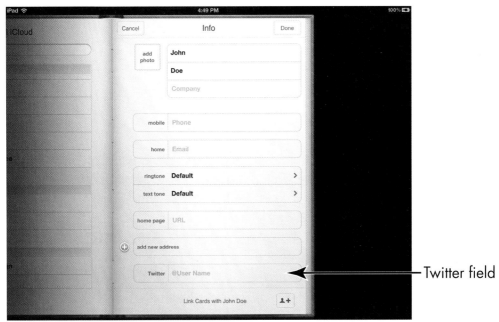

Twitter field

Figure 18-10

6. Tap Done, and the information is saved. The account is now displayed when you select the contact, and you can send a tweet, Facebook, or other message by simply tapping the username for a service and choosing the appropriate command (such as Tweet, as shown in **Figure 18-11**).

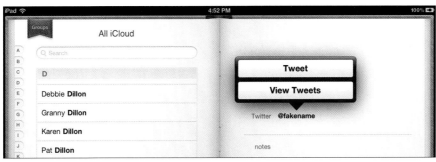

Figure 18-11

Designate Related People

1. You can quickly designate family relations in a contact record if those people are saved to Contacts. Tap a contact and then tap Edit.

2. Scroll down the record and tap Add Field.

3. Tap Related People (see **Figure 18-12**). A new field labeled *Mother* appears.

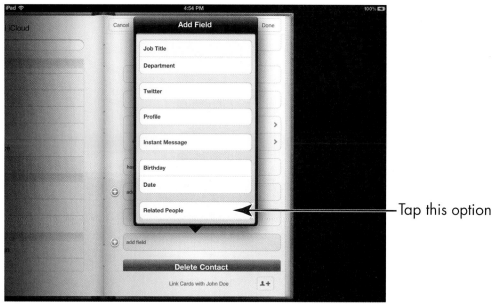

Tap this option

Figure 18-12

4. Tap the label Mother, and a list of other possible relations appears. Tap one to change the label if you wish.

5. Tap the blue arrow in the field, and your contact list appears. Tap a person's name, and it appears in the field. A new blank field also appears (see **Figure 18-13**).

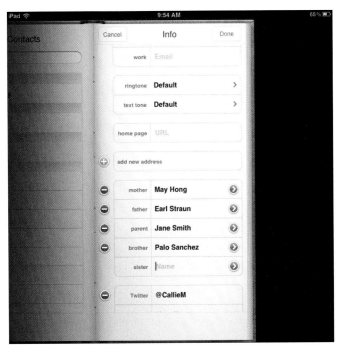

Figure 18-13

 After you add relations to a contact record, when you select the person in the Contacts main screen, all the related people for that contact are listed there.

Set Ringtones

1. If you want to hear a unique tone when you receive a FaceTime call from a particular contact, you can set up this feature in Contacts. For example, if you want to be sure you know instantly if your spouse, sick friend, or boss is calling, set a unique tone for that person. Tap to add a new contact or select a contact in the list of contacts and tap Edit.

2. Tap the Ringtone field, and a list of tones appears (see **Figure 18-14**). You can also tap Buy More Tones to buy additional ringtones from Apple.

Figure 18-14

3. Tap a tone, and it previews. When you hear one you like, tap Save.

4. Tap Done to close the contact form.

 You can set a custom tone for FaceTime calls and text messages through Settings⇨Sounds.

 If your Apple devices are synced via iCloud, setting a unique ringtone for an iPad contact also sets it for your iPhone and iPod touch, as well as FaceTime on a Mac. See Chapter 3 for more about iCloud.

Search for a Contact

1. With Contacts open, tap in the Search field at the top of the left page (see **Figure 18-15**). The onscreen keyboard opens.

Tap in the
Search field

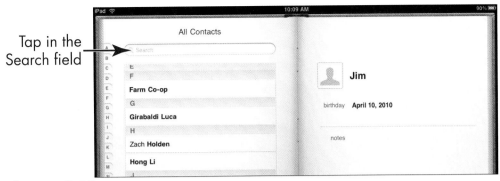

Figure 18-15

2. Type the first letter of either the first or last name or company; all matching results appear, as shown in **Figure 18-16.** In the example, pressing *N* displays *Nancy Boysen, Nettie Dillon,* and *Space Needle* in the results, all of which have *N* as the first letter of the first or last part of the name.

Search
results

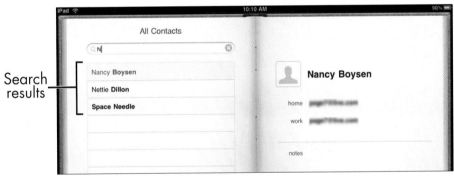

Figure 18-16

3. Tap a contact in the results to display that person's information on the page on the right (refer to **Figure 18-16**).

You can't search by phone number, website, or address in Contacts at the time of this writing, though you can search by these criteria using Spotlight Search (the Search function for iPad described in Chapter 2). We can only hope that Apple adds this functionality in future versions of the app!

You can also use the alphabetical listing to locate a contact. Tap and drag to scroll down the list of contacts on the All Contacts page on the left. You can also tap on any tabbed letter along the left side of the page to scroll quickly to the entries starting with that letter.

Go to a Contact's Website

1. If you entered website information in the Home Page field of a contact record, it automatically becomes a link in the contact's record. Tap the Contacts app icon on the Home screen to open Contacts.

2. Tap on a contact's name to display the person's contact information on the page at the right, and then tap the link in the Home Page field (see **Figure 18-17**).

3. The Safari browser opens with the web page displayed (see **Figure 18-18**).

 You can't go directly back to Contacts after you follow a link to a website. You have to press the Home button and then tap the Contacts app icon again to re-enter the application or use the multitasking feature by double-pressing the Home button and choosing Contacts from the icons that appear along the bottom of the screen. However, if you have gesture support turned on in General Settings, you can do the four-finger swipe to the left to return to the app you just left and keep swiping to go to the apps on the multitasking bar in sequence.

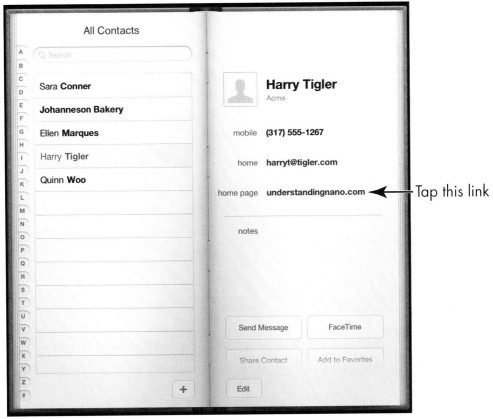

Figure 18-17

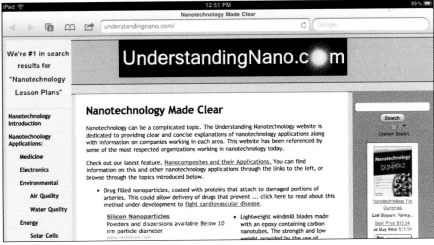

Figure 18-18

Address E-mail Using Contacts

1. If you entered an e-mail address for a contact, the address automatically becomes a link in the contact's record. Tap the Contacts app icon on the Home screen to open Contacts.

2. Tap a contact's name to display the person's contact information on the page at the right, and then tap the e-mail address link (labeled *Home* in the example shown in **Figure 18-19**).

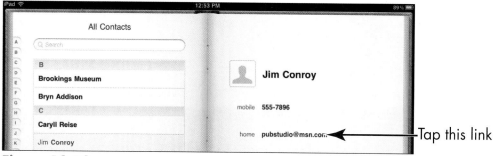

Tap this link

Figure 18-19

3. The New Message dialog appears, as shown in **Figure 18-20**. Initially the title bar of this dialog reads New Message, but as you type a Subject, New Message changes to the specific title as shown in this example.

Cancel	Check this out	Send

To: pubstudio@msn.com

Cc/Bcc:

Subject: Check this out

I like this new website. Try it!

IPadMadeClear.com

Sent from my iPad

Figure 18-20

4. Use the onscreen keyboard to enter a subject and message.

5. Tap the Send button. The message goes on its way!

Share a Contact

1. After you've entered contact information, you can share it with others via an e-mail message. With Contacts open, tap a contact name to display its information.

2. On the information page, tap the Share Contact button (refer to **Figure 18**-4). In the dialog that appears, tap either Email or Message. A New Message form appears.

3. In the e-mail New Message form, shown in **Figure 18-21**, use the onscreen keyboard to enter the recipient's e-mail address. *Note:* If the person is saved in Contacts, just type his or her name here. If you were sending a Message, you'd enter an iMessage contact's info in the To line along with a message.

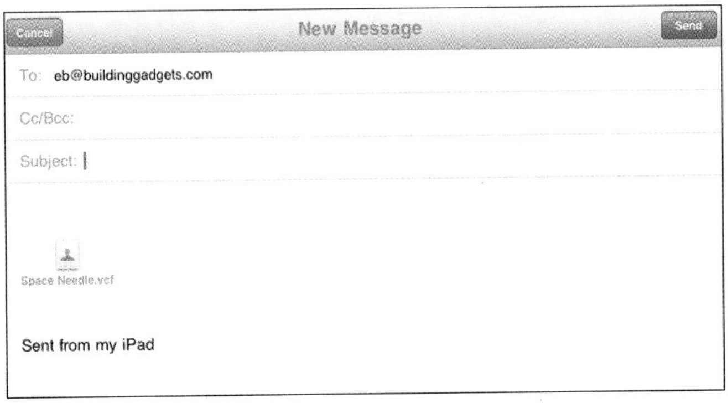

Figure 18-21

4. Enter information in the Subject field.

5. If you like, enter a message and then tap the Send button. The message goes to your recipient with the contact information attached as a `.vcf` file. (This *vCard* format is commonly used to transmit contact information.)

 When somebody receives a vCard containing contact information, he or she needs only to click (or tap) the attached file to open it. At this point, depending on the recipient's e-mail or contact management program, he can perform various actions to save the content. Other Mac, iPhone, iPod touch, or iPad users can easily import `.vcf` records into their own Contacts apps. Even PC users can do this if their contact management program supports .vcf records.

View a Contact's Location in Maps

1. If you've entered a person's address in Contacts, you have a shortcut for viewing that person's location in the Maps application. Tap the Contacts app icon on the Home screen to open it.

2. Tap the contact you want to view to display his information.

3. Tap the address. Maps opens and displays a map to the address (see **Figure 18-22**).

 This task works with more than your friends' addresses. You can save information for your favorite restaurant or movie theater or any other location and use Contacts to jump to the associated website in the Safari browser or to the address in Maps. For more about using Safari, see Chapter 5. For more about the Maps application, see Chapter 15.

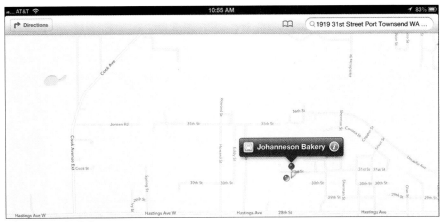

Figure 18-22

Delete a Contact

1. When it's time to remove a name or two from your Contacts, it's easy to do. With Contacts open, tap the contact you want to delete.

2. On the information page on the right (refer to **Figure 18-4**), tap the Edit button.

3. On the Info page that appears, drag your finger upward to scroll down and then tap the Delete Contact button at the bottom (see **Figure 18-23**).

4. The confirming dialog shown in **Figure 18-24** appears; tap the Delete button to confirm the deletion.

 During this process, if you change your mind before you tap Delete, tap the Cancel button in Step 4. But be careful: After you tap Delete, there's no going back!

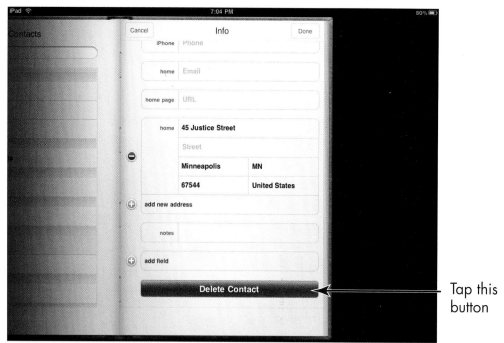

Tap this button

Figure 18-23

Tap this button

Figure 18-24

Talking to Your iPad with Siri

*O*ne of the biggest changes in iOS 6 for iPad is Siri, a personal assistant feature that responds to spoken commands using a third-generation iPad. Siri first appeared with iPhone 4S, and now with Siri on your iPad, you can ask for nearby restaurants, and a list appears. You can dictate your e-mail messages rather than typing them. Calling your mother is as simple as saying, "Call Mom." Want to know the capital of Rhode Island? Just ask. Siri checks an online database to answer questions ranging from the result of a mathematical calculation to the size of Jupiter.

Activate Siri

When you first go through the process of setting up your third-generation iPad, making settings for your location, using iCloud, and so on, at one point you will see the screen in **Figure 19-1.** To activate Siri at this point, just tap Use Siri and then tap Next. As you begin to use your iPad, it reminds you about using Siri by displaying a message.

Get ready to . . .

➡ Activate Siri

➡ Understand All that Siri Can Do

➡ Call Contacts via FaceTime

➡ Create Reminders and Alerts

➡ Add Tasks to Your Calendar

➡ Play Music

➡ Get Directions

➡ Ask for Facts

➡ Search the Web

➡ Send E-mail or Messages

➡ Get Helpful Tips

Figure 19-1

If you didn't activate Siri during the registration process, you can use Settings to turn Siri on by following these steps:

1. Tap the Settings icon on the Home screen.

2. Tap General, and then tap Siri (see **Figure 19-2**).

3. In the dialog in **Figure 19-3,** tap the On/Off button to turn Siri on.

Tap General...   then tap Siri

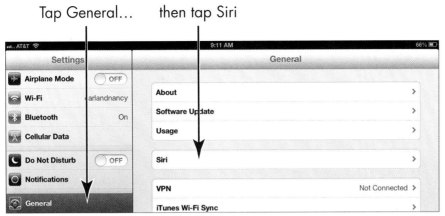

Figure 19-2

Make sure this is set to On

Figure 19-3

4. If you wish to change the language Siri uses, tap Language and choose a different language in the list that appears.

 If you only want Siri to verbally respond to your requests when iPad isn't in your hands, Tap Voice Feedback and choose Handsfree Only. Here's how this setting works and why you might want to use it: In general, if you're holding your iPad, you can read responses on the screen, so you might not want to have your tablet talk to you out loud. However, if you are, say, puttering with an electronics project, you may want to speak requests for mathematical calculations and hear the answers rather than having to read them. In such situations, Handsfree is a useful setting.

 Siri is only available on iPad when you have Internet access, but remember that cellular data charges could apply if that connection is via 3G/4G. In addition, Apple warns that available features may vary by area.

Understand All that Siri Can Do

Siri allows you to interact with many apps on your iPad by voice. You can pose questions or ask to do something like make a FaceTime call or add an appointment to your calendar, for example. Siri can also search the Internet or use an informational database called Wolfram Alpha to provide information on just about any topic. You don't have to be in an app to make a request involving another app.

Siri is the technology behind the iPad's Dictation feature. When you have the onscreen keyboard open, note that it contains a microphone key you can tap to begin or end dictation. This works in any app that uses the onscreen keyboard.

Siri requires no preset structure for your questions; you can phrase things in several ways. For example, you might say, "Where am I?" to see a map of your current location, or you could say, "What is my current location?" or "What address is this?" and get the same results.

Siri responds to you both verbally and with text information, in a form as with e-mail (see **Figure 19**-4), or in a graphic display for some items such as maps. When a result appears, you can tap it to make a choice or open a related app.

Figure 19-4

Siri works with FaceTime, Music, Messages, Reminders, Calendar, Maps, Mail, Clock, Contacts, Notes, and Safari. In the following tasks, I provide a quick guide to some of the most useful ways you can use Siri.

Note that no matter what kind of action you wish to perform, first press and hold the Home button until Siri opens (see **Figure 19-5**). Remember that this works only with third-generation iPads with iOS 6 installed. The rest of this chapter assumes you're working with a third-generation iPad with iOS 6.

Figure 19-5

Call Contacts via FaceTime

First make sure the people you call are entered in your Contacts app and include their phone number in their records. If you want to call somebody by stating your relationship to her, such as "Call sister," be sure to enter that relationship in the related field in her contact record and make sure that the settings for Siri (refer to **Figure 19-3**) include your contact name in the My Info field. (See Chapter 18 for more about creating contact records.)

1. Press and hold the Home button until Siri appears.

2. Speak a command such as "Make a FaceTime call to Earl" or "FaceTime Mom."

3. If you have two contacts who might match a spoken name, Siri responds with a list of possible matches (see **Figure 19-6**). Tap one in the list or state the correct contact's name to proceed.

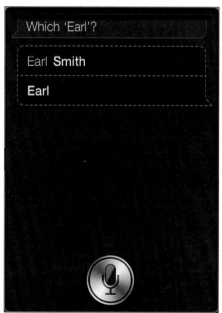

Which 'Earl'?

Earl **Smith**

Earl

Figure 19-6

4. The call is placed. To end it before it completes, you can press the Home button and then tap End.

 To cancel any spoken request, you have four options: You can say, "Cancel," tap the Microphone button on the Siri screen, press the Home button, or tap anywhere on the screen outside the Siri panel.

Create Reminders and Alerts

1. You can also use Siri with the Reminders app. To create a reminder, press and hold the Home button and then speak a command, such as "Remind me to call Dad on Thursday at 10 a.m." or "Wake me up tomorrow at 7 a.m."

2. A preview of the reminder is displayed (see **Figure** 19-7), and Siri asks you if it should create the reminder. Tap or say "Confirm" to create it or tap or say "Cancel."

Figure 19-7

3. If you want a reminder ahead of the event you created, activate Siri and speak a command such as "Remind me tonight about the play on Thursday at 8 p.m." Siri creates a second reminder, which you can confirm or cancel.

Add Tasks to Your Calendar

1. You can also set up events on your Calendar using Siri. Press and hold the Home button and then speak a phrase such as "Set up meeting at 5 p.m. on July 23rd."

2. A sample calendar entry appears, and Siri asks if you want to confirm it.

3. If there's a conflict with the appointment, Siri tells you that there's already an appointment at that time (see **Figure 19-8**) and asks if you still want to set up the new appointment. You can say "Yes" or "Cancel" at that point or tap the Yes or Cancel button.

Figure 19-8

Play Music

1. Press and hold the Home button until Siri appears.

2. To play music, speak a command, such as "Play music" or "Play 'As Time Goes By'" to play a specific song or album.

3. When music is playing, use commands, such as "Pause music," "Next track," or "Stop music" to control playback.

 One of the beauties of Siri is that you don't have to follow a specific command format as you do with some other voice command apps. You could say "Play the next track" or "Next track" or "Jump to the next track on this album" and Siri will get your meaning.

Get Directions

You can use the Maps app and Siri to find your current location, find nearby businesses such as restaurants or a bank, or get a map of another location.

Here are some of the commands you can try to get directions or a list of nearby businesses:

➡ **"Where am I?"**

Siri displays a map of your current location. If you have a Wi-Fi–only iPad, this location may be approximate.

➡ **"Where is Apache Junction, Arizona?"**

Siri displays a map of that city.

➠ "Find restaurants."

Siri displays a list of restaurants near your current location as in **Figure 19-9;** tap one to display a map of its location.

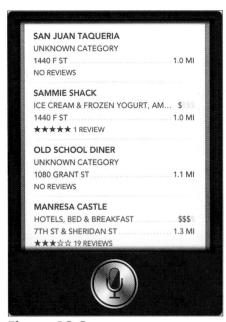

SAN JUAN TAQUERIA
UNKNOWN CATEGORY
1440 F ST . . . . 1.0 MI
NO REVIEWS

SAMMIE SHACK
ICE CREAM & FROZEN YOGURT, AM... $$$$
1440 F ST . . . . 1.0 MI
★★★★★ 1 REVIEW

OLD SCHOOL DINER
UNKNOWN CATEGORY
1080 GRANT ST . . . . 1.1 MI
NO REVIEWS

MANRESA CASTLE
HOTELS, BED & BREAKFAST . . . . $$$$
7TH ST & SHERIDAN ST . . . . 1.3 MI
★★★☆☆ 19 REVIEWS

Figure 19-9

➠ "Find Bank of America."

Siri displays a map with the location of that business (or in some cases several nearby locations, such as a bank branch and all ATMs) indicated.

After a location is displayed in a map, tap the information button on the location's label to view its address, phone number, and website address, if available.

Ask for Facts

Wolfram Alpha is a self-professed online computational knowledge engine. That means it's more than a search engine because it provides specific information about a search term rather than multiple search results. If you want facts without having to spend time browsing websites to find those facts, Wolfram Alpha is a very good resource.

Siri uses Wolfram Alpha to look up facts in response to questions, such as "What is the capital of Kansas?", "What is the square root of 2003?", or "How large is Mars?" Just press and hold the Home button and ask your question; Siri consults Wolfram Alpha and returns a set of relevant facts.

You can also get information about the weather, stocks, or the time. Just say a phrase like one of these to get what you need:

⟹ **"What is the weather?"**

This shows the weather report for your current location. If you want weather in another location, just specify the location in your question.

⟹ **"What is the price of Apple stock?"**

Siri tells you the current price of the stock or the price of the stock when the stock market last closed. (Let's hope you own some.)

⟹ **"What time is it?"**

Siri tells you the time in your time zone and displays a clock (see **Figure 19-10**).

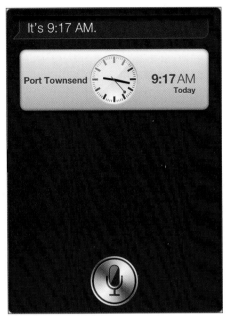

Figure 19-10

Search the Web

Siri can use Wolfram Alpha to respond to specific requests such as "Who is the Queen of England?" but Siri searches the web if you ask more general requests for information.

For example, if you speak a phrase such as "Find a website about birds" or "Find information about the World Series," Siri can respond in a couple of ways. The app can simply display a list of search results using the default search engine specified in your settings for Safari or suggesting, "If you like, I can search the web for such-and-such." In the first instance, just tap a result to go to that website. In the second instance, you can confirm that you want to search the web or cancel.

Send E-mail or Messages

You can create an e-mail or an instant message using Siri. For example, if you say, "E-mail Jack Wilkes," a form opens already addressed to that contact. Siri asks you the subject and what to say in the message; speak your message and then say, "Send" to speed your message on its way.

Siri also works with the iMessage feature. Tap Siri and say "Message Sarah." Siri creates a message and asks what you want to say. Say "Tell Sarah I'll call soon" and Siri creates a message for you to approve and send.

 It's hard to stump Siri. For example, at this point, Siri can't tweet unless you have downloaded and set up the Twitter app. But if you try to speak a tweet without it installed, she gives you a link to tap to install the app!

Get Helpful Tips

I know you're going to have a wonderful time learning the ins and outs of Siri, but before I close this chapter, here are some tips to get you going:

⟹ **If Siri doesn't understand you:** When you speak a command and Siri displays what it thought you said, if it misses the mark, you have a few options. To correct a request you've made, you can tap the bubble containing the command Siri heard and edit it by typing or tapping the microphone key on the onscreen keyboard and dictating the correct information. If a word is underlined in blue, it's a possible error. Tap the word and then tap an alternative that Siri suggests. You can also simply speak to Siri and say something like, "I meant Sri Lanka" or "No, send it to Sally." If even corrections aren't working, you may need to restart your iPad to reset the software.

➡ **Using Find My Friends:** You can download a free app from the App Store called Find My Friends that allows you to ask Siri to locate your friends geographically, if they are carrying a device with GPS turned on.

➡ **Getting help with Siri:** To get help with Siri features, just press and hold the Home button and ask Siri, "What can you do?"

Making Notes

*N*otes is the built-in application that you can use to do everything from jotting down notes at meetings to keeping to-do lists. It isn't a robust word processor (such as Apple Pages or Microsoft Word) by any means, but for taking notes on the fly, jotting down to-do lists, or writing or speaking a poem using the Dictation feature while you sit and sip a cup of tea on your deck, it's a great option.

In this chapter, you see how to enter and edit text in Notes and how to manage notes by navigating among them, searching for content, and e-mailing, deleting, and printing notes.

Open a Blank Note and Enter Text

1. To get started with Notes, tap the Notes app icon on the Home screen. If you've never used Notes, it opens with a new, blank note displayed. (If you have used Notes, it opens to the last note you were working on. If that's the case, you might want to jump to the next task to create a new, blank note.) Depending on how your iPad is oriented, you see the view shown in **Figure 20-1** (portrait) or **Figure 20-2** (landscape).

Chapter 20

Get ready to . . .

➡ Open a Blank Note and Enter Text

➡ Create a New Note

➡ Use Copy and Paste

➡ Display the Notes List

➡ Move among Notes

➡ Search for a Note

➡ E-mail a Note

➡ Delete a Note

➡ Print a Note

Figure 20-1

2. Tap the blank page. The onscreen keyboard, shown in
Figure 20-3, appears.

 3. Tap keys on the keyboard to enter text (or, if you're using
third-generation iPad, tap the Dictation key to speak your
text; refer to **Figure 20-3** to find the Dictation key).

 If the Dictation key isn't available on your third-generation iPad, go to Settings➪General➪Keyboard and
tap Dictation to turn it on.

Figure 20-2

Dictation key

Figure 20-3

.?123 **4.** If you want to enter numbers or symbols, tap either of the keys labeled *.?123* on the keyboard. The numerical keyboard, shown in **Figure 20-4,** appears. Whenever you want to return to the alphabetic keyboard, tap either of the keys labeled *ABC*.

Figure 20-4

5. To capitalize a letter, tap a Shift key (one with the upward-pointing arrow on it) at the same time as you tap the letter. If you activate the Enable Caps Lock feature in General Keyboard Settings, you can also turn Caps Lock on by double-tapping the Shift key; tap the key once again to turn the feature off.

6. When you want to start a new paragraph or a new item in a list, tap the Return key.

7. To edit text, tap to the right of the text you want to edit and either use the Delete key to delete text to the left of the cursor or enter new text.

 If you use the Dictation feature, everything you say is sent to Apple to be changed into text. If you're not comfortable with that, you may want to disable the Dictation feature. For more about Dictation, see Chapter 4.

 When you have the numerical keyboard displayed (refer to **Figure 20-4**), you can tap either of the keys labeled #+= to access more symbols, such as the percentage sign or the euro symbol, or additional bracket styles. Pressing and holding certain keys displays alternative characters.

No need to save a note — it's kept automatically until you delete it.

 You can choose from a very small selection of fonts for your notes by going to the Notes item in Settings.

Create a New Note

 1. With one note open, to create a new note, tap the New Note button — the one with the plus sign (+) on it — in the top-right corner.

2. A new, blank note appears (refer to **Figure 20-1**). Enter and edit text as described in the previous task.

 If your iPad is in portrait orientation and you want to display the list of saved notes beside the current note, switch to landscape orientation. You can also tap the Notes button in portrait orientation to see a drop-down list of notes.

Use Copy and Paste

1. The Notes app includes two essential editing tools you're probably familiar with from other word processors: copy and paste. With a note displayed, press and hold your finger on a word. The toolbar shown in **Figure 20-5** appears.

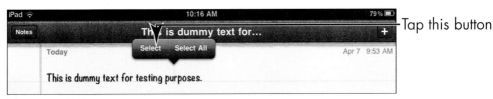

Figure 20-5

2. Tap the Select button. The toolbar shown in **Figure 20-6** appears.

Tap this button

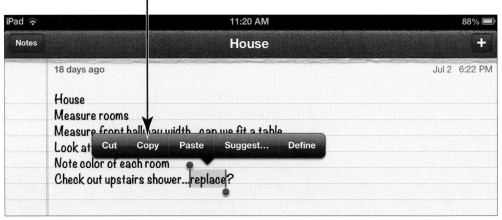

Figure 20-6

3. Tap the Copy button.

4. Press and hold your finger in the document at the spot where you want to place the copied text.

5. On the toolbar that appears (see **Figure 20-7**), tap the Paste button. The copied text appears.

Tap this option

Figure 20-7

If you want to select all text in a note to either delete or copy it, tap the Select All button on the toolbar shown in **Figure 20-5.** All text is selected and the toolbar shown in **Figure 20-6** appears again. Tap a button to cut or copy the selected text.

 To get an alternate spelling suggestion, you can tap Suggest in the menu shown in **Figure 20-6.**

 To extend a selection to adjacent words, press one of the little handles that extend from the selection and drag to the left or right.

 To delete text, you can also choose text using the Select or Select All command and then press the Delete key on the onscreen keyboard.

Display the Notes List

1. Tap the Notes app icon on the Home screen to open Notes.

2. In landscape orientation, a list of notes appears by default on the left side of the screen (refer to **Figure 20-2**). In portrait orientation, you can display this list by tapping the Notes button in the top-left corner of the screen; the notes list appears, as shown in **Figure 20-8.**

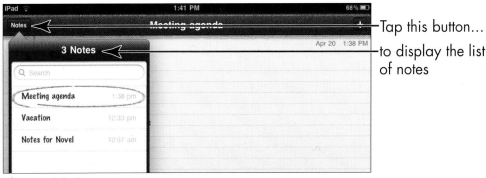

Tap this button...

to display the list of notes

Figure 20-8

3. Tap any note on the list to display it.

 Notes names your note using the first line of text. If you want to rename a note, first display the note, tap at the end of the first line of text, and then tap the Delete key on your onscreen keyboard to delete the old title or tap before the current initial text and enter a new title, which becomes the name of your note in the notes list.

Move among Notes

1. If you want to look for a note based on how long ago you created it, you should know that notes are stored with the most recently created or modified notes at the top of the notes list. Older notes fall toward the bottom of the list. The date you last modified a note is also listed in the notes list to help you out. You have a couple of ways to move among notes you've created. Tap the Notes app icon on the Home screen to open Notes.

2. With the notes list displayed (you can either turn your iPad to landscape orientation or tap the Notes button in portrait orientation; see the previous task for more on viewing the notes list), tap a note to open it.

3. To move among notes, tap the Next or Previous button (the right- or left-facing arrow at the bottom of the Notes pad, as shown in **Figure 20-9**).

Tap either of these buttons

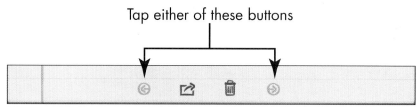

Figure 20-9

Notes lets you enter multiple notes with the same
title — which can cause confusion, so it's a good idea
to name your notes uniquely!

Search for a Note

1. You can search to locate a note that contains certain text.
The Search feature lists only notes that contain your
search criteria; it doesn't highlight and show you every
instance of the word or words you enter. Tap the Notes
app icon on the Home screen to open Notes.

2. Either hold the iPad in landscape orientation or tap the
Notes button in portrait orientation to display the notes
list (refer to **Figure 20-8**).

3. Tap in the Search field at the top of the notes list (see
Figure 20-10). The onscreen keyboard appears.

Tap here to display the onscreen keyboard

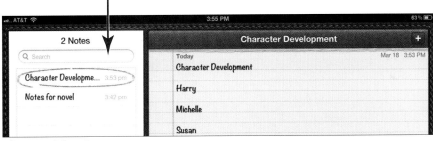

Figure 20-10

4. Begin to enter the search term. All notes that contain
matching words appear on the list, as shown in
Figure 20-11.

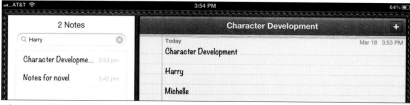

Figure 20-11

5. Tap a note to display it, and then locate the instance of the matching word the old-fashioned way — by skimming to find it.

E-mail a Note

1. If you want to share what you wrote with a friend or colleague, you can easily e-mail the contents of a note. With a note displayed, tap the Menu button at the bottom of the screen, as shown in **Figure 20-12**.

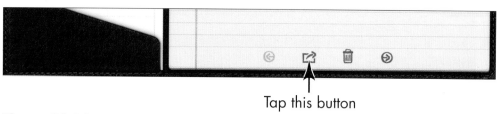

Tap this button

Figure 20-12

2. Tap Mail. In the e-mail form that appears (see **Figure 20-13**), type one or more e-mail addresses in the appropriate fields. At least one e-mail address must appear in the To field.

3. If you need to make changes to the subject or message, tap in either area and make the changes by using either the onscreen keyboard or the Dictation feature (on a third-generation iPad).

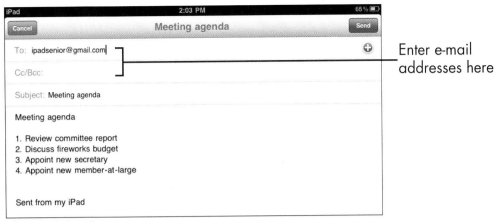

Figure 20-13

4. Tap the Send button, and your e-mail goes on its way.

 You can tap the button with a plus sign (+) on it in the top-right corner of the e-mail message form to display your contacts list and choose recipients from it. This method works only with contacts for whom you've added an e-mail address. See Chapter 18 for more about using the Contacts app.

 To cancel an e-mail message and return to Notes without sending it, tap the Cancel button in the e-mail form and then tap Delete Draft on the menu that appears. To leave a message but save a draft so that you can finish and send it later, tap Cancel and then tap Save Draft. The next time you tap the e-mail button with the same note displayed in Notes, your draft appears.

Delete a Note

1. There's no sense in letting your notes list get cluttered, making it harder to find the ones you need. When you're done with a note, it's time to delete it. Tap the Notes app icon on the Home screen to open Notes.

2. With the iPad in landscape orientation, tap a note in the notes list to open it.

3. Tap the Trash Can button, shown in **Figure 20-14.**

Tap this button

Figure 20-14

4. Tap the Delete Note button that appears (see **Figure 20-15**). The note is deleted.

Tap this button

Delete Note

Figure 20-15

Notes is a nice little application, but it's limited. It offers no formatting tools or ways to print the content you enter unless you have an AirPrint compatible printer. You can't paste pictures into Notes (you can try, but it won't work: only the filename appears, not the image). So, if you've made some notes and want to graduate to building a more robust document in a word processor, you have a couple of options. You can let iCloud sync your iPad Notes with the Notes app on your Mac if it used the Mountain Lion OS and then work with text from there. You can also buy the Pages word processor application for iPad, which costs about $9.99, and copy your note (using the copy-and-paste feature discussed earlier in this chapter). Alternatively, you can send the note to yourself in an e-mail message. Open the e-mail and copy and paste its text into a full-fledged word processor, and you're good to go.

Print a Note

1. If you have an AirPrint-enabled printer, you can print your notes. With Notes open and the note you want to print displayed, tap the Menu icon at the bottom of the screen.

2. In the icons displayed (see **Figure 20-16**), tap Print.

Tap this option

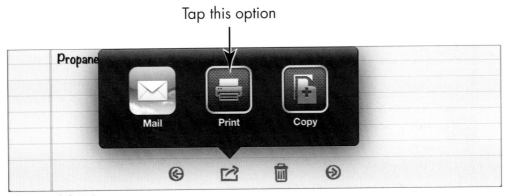

Figure 20-16

3. In the Print dialog that appears, shown in **Figure 20-17**, tap Select Printer to display a list of available printers. Tap the one you want to use.

Tap here

Figure 20-17

4. Tap the + button in the Copy field to print more than one copy.

5. Tap Print.

 See Chapter 5 for more about AirPrint-compatible printers.

Troubleshooting and Maintaining Your iPad

*i*Pads don't grow on trees — they cost a pretty penny. That's why you should learn how to take care of your iPad and troubleshoot any problems it might have so that you get the most out of it.

In this chapter, I provide some advice about the care and maintenance of your iPad, as well as tips about how to solve common problems, update iPad system software, and even reset the iPad if something goes seriously wrong. In case you lose your iPad, I even tell you about a feature that helps you find it — or even disable it if it has fallen into the wrong hands. Finally, you get information about backing up your iPad settings and content using iCloud.

Keep the iPad Screen Clean

If you've been playing with your iPad, you know that it's a fingerprint magnet (despite Apple's claim that the iPad has a fingerprint-resistant screen). Here are some tips for avoiding fingerprint marks and cleaning your iPad screen:

Get ready to . . .

- ➡ Keep the iPad Screen Clean
- ➡ Protect Your Gadget with a Case
- ➡ Extend Your iPad's Battery Life
- ➡ Find Out What to Do with a Nonresponsive iPad
- ➡ Make the Keyboard Reappear
- ➡ Update Software
- ➡ Restore the Sound
- ➡ Get Support
- ➡ Find a Missing iPad
- ➡ Back up to iCloud

➡ **Use a stylus instead of your fingers.** You can buy a stylus for as little as $2 and use it to tap the screen. You may even find it's more accurate than your fingers when using the onscreen keyboard.

➡ **Use a dry, soft cloth.** You can get most fingerprints off with a dry, soft cloth such as the one you use to clean your eyeglasses or a cleaning tissue that's lint- and chemical-free. Or try products used to clean lenses in labs, such as Kimwipes or Kaydry, which you can get from several major retailers such as Amazon.

➡ **Use a slightly dampened soft cloth.** To get the surface even cleaner, very slightly moisten the soft cloth. Again, make sure that whatever cloth material you use is free of lint.

➡ **Remove the cables.** Turn off your iPad and unplug any cables from it before cleaning the screen with a moistened cloth.

➡ **Avoid too much moisture.** Avoid getting too much moisture around the edges of the screen, where it can seep into the unit.

➡ **Never use household cleaners.** They can degrade the coating that keeps the iPad screen from absorbing oil from your fingers.

 Do *not* use premoistened lens-cleaning tissues to clean your iPad screen. Most wipe brands contain alcohol, which can damage the screen's coating.

Protect Your Gadget with a Case

Your screen isn't the only element on the iPad that can be damaged, so consider getting a case for it so you can carry it around the house or around town safely. Besides providing a bit of padding if you drop the device, a case makes the iPad less slippery in your hands, offering a better grip when working with it.

Several types of cases are available for iPad, and more are showing up all the time. You can choose the Smart Cover, from Apple, for example ($39 for polyurethane or $69 for leather), which covers the screen only; the Smart Case from Apple, which covers both the front and back ($49 in polyurethane); or a cover from another manufacturer, such as Tuff-Luv (www.tuff-luv.com) or Griffin (www.griffin technology.com) that comes in materials ranging from leather to silicone (see **Figures 21-1** and **21-2**).

Figure 21-1

Figure 21-2

Cases range from a few dollars to $70 or more for leather (with some outrageously expensive designer cases upward of $500). Some provide a cover for the screen and back (refer to **Figure 21-1**), and others protect only the back and sides (refer to **Figure 21-2**) or, in the case of Smart Cover, only the screen. If you carry your iPad around much, consider a case with a screen cover to provide better protection for the screen or use a screen overlay, such as InvisibleShield from Zagg (www.zagg.com).

Extend Your iPad's Battery Life

The much-touted 10-hour battery life of the iPad is a wonderful feature, but you can do some things to extend it even further. Here are a few tips to consider:

➥ **Keep tabs on remaining battery life.** You can estimate the amount of remaining battery life by looking at the Battery icon on the far-right end of the Status bar, at the top of your screen.

➥ **Use standard accessories to charge your iPad most effectively.** When connected to a Mac computer for charging, the iPad can slowly charge; charging the iPad on certain PC connections, on the other hand, slowly *drains* the battery. Even so, the most effective way to charge your iPad is to plug it into a wall outlet using the Dock Connector to USB Cable and the 10W USB Power Adapter that comes with your iPad (see **Figure 21-3**).

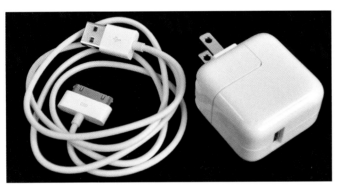

Figure 21-3

⟹ **The fastest way to charge the iPad is to turn it off while charging it.**

⟹ **Your battery may *lose* power if you leave it connected to the USB port on an external keyboard.**

⟹ **The Battery icon on the Status bar indicates when the charging is complete.**

 Your iPad battery is sealed in the unit, so you can't replace it, as you can with many laptops or cellphone batteries. If the battery is out of warranty, you have to fork over more than $100, possibly, to get a new one. See the "Get Support" task, later in this chapter, to find out where to get a replacement battery.

Apple has introduced AppleCare+. For $99 you get two years of coverage, which even covers you if you drop or spill liquids on your iPad. (Apple covers up to two incidents of accidental damage.) If your iPad has to be replaced, it will cost you only $49, rather than the $250 it used to cost with garden variety AppleCare. You can purchase AppleCare+ when you buy your iPad or within a month of the date of purchase. See www.apple.com/support/products/ipad.html for more details.

Find Out What to Do with a Nonresponsive iPad

If your iPad goes dead on you, it's most likely a power issue, so the first thing to do is to plug the Dock Connector to USB Cable into the 10W USB Power Adapter, plug the 10W USB Power Adapter into a wall outlet, plug the other end of the Dock Connector to USB Cable into your iPad, and charge the battery.

Another thing to try — if you believe that an app is hanging up the iPad — is to press the Sleep/Wake button for a couple of seconds. Then press and hold the Home button. The app you were using should close.

You can always try the tried-and-true reboot procedure: On the iPad, press the Sleep/Wake button on top until a red slider appears. Drag the slider to the right to turn off your iPad. After a few moments, press the Sleep/Wake button to boot up the little guy again.

If the situation seems drastic and none of these ideas works, try to reset your iPad. To do this, press the Sleep/Wake button and the Home button at the same time until the Apple logo appears onscreen.

Make the Keyboard Reappear

When you're using a Bluetooth keyboard, your onscreen keyboard doesn't appear. The physical keyboard has, in essence, co-opted keyboard control of your device. To use your onscreen keyboard after connecting a Bluetooth keyboard, you can turn off the Bluetooth keyboard by turning off Bluetooth in the iPad's General settings, or by moving the keyboard out of range or switching the keyboard off. Your onscreen keyboard should reappear.

Update Software

1. Apple occasionally updates the iPad system software to fix problems or offer enhanced features. You can also open Settings, tap General, and then tap Software Update to update your software. If you're not using the iCloud feature, which updates your iOS automatically, or you prefer to look for updates yourself using iTunes, you should start by connecting your iPad to your computer.

2. On your computer, open the iTunes software you installed. (See Chapter 3 for more about this topic.)

3. Click on your iPad in the iTunes source list on the left.

4. Click the Summary tab, shown in **Figure 21-4.**

5. Click the Check for Update button. iTunes displays a message telling you whether a new update is available.

Click on your iPad...   then click the Summary tab

Figure 21-4

6. Click the Update button to install the newest version.

 If you're having problems with your iPad, you can use the Update feature to try to restore the current version of the software. Follow the preceding set of steps, and then click the Restore button instead of the Update button in Step 6.

 You can also use the iTunes Wi-Fi Sync feature through the General Settings to sync wirelessly to a computer that has iTunes installed.

Restore the Sound

On the morning I wrote this chapter, as my husband puttered with our iPad, its sound suddenly (and ironically) stopped working. We gave ourselves a quick course in sound recovery, so now I can share some tips with you. Make sure that

⟶ **You haven't touched the volume control keys on a physical keyboard connected to your iPad via**

Bluetooth. They're on the right side of the top row (see **Figure 21-5**). Be sure not to touch one and inadvertently mute the sound.

➡ **You haven't flipped the Side Switch.** If you have the Side Switch set up for the Silent feature, moving the switch mutes sound on the iPad.

The volume control keys

Figure 21-5

➡ **The speaker isn't covered up.** It may be covered in a way that muffles the sound.

➡ **A headset isn't plugged in.** Sound won't play over the speaker and the headset at the same time.

➡ **The volume limit is set to Off.** You can set up the volume limit in the Music settings to control how loudly your music can play (which is useful if you have teenagers around). Tap the Settings icon on the Home screen and then, on the left side of the screen, tap Music and use the Volume Limit control (see **Figure 21-6**) to turn off the volume limit.

Make sure this is set to Off

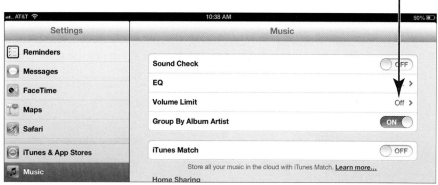

Figure 21-6

 When all else fails, reboot. This strategy worked for us — just press the Sleep/Wake button until the red slider appears. Press and drag the slider to the right. After the iPad turns off, press the Sleep/Wake button again until the Apple logo appears, and you may find yourself back in business, sound-wise.

Get Support

Every new iPad comes with a year's coverage for repair of the hardware and 90 days of free technical support. Apple is known for its helpful customer support, so if you're stuck, I definitely recommend that you try it out. Here are a few options you can explore for getting help:

➠ **The Apple Store:** Go to your local Apple Store (if one is handy) to see what the folks there might know about your problem.

➠ **The Apple support website:** It's at www.apple. com/support/ipad (see **Figure 21-7**). You can find online manuals, discussion forums, and downloads, and you can use the Apple Expert feature to contact a live support person by phone.

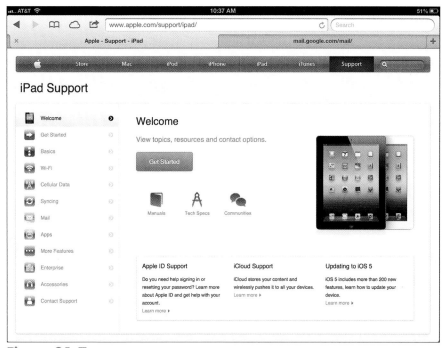

Figure 21-7

⟶ **The *iPad User Guide*:** You can use the bookmarked manual on the Safari browser to visit `http://manuals.info.apple.com/en_us/ipad_user_guide.pdf` and open a more robust version of the user guide that comes with your iPad.

⟶ **The Apple battery replacement service:** If you need repair or service for your battery, visit `www.apple.com/batteries/replacements.html`. Note that your warranty provides free battery replacement if the battery level dips below 50 percent and won't go any higher during the first year you own it. If you purchase the AppleCare service agreement, this is extended to two years.

 Apple recommends that you have your iPad battery replaced only by an Apple Authorized Service Provider.

Find a Missing iPad

You can take advantage of the Find My iPad feature to pinpoint the location of your iPad. This feature is extremely handy if you forget where you left your iPad or someone walks away with it. Find My iPad not only lets you track down the critter, but also lets you wipe out the data contained in it if you have no way to get the iPad back.

Follow these steps to set up the Find My iPad feature:

1. Tap the Settings icon on the Home screen.

2. In the Settings pane, tap iCloud.

3. In the iCloud settings that appear, tap the On/Off button for Find My iPad to turn the feature on (see **Figure 21-8**). Tap Allow on the Find My iPad dialog that appears.

Set this to On

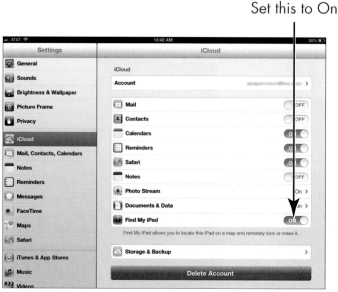

Figure 21-8

4. From now on, if your iPad is lost or stolen, you can go to http://icloud.com from your computer and enter your ID and password.

5. The Find My iPad screen appears with your iPad's location noted on a map.

6. To erase all information from the iPad in a process called wiping, click the Remote Wipe button (see **Figure 21-9**). Remember that this will erase all content, such as contacts, music, notes, and so on, for good. To lock the iPad from access by others, click the Remote Lock button.

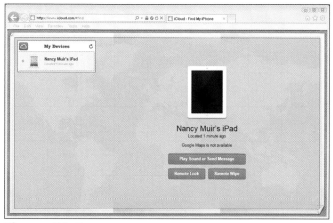

Figure 21-9

 You can also click Play Sound or Send Message to send whoever has your iPad a note saying how to return it to you — or that the police are on their way, if it has been stolen! If you choose to play a sound, it plays for two minutes, helping you track down anybody holding your iPad who is within earshot.

Backup to iCloud

You used to be able to back up your iPad content only using iTunes, but with Apple's introduction of iCloud with iOS 5, you can back up via a Wi-Fi network to your iCloud storage. You get 5GB of storage (not including iTunes-bought music, video, apps, and electronic books or music you've copied into the cloud via the paid subscription service, iTunes Match) for free or you can pay for increased levels of storage (10GB for $20 a year, 20GB for $40 a year, or 50GB for $100 a year).

1. To perform a backup to iCloud, first set up an iCloud account (see Chapter 3 for details on creating an iCloud account) and then tap Settings on the Home Screen.

2. Tap iCloud and then tap Storage & Backup (see **Figure 21-10**).

Tap this option

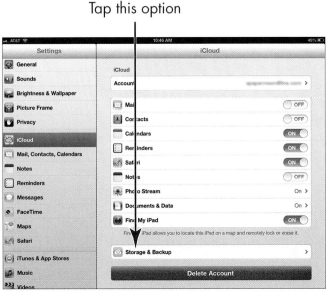

Figure 21-10

3. In the pane that appears (see **Figure 21-11**) tap the iCloud Backup On/Off switch to enable automatic backups. To perform a manual backup, tap Back Up Now. A progress bar shows how your backup is moving along.

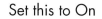
Set this to On

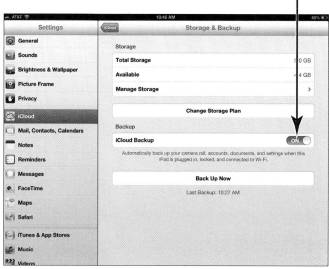

Figure 21-11

Index

• A •

A5X dual-core chip, 10

ABC, video content from, 158

Accept Cookies option, Safari, 111–112

accessibility features

  AssistiveTouch feature, 84–85

  brightness of screen, 70–71, 188

  Dictation feature. *See* Dictation feature

  Large Text feature, 83

  Speak Auto-text feature, 81–82

  VoiceOver feature, 75–79

  volume of ringers and alerts, 79–80

  wallpaper, 71–72

  white text on black, 74–75, 188, 189

  Zoom feature, 72–74

accessories, 19–22

Activity icon, on Status bar, 47

adding

  clocks, 299–300

  tasks to Calendar app with Siri, 344

address, e-mail, 121, 123

address book. *See* Contacts app

Address field, Safari, 95–96

Air Video, 159

Air Video Server, 159

AirPlay feature, 242

AirPlay technology, 215–216

AirPort-enabled wireless speakers, 215

AirPrint Activator 2 app, 22, 112

AirPrint technology, 22, 112

alarms, setting in Clock app, 300–301

albums, music

  buying, 154–156

  playing, 210–212

  viewing in Music library, 206–207

albums, photo

  creating in Camera Roll folder, 227–228

  imported photos in, 222

  slideshows of, 233

  viewing, 223–224

alerts. *See also* Calendar app

  for calendar events, 291–293

  creating with Siri, 343–344

  deleting, 315

  icons for, on Home screen, 313

  jumping to other apps from, 314

  types of, 311–313

  viewing in Notification Center, 313–314

  volume of, 79–80

AOL account, 116–117

App Store app

  buying apps, 166–167

  buying games, 247, 253–254

  described, 51

  recommended apps, list of, 162–163

  searching, 164–166

Apple AirPrint technology, 22, 112
Apple Component AV Cable, 21
Apple Composite AV Cable, 21
Apple Digital AV Adapter, 14, 21, 242
Apple ID, 18
Apple Store
  buying iPad at, 18–19
  customer support from, 374
  registering iPad at, 17, 30
Apple TV, 242
Apple Wireless Keyboard, 21
AppleCare+ coverage, 370
appointments. *See* events
apps. *See also* specific apps
  buying, 166–167
  deleting, 170–172
  described, 161
  icons for, on Home screen, 30, 31,
    47–52, 167–169
  from iPhone, using on iPad, 164
  jumping to, from alerts, 314
  list of, built-in to iPad, 47–52
  list of, optimized for Retina display, 164
  list of, recommended, 162–163
  multiple open, moving between, 43–44
  organizing in folders, 169–170
  for periodicals, downloading, 199–201
  syncing from other devices with
    iCloud, 159–160
  tweeting from, 140–141
  unresponsive, closing, 370
  updating, 172–173
Apps settings, iTunes, 59
AssistiveTouch Control Panel, 70
AssistiveTouch feature, 84–85
AT&T data plans, 15–17

audio media. *See* audiobooks; music;
    podcasts
audiobooks
  buying, 154–156
  finding in iTunes Store, 148–152
  playing. *See* Music app
  previewing before buying, 152–154
autocapitalizations, spoken, 81–82
autocorrections, spoken, 81–82
AutoFill option, Safari using, 97

• *B* •

backing up iPad contents to iCloud,
    14, 378–379
Badge App Icons, 313
battery
  charging, 56–57
  life of, extending, 368–370
  replacing, 369, 375
Battery Life icon, on Status bar, 47, 368
Bcc field, Mail, 123, 124
Belkin HDMI devices, 14
blind carbon copies (Bcc) of e-mails,
    123, 124
Bluetooth icon, on Status bar, 47
bookmarks
  in e-books, 191–194
  in maps, 268, 270–272
  in Safari, 102–104
books. *See* audiobooks; e-books
Books settings, iTunes, 59
Bookshelf
  organizing in collections, 198–199
  viewing books in, 184–186, 196–197
brightness of screen, 70–71, 188
browser. *See* Safari app
buttons on iPad, 24–26. *See also* specific
    buttons

• C •

cables
  Apple Component AV Cable, 21
  Apple Composite AV Cable, 21
  Dock Connector to USB Cable,
    23, 25, 57, 59
Calendar app
  adding events using Siri, 290
  adding tasks with Siri, 344
  alerts, adding, 291–293
  contacts' birthdays in, 296
  Day View, 284
  described, 49, 283
  e-mail calendars, sharing, 296
  events (appointments), adding, 288–289
  events (appointments), deleting,
    296–297
  events (appointments), editing, 298
  events (appointments), repeating,
    290–291, 298
  events (appointments), searching,
    293–294
  List view, 286–287
  Microsoft Exchange invitations,
    sharing, 293
  Microsoft Outlook calendar,
    sharing, 296
  Month view, 285, 286
  schedule, viewing, 284–287
  subscribing to online calendars,
    294–296
  Week view, 285
  Year view, 285–286
Camera app. See also cameras; Photos app
  described, 51
  recording videos, 44–46, 238–239
  taking photos, 44–46, 218–221
  tweeting from, 140
  viewing captured photos or videos, 46
Camera Connection Kit, iPad, 20, 221
Camera Roll folder. See also albums, photo
  creating albums in, 223–224
  organizing photos in, 227–228
  saving website photos in, 222–223
cameras. See also Camera app; Photos app
  controls for, 45
  described, 10, 44–46, 218, 237
  FaceTime app using, 133
  front- and rear-facing, switching
    between, 45, 139–140, 218, 238
  grid for, enabling, 45, 218
  locations of, 24, 25
  recording videos, 238–239
  taking photos, 218–221
  video and camera functions, switching
    between, 45, 238
Camera/Video slider, 45
Caps Lock feature, on keyboard, 38
carbon copies (Cc) of e-mails, 123, 124
care of iPad. See maintaining iPad
Case, iPad, 19
CBS news, video content from, 158
Cc field, Mail, 123, 124
cellular technology, 10, 15–17, 92
Clicker, video content from, 158
Clock app, 283
  adding clocks, 299–300
  deleting clocks, 299–300
  described, 50
  displaying, 298–299
  setting alarms, 300–301
  Stopwatch tab, 301–302
  Timer tab, 301–302
  World Clock, 299

closed-captioning, 242–243

color themes, for reading e-books, 188, 189

Component AV Cable, Apple, 21

Composite AV Cable, Apple, 21

computer requirements, 18, 28

Contacts app

  adding contacts, 318–320

  birthdays for contacts, displayed in Calendar app, 296

  calling contacts via FaceTime with Siri, 342–343

  deleting contacts, 335–336

  described, 50, 317

  e-mail addresses for contacts, 206

  Facebook information for contacts, 324–325

  location of contacts, viewing in Maps, 334–335

  phonetic name spellings for contacts, 320

  photos for contacts, assigning, 322–324

  relationships between contacts, 326–327

  ringtones for contacts, 327–328

  searching contacts, 328–330

  sending e-mail to contacts, 332–333

  sharing contacts, 333–334

  syncing contacts with e-mail accounts, 321–322

  Twitter information for contacts, 324–325

  website for contacts, going to, 330–331

conventions used in this book, 1

customer support, 374

• *D* •

Day View, Calendar app, 284

DealCatcher iPad Edition app, 163

Delete key, on keyboard, 37

Dictation feature

  described, 10, 38, 85–86

  for e-mail messages, 123

  for maps, 267

  for notes, 352, 354

  in Siri, 340

Dictation (microphone) key, on keyboard, 38, 85–86

dictionary, 195–196

Digital AV Adapter, Apple, 14, 21, 242

display. *See* screen

Do Not Disturb feature, 303, 315–316

Dock, iPad (accessory), 20, 57

Dock, on Home screen

  icons in, 30, 46–47

  scrolling left or right, 43

Dock Connector slot, 24, 25

Dock Connector to USB Cable, 23, 25, 57, 59

documentation, 22–23, 65–67

double-tapping, 33, 35, 72–73

dragging to scroll (swiping), 34, 44

dual-core A5X chip, 10

DVDO HDMI devices, 14

• *E* •

e-books

  bookmarks in, 191–194

  buying from App Store, 166–167

  buying from iBookstore, 178–181, 182–184

collections of, creating, 198–199
dictionary for, 195–196
highlighting, 191–194
interactive, creating, 177, 188–190
interactive, reading, 186–187
library of, organizing, 196–197
reading, brightness for, 188
reading, color themes for, 188, 189
reading, font for, 188–190
reading with iBooks app, 184–186
reading with Kindle app, 181
reading with Nook app, 181
samples of, viewing before buying, 181
searching, 190–191
sources for, 181–182
syncing from computer to iPad, 184
syncing from other devices with
    iCloud, 159–160
textbooks, My Notes in, 194–195
textbooks, Study Cards in, 194–195
e-mail account
  AOL, adding to iPad, 116–117
  calendars in, sharing, 296
  Gmail, adding to iPad, 116–117
  iCloud, adding to iPad, 116–117
  for iMessages, 142
  Microsoft Hotmail, adding to iPad,
      116–117
  POP3, adding to iPad, 118–121
  sending messages with Siri, 349
  Yahoo!, adding to iPad, 116–117
e-mail messages
  blind carbon copies (Bcc) of, 123, 124
  carbon copies (Cc) of, 123, 124
  deleted, viewing, 124
  deleting, 127

flagging, 121
formatting, 124–125
forwarding, 121–123
hiding address details for, 121
marking as unread, 121
organizing in folders, 127–128
reading, 120–121
replying to, 121–123
searching, 126
sending, 123–124
sending contact information in,
    333–334
sending links in, 110–111
sending locations in, 277–278
sending to contacts, 332–333
stopping retrieval of, 121
VIP List, 128–131
writing, 123–124, 124–125
enlarging or shrinking screen contents.
    See zooming
e-reader, 177. *See also* iBooks app
events (appointments). *See also* Calendar
    app; Reminders app
  adding, 288–289
  adding using Siri, 290
  alerts for, 291–293
  deleting, 296–297
  editing, 298
  repeating, 290–291, 298
  searching, 293–294

● *F* ●

face detection, 10
FaceTime app
  accepting or declining calls, 138–139
  adding callers to Favorites list, 139

FaceTime app *(continued)*
  calling contacts with Siri via, 342–343
  described, 11, 51, 133, 134–135
  enabling, 135
  ending calls, 138
  making calls, 135–137
  switching cameras during calls, 139–140
Favorites list. *See also* bookmarks
  in FaceTime app, 139
Find My Friends feature, 12, 350
Find My iPad feature, 376–377
finger motions. *See* screen
Flash, not supported, 158
flash drive, not supported, 14
flicking, 35, 78
Flickr + app, 163
folders. *See also* libraries
  for apps, 169–170, 171
  for e-mail messages, 124, 127–128
  for photos. *See* albums, photo; Camera Roll folder
  for Safari bookmarks, 104
fonts
  for e-books, 188–190
  for notes, 355
  white text on black, 74–75, 188, 189
four-finger flicking, 78

● *G* ●

Game Center app
  account for, creating, 248–249
  buying games, 247, 253–254
  described, 51, 247
  friends for, adding, 252–253
  friends for, playing games with, 258–259
  profile for, creating, 249–252

games
  battery life, benefits of, 256
  buying from App Store, 247, 253–254
  full-screen mode for, 256
  motion sensor and gyroscope for, 257
  playing against yourself, 257
  playing with Game Center friends, 258–259
  processor speed, benefits of, 255
  screen, benefits of, 255, 256
  speaker, benefits of, 256
GarageBand app, 163
global positioning system (GPS), 15, 17, 262–263
Gmail account, 116–117
Google calendar, subscribing to, 294–296
GPS (global positioning system), 15, 17, 262–263
GPS icon, on Status bar, 47
Griffin iPad cover, 368–369
Gruman, Galen (author)
  iBooks Author For Dummies, 187
Guided Access feature, 11, 70, 86–88
gyroscope, 257

● *H* ●

Handbrake utility, 159
HDMI devices, 14
headphone jack, 24, 26
hearing challenges. *See also* accessibility features
  Mono Audio feature, 80–81
  volume of ringers and alerts, 79–80
highlighting e-books, 191–194
history, Safari, 98–100
Home button, 24–25

Home screen
  alerts on app icons, 313
  app icons on, 30, 31, 47–52, 167–169
  AssistiveTouch control for, 84–85
  described, 30–31
  Dock icons on, 30, 46–47
  going to, 24–25
  organizing apps on, 167–169
  Sleep/Wake slider on, 52–53
  Status bar on, 35, 46–47
  website icons on, 107–108
Home Sharing feature (iTunes), 212
hotspots for Wi-Fi, 17

• *I* •

iBooks app
  bookmarking e-books, 191–194
  brightness of screen, 188
  buying e-books, 178–181, 182–184
  described, 52, 163, 177
  dictionary for, 195–196
  font size and type, 188–190
  highlighting e-books, 191–194
  reading e-books, 184–186
  searching e-books, 190–191
iBooks Author app, 178, 187
iBooks Author For Dummies
    (Gruman), 187
iBookstore, 178–181, 182–184
iCal, syncing with Reminders app,
    309–310
iCloud
  account for, 62–63, 116–117
  backing up iPad contents to,
    14, 378–379
  described, 17, 18, 61
  iOS updates from, 30, 42
  locating iPad using, 65

registering iPad using, 17
  requirements for, 28
  syncing with, 63–65, 159–160, 184,
    207, 296, 309–310
iCloud Tabs, 113–114
icons
  explained, 1
  on Home screen. *See* Home screen
IM (instant messaging), 133. *See also*
    Messages app
images. *See* photos
iMessage feature, 133, 141–146, 349. *See*
    also Messages app
iMovie app, 237
Info settings, iTunes, 59
instant messaging (IM), 133. *See also*
    Messages app
Internet browser. *See* Safari app
Internet connection
  3G and 4G cellular service for,
    10, 15–17, 92
  choosing, 15–17
  cost of, 15–17
  hotspot feature on smartphone for, 17
  requirements for, 17–18, 28
  Wi-Fi network for, 16–17, 28, 92–93
InvisibleShield screen overlay, 368
iOS
  new features of, 11
  updating, 30, 41–43, 371–372
  version of, 4, 10
iPad. *See also specific topics*
  accessories for, 19–22
  buying, 18–19
  choosing, 12–13
  color of, 12
  customer support, 374
  diagram of, 24

iPad (continued)
documentation for, 22–23, 65–67
Internet connection options. See
    Internet connection
iPad 2, 4, 13, 41–42
lost or stolen, locating, 65, 376–377
memory in, 13–15, 16
new features in, 10
original iPad, 4, 41–42
packaging for, 22–23
rebooting, 370, 374
registering, 17, 29–30
remotely erasing contents of, 377
remotely locking, 377
resetting, 370
return period for, 22
searching, 40–41
turning off, 53
turning on, 29–30
Wi-Fi + 3G model, 4, 15–17
Wi-Fi + 4G model, 4, 15–17
Wi-Fi only model, 4, 16–17
iPad Camera Connection Kit, 20, 221
iPad Case, 19
iPad Dock (accessory), 20, 57
iPad Dock, on Home screen
icons in, 30, 46–47
scrolling left or right, 43
iPad Keyboard Dock, 20–21
iPad Smart Cover, 19, 52, 367
iPad User Guide, 65–67, 375
iPhone, using apps from, 164
iPhoto app, 163
iSight camera, 10, 44, 218, 237. See also
    cameras
iTunes, on computer
Book library, syncing to iPad, 184
Home Sharing feature, 212
iPad settings in, 59

registering iPad with, 29–30
syncing with, 59–60
updating iOS from, 41–43
version of, 4, 18
iTunes app, on iPad
buying iTunes content, 148–152,
    154–156
described, 51
iTunes account for, 59
previewing items, 152–154
renting videos, 156–158
restricting purchases to, 156
searching iTunes Store, 148–152
signing in to iTunes, 148
iTunes Match service, 207
iTunes Store. See iTunes app, on iPad
iTunes U, 150

keyboard, onscreen
.?123 key, 37, 353
#+= key, 354
Caps Lock feature, 38
Delete key, 37
described, 36–39
Dictation (microphone) key, 38, 85–86
displaying after Bluetooth keyboard
    used, 371
hiding, 39
moving, 37
Return key, 37
Shift key, 38
splitting, 39–40
symbols, typing, 38, 354
keyboard, wireless, 20–21, 371
Keyboard Dock, iPad, 20–21
Kindle app, 181

• *L* •

Large Text feature, 83
libraries. *See also* folders
  Bookshelf, organizing in collections,
    198–199
  Bookshelf, viewing books in,
    184–186, 196–197
  Music library, searching, 208–210
  Music library, viewing, 206–207
  online, borrowing e-books from, 182
  Photo Library, saving website images
    in, 108, 222–223
links, following in Safari, 97
List view, Calendar app, 286–287

• *M* •

Mac. *See* computer requirements
magazines. *See* periodicals
magnifying glass (Search) icon, 40
Mail app
  Bcc field, 123, 124
  Cc field, 123, 124
  deleted messages, viewing, 124
  deleting messages, 127
  described, 12, 48
  To field, 121, 123, 124
  formatting messages, 124–125
  forwarding messages, 121–123
  Inbox, displaying, 120–121
  opening, 119
  organizing messages in folders, 127–128
  reading messages, 120–121
  replying to messages, 121–123
  Search field, 126
  sending messages, 123–124
  setting up e-mail accounts for, 116–117
  stopping retrieval of messages, 121
  Subject field, 124
  VIP List, 128–131
  writing messages, 123–124, 124–125
maintaining iPad. *See also*
    troubleshooting iPad problems
  AppleCare+ coverage, 370
  backing up iPad contents to iCloud,
    14, 378–379
  battery, replacing, 369, 375
  battery life, extending, 368–370
  case to protect iPad, 19, 367–368
  screen, cleaning, 28, 365–366
  updating iOS, 371–372
Maps app
  accuracy of, with different iPad models,
    15, 17, 262–263
  bookmarks, creating, 268, 270–271
  bookmarks, deleting, 271–272
  bookmarks, displaying list of, 270–271
  compass, displaying, 257
  contacts, assigning locations to,
    276–277
  contacts, viewing location in Maps,
    334–335
  current location, displaying on map,
    262–263
  described, 11, 50, 261
  directions, finding, 272–274
  getting directions with Siri, 345–346
  Hybrid view of maps, 263–264
  information about locations, 275–276
  pins, colors of, 269

Maps app *(continued)*
  pins, placing on map, 269–270
  printing maps, 265
  Satellite view of maps, 263–264
  searching for locations, 266–268
  sharing locations, 277–278
  Siri, 267
  Standard view of maps, 263
  Traffic indicators on maps, 264
  tweeting from, 140
  zooming maps, 265–266
media. *See* audiobooks; music; podcasts; videos
Mediquations Medical Calculator app, 163
memory, 13–15, 16
messages. *See* e-mail messages
Messages app
  clearing a conversation, 145–146
  described, 133
  iMessage account for, 142–145
  including photos or videos in messages, 145
microblog, Twitter as, 133, 140
microphone (Dictation) key, on keyboard, 38, 85–86
microphone on iPad, 24, 26
Microsoft Exchange, invitations from, 293
Microsoft Hotmail account, 116–117
Microsoft Outlook calendar
  syncing with Calendar app, 296
  syncing with Reminders app, 309–310
Mono Audio feature, 80–81
Month view, Calendar app, 285, 286
motion sensor, 257
movies. *See* videos
Movies settings, iTunes, 59
multitasking, 43–44

multi-touch display. *See* touchscreen technology
music
  buying, 154–156
  finding in iTunes Store, 148–152
  Ping social network for, 214–215
  playing, 210–212
  playing, status indicator for, 47
  playing with Siri, 345
  playing with slideshows, 232
  previewing before buying, 152–154
  searching Music library, 208–210
  from sources other than iTunes Store, 158–159
  streaming to other devices, 13, 215–216
  syncing from other devices with iCloud, 159–160, 207
  viewing Music library, 206–207
Music app
  described, 49, 205
  Music library, viewing, 206–207
  playing music, 210–212
  playlists, creating, 207–208
  searching Music library, 208–210
  shopping in iTunes Store, 207
  shuffle music, 212–213
  volume, adjusting, 213–214
Music library
  searching, 208–210
  viewing, 206–207
Music settings, iTunes, 59
My Notes, in textbooks, 194–195

• *N* •

Netflix, video content from, 158
New icon, in this book, 1
newspapers. *See* periodicals

Newsstand app
  buying issues of periodicals, 201–202
  described, 51, 177
  downloading periodical apps to,
    199–201
  reading periodicals, 202–203
Next arrow, Safari, 97
Nook app, 181
Notes app
  copying and pasting text from,
    355–357
  creating notes, 36, 351–355
  deleting notes, 361–363
  described, 49, 351
  e-mailing notes, 360–361
  fonts, setting, 355
  limitations of, 362–363
  list of notes, displaying, 357–358
  naming notes, 358, 359
  printing notes, 363–364
  scrolling through, 358–359
  searching notes, 359–360
Notification Center, 303, 311–314
numbers, typing, 38

● *0* ●

operating system
  for computer, 18
  for iPad. *See* iOS

● *p* ●

Pages word processor app, 362–363
Paint Studio app, 163
password, for Wi-Fi network, 93
PC. *See* computer requirements
PC Free feature, 30
PDF files, reading, 190

performance, 10
periodicals
  buying issues of, 201–202
  downloading to Newsstand app,
    199–201
  reading, 202–203
phone calls with video. *See*
    FaceTime app
Photo Booth app, 51, 218, 235–236
Photo Library, saving website images in,
    108, 222–223
Photo Stream feature, 11
photos
  albums for, creating, 227–228
  albums for, imported photos in, 222
  albums for, slideshows of, 233
  albums for, viewing, 223–224
  Camera Roll folder for, 222–223,
    227–228
  for contacts, 220, 322–324
  copying, 220
  copyright issues regarding, 108
  cropping, 226
  deleting, 220, 233–234
  editing, 225–227
  e-mailing, 220, 228–229
  enhancing, 226
  file formats supported, 218
  Flickr + app for, 163
  importing from other devices, 221–222
  instant messaging, 220, 228–229
  iPhoto app for, 163
  PhotoStream, sharing with, 229–230
  posting from Safari, 109–110
  printing, 220, 231
  red-eye, removing, 226
  rotating, 226
  sharing, 11

photos *(continued)*
  special effects for, 235–236
  streaming to other devices, 215–216
  taking, 218–221
  tweeting, 140, 220, 228–229
  viewing, 220, 223–225
  viewing in frame, while iPad
    locked, 233
  viewing in slideshow, 231–233
  as wallpaper, 220
  on websites, saving, 108, 222–223
Photos app. *See also* Camera app;
    cameras
  copying photos, 220
  deleting photos, 220, 233–234
  described, 50, 218
  editing photos, 225–227
  e-mailing photos, 220, 228–229
  instant messaging photos,
    220, 228–229
  photos for contacts, assigning, 220
  printing photos, 220, 231
  tweeting photos, 140, 220, 228–229
  viewing photos, 220, 223–225
  viewing slideshows, 231–233
  wallpaper, photos as, 220
Photos settings, iTunes, 59
PhotoStream, 229–230
pinching, 33, 35
Ping social network, 214–215
Play icon, on Status bar, 47
playlists, creating, 207–208
podcasts
  deleting, 244–245
  finding in iTunes Store, 150
  playing, 239–242
Podcasts settings, iTunes, 59
POP3 e-mail account, 118–121
power adapter. *See* USB Power Adapter

pressing and holding, 35, 36
Previous arrow, Safari, 96
printers, 21–22, 112–113
printing
  maps, 265
  notes, 363–364
  photos, 220, 231
  web pages, 112–113
Printopia app, 22, 112
privacy issues. *See* security and privacy
    issues
Private Browsing feature, Safari, 111–112
Project Gutenberg, 182

• Q •

Quote Level feature, 125

• R •

reader, electronic. *See* iBooks app; Safari
    Reader
Reading List, Safari, 104–105
Real-Time Stocks app, 163
rebooting iPad, 374
registering iPad, 29–30
Reminders app
  creating reminders with Siri, 343–344
  described, 49, 303
  syncing with other devices or calendars,
    309–310
  task lists, creating, 308
  tasks, creating, 304–305
  tasks, deleting, 310–311
  tasks, editing, 305–306
  tasks, marking as complete, 310–311
  tasks, priority of, 305
  tasks, scheduling a reminder for,
    306–307

Retina display, 10, 44, 164. *See also*
    screen
Return key, keyboard, 37
ringers, volume of, 79–80
ringtones, assigning to contacts,
    277, 327–328
rotating screen, 32

• *S* •

Safari app, 12. *See also* Internet
    connection
  Accept Cookies option, 111–112
  Address field, 95–96
  AutoFill for, 97
  bookmarks in, creating, 103–104
  bookmarks in, syncing, 103
  browsing history in, 98–100
  browsing web pages, 35–36, 95–98
  described, 48
  images, opening or copying, 35
  iPad User Guide, viewing, 65–67
  links, following, 35, 97
  links, sending in e-mail message,
    110–111
  opening, 93
  posting photos from, 109–110
  printing web pages, 112–113
  Private Browsing feature, 111–112
  reading websites like an e-reader,
    105–107
  saving images in Photo Library,
    108, 222–223
  saving websites as icons on Home
    screen, 107–108
  saving websites in Reading List,
    104–105
  searching the Web, 100–101
  tabbed browsing in, 97–98

  tweeting from, 140
  web address, entering, 95–96
  zooming, 35, 94–95
Safari Reader, 105–107
Saved Photos album. *See* Camera Roll
    folder
schedule. *See* Calendar app;
    Reminders app
screen. *See also* Home screen; keyboard,
    onscreen
  AssistiveTouch feature for, 84–85
  brightness of, 70–71, 188
  cleaning, 28, 365–366
  double-tapping, 33, 35, 72–73
  dragging to scroll (swiping), 34, 44
  finger motions for. *See* touchscreen
    technology
  flicking, 35, 78
  four- or five-finger swiping, 44
  four-finger flicking, 78
  glare from, reducing, 70
  keyboard on. *See* keyboard, onscreen
  new features in, 10
  pinching, 33, 35
  pressing and holding, 35
  protecting, 19, 31, 70, 367–368
  rotating, 32, 85
  rotation of, locking, 46, 47, 85
  selecting text, 35, 124, 357
  tapping, 33, 35, 78, 79
  three-finger double-tapping, 72–73
  three-finger flicking, 78
  three-finger tapping, 34, 79
  touchscreen technology for, 30–32
  two-finger flicking, 78
  two-finger tapping, 78
  VoiceOver feature for, 78–79
  wallpaper for, 71–72

screen *(continued)*
  white text on black, 74–75, 188, 189
  zooming. *See* zooming
screen protector, 70
Screen Rotation Lock icon, Status bar, 47
SD Card Reader, 221, 222
Search field, Mail, 126
Search (magnifying glass) icon, 40
security and privacy issues
  lost or stolen iPad, 65, 376–377
  Private Browsing feature, Safari,
    111–112
  with public Wi-Fi networks, 93
  remotely locking or erasing iPad, 377
selecting text, 35, 124, 357
sepia tint for screen, 188, 189
Settings for iPad, iTunes, 59
Settings icon, on iPad
  Accept Cookies option, 111–112
  Add Account option, 116, 118
  AssistiveTouch options, 84–85
  Auto-Brightness option, 70
  Auto-Lock option, 53
  Brightness option, 70
  described, 52
  FaceTime option, 135
  iCloud option, 61, 63–65
  iTunes Store options, 156
  Large Text option, 83
  Lock Rotation option, 46
  Messages options, 141–142
  Mono Audio option, 80–81
  Mute option, 46
  opening, 31
  Private Browsing option, 111–112
  Sounds options, 79–80
  Speak Auto-text option, 81–82
  Triple-Click Home option, 77

  Twitter option, 140
  VoiceOver option, 75–79
  wallpaper options, 71–72
  White on Black option, 74–75
  Zoom option, 72–74
Shift key, on keyboard, 38
shrinking or enlarging screen contents.
    See zooming
Side Switch, 25, 46
Siri
  activating, 337–340
  adding events using, 290
  adding tasks to Calendar app, 344
  calling contacts via FaceTime, 342–343
  creating reminders and alerts, 343–344
  described, 11, 212, 337, 349–350
  features of, 340–341
  getting directions in Maps app,
    345–346
  in Maps app, 267
  playing music, 345
  sending e-mail or messages, 349
  web searching, 348
  Wolfram Alpha, 347–348
Sleep mode, 25, 52–53
Sleep/Wake button, 25, 52–53
Sleep/Wake slider, on Home screen,
    52–53
slideshows, 231–233
Smart Cover, iPad, 19, 52, 367
songs. *See* music
sound
  speaker accessories, 215, 256
  speaker on iPad, 25–26
  troubleshooting, 372–374
  volume, setting. *See* volume
Speak Auto-text feature, 81–82
Speak Hints feature, 77

speaker accessories, 215, 256

speaker on iPad, 25–26

split keyboard, 39–40

Spotlight screen, 40–41

Spotlight Search feature, 126

Sprint data plans, 16

Status bar, 35, 46–47

Stopwatch tab (Clock app), 301–302

streaming content to other devices, 13, 215–216

Study Cards, in textbooks, 194–195

Subject field, Mail, 124

Sudoku Daily app, 162

Summary settings, iTunes, 59

support, 374–375

swiping (dragging to scroll), 34, 44

symbols, typing, 38, 354

syncing content from computer
  described, 18, 28, 59–60
  with iCloud, 63–65, 159–160, 184, 207, 296, 309–310
  with iTunes, 59–60, 103, 184, 296, 372

syncing content from e-mail accounts, 321–322

• T •

tabbed browsing, Safari, 97–98

tapping, 33, 35, 78, 79

text
  font or size of. See fonts; zooming
  selecting, 35, 124, 357

text messages. See also Messages app
  ringtones for, 277, 328
  sending locations in, 277–278
  sending photos in, 220, 228–229
  split keyboard for, 39–40

textbooks, 194–195

themes, setting, 188, 189

third-generation iPad. See iPad

three-axis accelerometer, 257

three-finger double-tapping, 72–73

three-finger flicking, 78

three-finger tapping, 34

Time, on Status bar, 47

Timer tab (Clock app), 301–302

Tip icon, in this book, 1

To field, Mail, 121, 123, 124

touchscreen technology, 30–32. See also screen

troubleshooting iPad problems. See also maintaining iPad
  customer support for, 374–375
  lost or stolen iPad, finding, 376–377
  onscreen keyboard, re-displaying, 371
  rebooting iPad, 370, 374
  remotely erasing iPad contents, 377
  remotely locking iPad, 377
  resetting iPad, 370
  sound, restoring, 372–374
  unresponsive iPad, 370
  updating iOS, 371–372

Tuff-Luv iPad cover, 367

TV shows. See also videos
  buying, 154–156
  closed-captioning for, 242–243
  deleting, 244–245
  finding in iTunes Store, 148–152
  playing, 239–242
  from sources other than iTunes Store, 158–159

TV Shows settings, iTunes, 59

tweets
  from iPad apps, 140–141
  sending locations in, 277–278
  sending photos in, 220, 228–229

Twitter account
  for contacts, assigning, 324–325
  enabling on iPad, 140
  signing up for, 140

Twitter app, 133, 140–141

two-finger tapping, 78

typing. *See* keyboard, onscreen

typing challenges

  AssistiveTouch feature, 84–85

  Dictation feature. *See* Dictation feature

Typing Feedback feature, 77

• U •

undo an action, 227

updates for this book, 5

USB port

  not available on iPad, 14

  requirements for, on computer, 18

USB Power Adapter, 23

USB stick, not supported, 14

User Guide, iPad, 65–67

UStream, video content from, 158

• V •

Verizon data plans, 15–17

videos

  buying, 154–156

  chapters of, going to, 243–244

  closed-captioning for, 242–243

  deleting, 244–245

  finding in iTunes Store, 148–152

  Flash for, not supported, 158

  in iTunes, syncing to iPad, 245

  non-iPad formats, converting, 159

  phone calls with video. *See* FaceTime app

  playing, 239–242

  playing, status indicator for, 47

  previewing before buying, 152–154

  recording, 238–239

  renting, 156–158

  from sources other than iTunes Store, 158–159

  streaming to other devices, 13, 215–216

Videos app

  deleting videos, 244–245

  described, 48, 237

  playing videos, 239–242

ViewSonic HDMI devices, 14

VIP List, 128–131

virtual private network. *See* VPN

visual challenges. *See also* accessibility features

  brightness of screen, 70–71

  Large Text feature, 83

  sepia tint, 188, 189

  Speak Auto-text feature, 81–82

  VoiceOver feature, 75–79

  wallpaper, 71–72

  white text on black, 74–75, 188, 189

  Zoom feature, 72–74

VoiceOver feature, 75–79

volume. *See also* sound

  adjusting, in Music app, 213–214

  muting, 46

  of ringers and alerts, 79–80

  volume rocker switch for, 26

VPN (virtual private network), 47

VPN icon, on Status bar, 47

• W •

Wake button. *See* Sleep/Wake button

wallpaper, 71–72

web address, entering in Safari, 95–96

Web Clips feature, 107–108

websites
ABC, video content from, 158
Air Video, 159
Apple Store, 19
Apple support, 374
AppleCare+ coverage, 370
apps optimized for Retina display, 164
AT&T data plans, 16
battery service, 375
CBS news, video content from, 158
Clicker, video content from, 158
of contacts, going to, 330–331
Griffin iPad cover, 367–368
Handbrake utility, 159
iOS updates, 43
for iPad, 5
for iPad Cheat Sheet, 53
iPad User Guide, 67, 375
iTunes, 18
iTunes Match service, 207
Netflix, video content from, 158
Sprint data plans, 16
for this book, 5
Tuff-Luv iPad cover, 367
Twitter, 140
UStream, video content from, 158
Verizon data plans, 16
Zagg InvisibleShield screen
overlay, 368

Week view, Calendar app, 285
white text on black, 74–75, 188, 189
Wi-Fi + 3G model, 4, 15–17
Wi-Fi + 4G model, 4, 15–17
Wi-Fi icon, on Status bar, 47
Wi-Fi network, 16–17, 28, 92–93
Wi-Fi only model, 4, 16–17
Wireless Keyboard, Apple, 20–21
Wolfram Alpha, 347–348
World Clock, 299

● *Y* ●

Yahoo! account, 116–117
Yahoo! calendar, subscribing to,
294–296
Year view, Calendar app, 285–286

● *Z* ●

Zagg InvisibleShield screen overlay, 368
zooming. *See also* fonts
finger motions for, 33, 35, 94–95
Large Text feature, 83
for maps, 265–266
for PDF files, 190
Zoom feature for, 72–74